Encyclopaedic History of India Series

DECLINE OF MUGHAL EMPIRE

Dr. Mahesh Vikram Singh
Professor, Deptt. of History
Mahatma Gandhi Kashi Vidyapeeth
Varanasi (UP)

Dr. Brij Bhushan Shrivastava
Head of Deptt., Ancient History, Archeology & Culture
SMMTPG College, Ballia (UP)

CENTRUM PRESS
NEW DELHI-110002 (INDIA)

CENTRUM PRESS
H.O.: 4360/4, Ansari Road, Daryaganj,
New Delhi-110002 (India)
Tel: 23278000, 23261597, 23255577, 23286875
B.O.: No. 1015, Ist Main Road, BSK IIIrd Stage,
IIIrd Phase, IIIrd Block, Bangalore-560085 (INDIA)
Tel: 080-41723429
Email: centrumpress@gmail.com
Visit us at: www.centrumpress.com

Decline of Mughal Empire

First Edition, 2011

ISBN 978-93-80836-80-5

PRINTED IN INDIA

Printed at Mehra Offset Press, Delhi

DECLINE OF MUGHAL EMPIRE

प्रो. विपिन चंद्रा
अध्यक्ष
Prof. Bipan Chandra
Chairman

नेशनल बुक ट्रस्ट, इंडिया
नेहरू भवन
5 इंस्टीट्यूशनल एरिया, फेज़-II, वसंत कुंज, नई दिल्ली-110 070
फोन/ Phone: 011-26121880 फैक्स/ Fax: 011-26121883

NATIONAL BOOK TRUST, INDIA
Nehru Bhawan
5 Institutional Area, Phase II, Vasant Kunj, New Delhi-110 070
ई-मेल / E-mail: chairman@nbtindia.org.in
वेबसाइट / Website: www.nbtindia.org.in

FOREWORD

The term 'history' is derived from the Greek word 'historia' that means knowledge acquired through investigation. Obviously, this knowledge can be correct if the method of investigation is objective and not vitiated by any kind of bias. In other words, if the study of human past is comprehensive and obtained through scientific inquiry, it can provide perspective on the present day problems and help one plan for the future.

A true historian has to identify the sources that can be most useful in a given context. Documents, coins, archaeology, anthropology, geography, travel accounts, oral traditions, mythology and so on can be useful but they can be used only after their veracity is tested and they are critically examined. They should be checked and counter-checked.

Over the centuries, one finds the study and writing of history vitiated by biases. There are numerous instances in which historical data have been distorted to support or oppose certain preconceived ideas and purposes. Strictly speaking such history is just like fiction to accord with preconceived notions and serve some ulterior purposes.

The study of the past has never been static. Conclusions go on changing because of the discovery of new materials and tools of investigation. To give a concrete example, the carbon 14 or radiocarbon dating test has revolutionized the study of civilizations and settlements, especially of prehistoric times, for which written documents, coins, etc. are seldom available. This method has enabled historians to determine more accurately than before the time period of a particular civilization or settlement. This method was discovered only 70 years ago by American scientists.

In our country, excavations brought to light the Indus Valley Civilization and its various features, hitherto unknown. Similarly, no complete text of Kautilya's Arthashastra was available before it was discovered by Shamasastry, the chief of the Mysore Government Oriental Library in the first decade of the last century. Likewise, people's knowledge of the history of the Buddhist period got extended after excavations at Sarnath and the ruins of the Asokan period at Patna. In the future, if the Harappan inscriptions are deciphered, our knowledge of the Indus Valley Civilization will increase enormously. All these instances underline the fact that our knowledge of history is never static and its frontiers go on extending.

In the light of what has been said above the encyclopedic history is going to be of great help to students interested in Indian history. It is comprehensive and as far as possible free from biases. It includes the latest materials, and objective conclusions.

Prof . Bipan Chandra
Professor Emeritus, JNU
Chairman, National Book Trust, India

Contents

Preface

The people of India have had a continuous civilization since 2500 B.C., when the inhabitants of the Indus River valley developed an urban culture based on commerce and sustained by agricultural trade. This civilization declined around 1500 B.C., probably due to ecological changes. During the second millennium B.C., pastoral, Aryan-speaking tribes migrated from the northwest into the subcontinent. As they settled in the middle Ganges River valley, they adapted to antecedent cultures.

The political map of ancient and medieval India was made up of myriad kingdoms with fluctuating boundaries. In the 4th and 5th centuries A.D., northern India was unified under the Gupta Dynasty. During this period, known as India's Golden Age, Hindu culture and political administration reached new heights. Islam spread across the Indian subcontinent over a period of 500 years. In the 10th and 11th centuries, Turks and Afghans invaded India and established sultanates in Delhi. In the early 16th century, descendants of Genghis Khan swept across the Khyber Pass and established the Mughal (Mogul) Dynasty, which lasted for 200 years. From the 11th to the 15th centuries, southern India was dominated by Hindu Chola and Vijayanagar Dynasties. During this time, the two systems—the prevailing Hindu and Muslim—mingled, leaving lasting cultural influences on each other.

The first British outpost in South Asia was established in 1619 at Surat on the northwestern coast. Later in the century, the East India Company opened permanent trading stations at Madras, Bombay, and Calcutta, each under the protection of native rulers. The British expanded their influence from these footholds until, by the 1850s, they controlled most of present-day India, Pakistan, and Bangladesh. In 1857, a rebellion in north India led by mutinous Indian soldiers caused the British Parliament to transfer all political power from the East India Company to the Crown. Great Britain began administering most of India directly while controlling the rest through treaties with local rulers.

In the late 1800s, the first steps were taken toward self-government in British India with the appointment of Indian councillors to advise the British viceroy and the establishment of provincial councils with Indian members; the British subsequently widened participation in legislative councils. Beginning in 1920, Indian leader Mohandas K. Gandhi transformed the Indian National Congress political party into a mass movement to campaign against British colonial rule.

—*Authors*

1

Disintegration of the Empire

Muhammad Shah died in 1748, a few weeks after this last victory. His long reign had seen a growing paralysis in imperial power, of which the most visible symptom was the establishment of hereditary viceroyalties in the major provinces of the empire. The pattern was one that had been seen before in India history: as the central power weakened, either as a cause or a result the outlying provinces assumed independent status. These states were the administrative units of the Mughal empire, but they were also the traditional "nuclear" regions of Indian history, defined by geography, language, and past traditions.

The provincial governors long continued to demonstrate the symbolic function of the Mughal emperor by their desire to gain his recognition for their rule, but from the time of Muhammad Shah they sought such recognition after, not before, their seizure of power. In the Punjab, largely because of the intervention of external forces from the northwest, independent kingdoms were not formed in the middle of the eighteenth century, but elsewhere the process of the disintegration of central authority was complete. In the Deccan, Oudh, Bengal, and to some extent Rohilkhand, large principalities over which the central government of Delhi had only nominal authority came into existence. By depriving the empire of financial resources, even though they continued to send an annual tribute to Delhi, and by reducing the possibility of united action, these kingdoms lessened the chances of the empire's survival when attacks came from without.

The most important of the new principalities was Hyderabad, made up of six subas of the Deccan, which at this time had a revenue of sixteen crores of rupees, compared with seventeen crores from the other twelve provinces of the Mughal empire. As already noted, the founder of the state was Nizam-ul-Mulk, who had been made viceroy of the Deccan by Farrukhsiyar in 1714, and wazir of the empire by Muhammad Shah in 1722. On his return to the Deccan in 1724, he began to build up a strong state, although still offering assistance to the emperor. At his death in 1748, he passed on a well-administered state that continued to be a center of Muslim culture in the Deccan for two centuries.

In Bengal, power passed into the hands of two remarkable men, Murshid Quli Khan and Alivardi Khan. Under these able administrators Bengal was among the most peaceful and prosperous areas of India, and paid an annual tribute of ten million rupees to the Delhi court.

In the Punjab, the Sikhs used Nadir Shah's invasion in 1739 as an opportunity to attack Mughal authority; but the able governor, Zakariya Khan, crushed them. After his death in 1745 the province passed out of effective Mughal control.

Sind does not figure greatly in Mughal history, and authority had always tended to reside in the hands of local chiefs. The most important of these belonged to the Kalhara family, descendants of the disciples of a sixteenth-century spiritual leader. Through the course of the next hundred years they built up great land holdings, and by the beginning of the eighteenth century were recognized as governors of a large area of Upper Sind. Muhammad Shah completed the process in 1736 by conferring on the chief of the Kalharas a title that acknowledged his control of the whole province of Sind.

Cultural Life

Against this picture of a disintegrating empire must be set the undoubted fact that Muhammad Shah's reign was a time of very considerable cultural activity. Urdu, which had gained admission in the literary and cultural circles of the metropolis only a few years before the beginning of Muhammad Shah's reign, was a fully developed literary language at its end. A new school of music grew up around the Mughal court, and the names of Sadarang and his brother occupy a high place in the evolution of khiyal, which was to supersede all other varieties of Hindustani music. Indian dancing, freed from the atmosphere of the temple, became an art ministering to human pleasure. A new style of painting, closely related to the rise of Urdu literature, brought fresh vigor to the tradition of pictorial art. Indian astronomy also reached a new level of excellence in this period, as indicated by the magnificent astronomical instruments at Delhi and Ujjain. The creator of these works, Maharaja Jai Singh of Jaipur, was Muhammad Shah's governor in Malwa from 1728 to 1734.

Most significant of all the cultural activities of Muhammad Shah's reign was the beginning of the work of Shah Waliullah (1703–1762), the greatest Islamic scholar India ever produced. That the political disintegration of Islamic power in the eighteenth century was not accompanied by a religious collapse was largely due to his work; and more than anyone else, he is responsible for the religious regeneration of Indian Islam.

Shah Waliullah received his training from his father, who as a theologian, Sufi, and philosopher combined in his own person these three main strands of Indian Islam. He was in his teens when he started teaching in his father's madrasah. He continued this for twelve years, after which he left for Arabia for higher studies and for performing the Hajj. He was in Arabia for nearly fourteen months, pursuing his studies under famous teachers at Mecca and Medina.

During his stay at Mecca, Shah Waliullah saw a vision in which the Holy Prophet informed him that he would be instrumental in the organization of a section of the Muslim community. Friends urged him to stay in Hijaz, and not to return to the unsettled conditions of India, but he was convinced that his mission was to work there. He returned to Delhi in 1732, and began what was to be his life's work. He had been a teacher before he went to Arabia, and while he resumed his occupation, he no longer followed the traditional methods of instruction. He trained pupils in different branches of Islamic knowledge, then entrusted them with the teaching of the students, while he devoted himself to writing. Before his death in 1762, he had completed practically a library of standard works in all branches of "Islamic sciences" of the type particularly suited to the Indian conditions.

Shah Waliullah's most important single work was his translation of the Quran into simple Persian, the literary language of Muslim India. Translations had been attempted earlier, but they either were incidental to a voluminous commentary, or did not gain wide acceptance. After some opposition Shah Waliullah's translation became popular, either because of the translator's eminence in religious circles, or because his translation was connected with a broad-based movement aimed at bringing the knowledge of the Quran within the reach of the average, literate Indian Muslim. Shah Waliullah's action, which involved not only scholarship, but also imagination and great moral courage, smoothed the way for others. Within sixty years his two sons prepared their Urdu translations—one completely literal and following the Arabic sentence-structure, and the other idiomatic and in accordance with Urdu usage. Not only did his sons follow his example, but in course of time, so did scores of others; and it is because of his initiative that, outside the Arabic-speaking countries, Muslims in India and Pakistan have taken the lead in the study and propagation of the Quran.

Not less important was his balanced understanding and fair-minded approach to different religious questions. In his day Indian Islam was rent by controversies and conflicts between the Shia and the Sunni, the Sufi and the Mullah, the Hanafi and the Wahhabi, the Mujaddidi and the Wahdat-al-Wajudi, and the Mu'tazali and the Asha'ari. To Shah Waliullah, *adl* (justice, equity) was the prime virtue and the basis of civilized existence, and he studied the writings of all schools of thought, trying to understand the attitudes of each of them. He then wrote authoritative volumes expounding what was just and acceptable to different points of view. In this way, by working out a system of thought on which all but the extremists could agree, he helped to provide a spiritual basis for national cohesion and harmony.

Shah Waliullah's success was also due to his able and devoted successors. One of his grandsons was the great reformer Shah Ismail Shahid. Three of his sons were leading scholars and writers, including Shah Abdul Aziz, who dominated Delhi religious life for nearly fifty years. The brothers taught and trained a large body of men who carried the message of Shah Waliullah to all parts of India. Their students and successors organized jihad against persecution of Islam by the Sikhs in the northwest, brought about a revival of Islam in Bengal, and were held in equal veneration by Sir Sayyid Ahmed Khan, the leader of the Aligarh movement, and Maulana Muhammad Qasim, the founder of the Deoband seminary.

While Islam is not organized along national lines, owing to historic, racial, linguistic, and geographic factors, a variety of schools and viewpoints have gained prominence in different Muslim countries. In Iran, for example, the Shia form of Islam is the national religion, while in the desert of Najd, Wahhabi puritanism is dominant. Similarly, different countries have adopted, according to their peculiar developments, different schools of law—the Shafii, the Hanbali, the Maliki, and the Hanafi. If the beliefs, the legal traditions, and the religious tendencies of modern Muslim India and Pakistan were to be examined from this point of view, it would be seen that the foundation of the religious structure which is dominant there was laid by Shah Waliullah.

Shah Muhammad's Successors

Looking at Shah Muhammad's reign, the author of the late eighteenth-century history, *Siyar-ul-Mutakhkhirin*, declared: "In his reign the people passed their lives in ease, and the empire outwardly retained its dignity and prestige. The foundations of the Delhi monarchy were really rotten, but Muhammad Shah by his cleverness kept them standing. He may be called the last of the rulers of Babur's line, as after him the kingship had nothing but the name left to it." The records of the last fifty years of the century suggest no reason for challenging this melancholy verdict. After Muhammad Shah's death, Prince Ahmad Shah (r.1748–1754), the hero of the battle of Sirhind, ascended the throne, and although he was a well-meaning and active young man, he could effect no improvement in government affairs. His appointment of Safdar Jang as wazir was especially unfortunate. An opportunist whose measures helped to destroy the Mughal empire, Safdar Jang seems to have been motivated by two aims. One was to humiliate any relatives of his predecessors in the wizarat; the other was to drive out all Afghans from positions of authority.

Safdar's policy brought him in conflict with the principal Turani families, but his initial difficulties came from the royal favorites headed by the chief eunuch, Javed Khan, and the emperor's mother. Safdar Jang had Javed Khan assassinated in August, 1752, but then the emperor started favoring Ghazi-ud-din, a grandson of Nizam-ul-Mulk, and a clever but completely unscrupulous youth of eighteen. Safdar Jang lost the support of the emperor, and in May, 1753, though still the wazir of the realm, rebelled against his master. Ghazi-ud-din organized the opposition to Safdar Jang, and with his usual lack of scruples, whipped up Shia-Sunni and Afghan-Irani differences to gain supporters. Safdar was defeated and forgiven; but realizing that the best field for the satisfaction of his ambitions was away from the capital, withdrew to Oudh. Ghazi-ud-din was now all-powerful at the capital. This was dramatically attested when the emperor, who had soon become estranged from him, sought to have him removed from the court. With the help of the Maratha chiefs, Ghazi-ud-din made himself wazir and in June, 1754, deposed the emperor.

The man placed on the throne in 1754 as Alamgir II was a son of Jahandar Shah. A man of good intentions, his adoption of Aurangzeb's title was an indication of his desire to follow in his great predecessor's footsteps, but the situation in the empire was beyond his control. The Marathas, who had grown more powerful because of their collaboration with Ghazi-ud-din, now dominated the whole of northern India. In 1758 they occupied Lahore and drove out Taimur Shah, the son and viceroy of the Afghan ruler, Ahmad Shah Abdali. This was the high-water mark of the Maratha expansion. "Their frontier extended on the north to the Indus and the Himalaya, and in the south nearly to the extremity of the peninsula; all the territory within those limits which was not their own, paid tribute." The whole of this great power was wielded by one hand, that of the Peshwa, who talked of placing Bishvas Rao on the Mughal throne.

Maratha dreams, however, received a shattering blow. The expulsion of Taimur Shah provoked the wrath of Ahmad Shah Abdali, who was joined in the war against the Marathas by the principal Muslim nobles of North India. The main battle was fought at Panipat on June 14, 1761. This was the most desperate of the three historic battles of Panipat (the first fought by Babur in 1526, and the second by Humayun in 1556), and its results were of great significance for Indian history. The Marathas were completely defeated, and while their chiefs retained power in Central India, the centralizing power of the Peshwa was destroyed. Panipat meant that whoever succeeded the Mughals on the throne of Delhi, it would not be the Marathas. Ahmad Shah Abdali's own design of building up an Afghan empire in India was frustrated by the impetuosity of his soldiers, who hated the heat of the plains and clamored for an immediate return to Kabul with their plunder.

Since they had been away from their homes for a long time and were on the verge of mutiny, Ahmad Shah had to abandon his dreams and return to his own country.

Ghazi-ud-din had put Alamgir II to death in 1759, replacing him with a puppet, but after the battle of Panipat, Ahmad Shah nominated a son of Alamgir II as emperor, with the title of Shah Alam (1761–1803). In the struggles that followed, Ghazi-ud-din lost power and fled from the capital. The administration of the shrunken empire—by now reduced to little more than the area around Delhi—was in the hands of Najib-ud-daula. It was he who had organized the Muslim confederacy that defeated the Marathas at Panipat, and he remained loyal throughout his life to the Mughal emperor. This was all the more remarkable since Shah Alam was absent from Delhi almost continuously until 1772. Najib's main task was to maintain order in the Mughal domain around Delhi. After the battle of Panipat the Marathas were quiescent for some time, but the Jats and the Sikhs began to threaten the integrity of the remaining imperial territories. Najib defeated the Jats and killed their leader, Suraj Mal, but he was less successful with the Sikhs. They were kept from creating too much trouble, however, by an internal split between two groups.

Rise of British Power

Meanwhile, far-reaching developments had taken place outside the capital. Alivardi Khan, the able governor of Bengal, died on April 10, 1756, and was succeeded by his grandson, Mirza Muhammad, better known as Siraj-ud-daula. The disruptive forces which had been kept under check by Alivardi got out of hand and overwhelmed the government. Alivardi's commander-in-chief, Mir Jafar, to whom his half-sister was married, started plotting against Siraj-ud-daula, and for a short time was removed from the command. Another reason for weakness was the existence of the East India Company, which had established at Calcutta not only a commercial, but a political center. A third was the attitude of the Hindu zamindars, bankers, and officials who, always influential in Bengal, had grown very powerful since the days of Murshid Quli Khan.

Alivardi Khan made no distinction between the Hindus and the Muslims. He had gained his position with the support of the Hindu notables, and they shared the government with him. This had not reconciled them to a Muslim ruler; or perhaps they recognized that a new power might soon overthrow his rule, and they wanted to be on the winning side. In any case, as an official of the East India Company had written two years before Alivardi's death: "[Hindu] rajas and inhabitants were disaffected to the Moor government and secretly wished for a change and opportunity of throwing off their tyrannical yoke." These three forces sealed the fate of Siraj-ud-daula. The familiar story of British activities need not be told here, but the role of the treacherous Mir Jafar, generally held responsible for the fate of Siraj, was comparatively a minor one. More significant was the alliance of the Hindu merchants with the East India Company. This new alignment, as much as any single factor, must be taken into account in explaining the end of Muslim rule in Bengal.

The battle fought at Plassey, a few miles outside Murshidabad, has been called by a modern British writer "the most miserable skirmish ever to be called a decisive battle." An army of which the commander-in-chief had been won over and took no part in the battle, can hardly offer spirited contests. Siraj-ud-daula's Hindu paymaster, Mir Madan, however, was loyal to the nawab, and fell in action. Clive's spirited leadership and British organization, coupled with the help they received from the powerful local elements, resulted in the rout and flight of Siraj-ud-daula. On June 28, 1757, Clive installed Mir Jafar on the masnad of Murshidabad and four days later Siraj-ud-daula was executed.

The legal position in Bengal had not changed with the British victory at Plassey, for the nawab was still in charge of the administration. But the officials of the East India Company expected him to do their bidding, and a clash was inevitable if a nawab sought to impose policies counter to British interests. The clash came when Nawab Mir Qasim, who had succeeded the incompetent Mir Jafar, tried to collect internal revenue from the English traders. According to an agreement, only the East India Company itself was to be free from the tax; in practice, every company servant traded on his own account and refused to pay any duty. In desperation, since his revenues were disappearing, Mir Qasim abolished all internal duties, thus removing the English advantage over the Indian traders. The British refused to accept this, and Mir Qasim left Bengal to organize an attack on the British. Support of a half-hearted kind came from Emperor Shah Alam and

Shuja-ud-daula, the wazir of Oudh, who had followed the general pattern of the time by establishing himself as a semi-independent ruler. The Mughal and the British forces met at Buxar in October, 1764, and while the British suffered fairly heavy losses, they won a clear victory. The results of the battle of Buxar were more far-reaching than those of Plassey. Even before the battle the British had attempted to facilitate the military task by diplomatic means, and the newly crowned Shah Alam was only a fugitive from Delhi, but the East India Company had gained a victory against what appeared to be the combined army of the emperor and the rulers of Bengal and Oudh. It gave greater prestige to British arms than had the earlier victory over a provincial government. It also altered Shuja-ud-daula's course of action. Henceforth dependence on the British became a cardinal point of his policy, and Oudh was, for all practical purposes, drawn into the orbit of the British influence. Most important of all, Emperor Shah Alam was forced to give the East India Company the diwani, or civil government, of Bengal, Bihar, and Orissa in return for the districts of Allahabad and Kora and an annual payment of two and a half million rupees. This provided the legal basis for British rule in Bengal.

Emperor Shah Alam remained in Allahabad for some years after the battle of Buxar, but he returned to Delhi in 1772, after the death of his wazir, Najib-ud-daula, who had been the actual ruler of the city for a decade. Motivated either by his own greed for money, or under the influence of the Marathas, who were supporting him for their own ends, Shah Alam attacked Zabita Khan, the powerful son of Najib-ud-daula, who was the leader of the Rohilla Afghans who had established themselves to the east of Delhi. In one punitive expedition against the family stronghold of Ghausgarh, Zabita Khan's relatives were treated with great cruelty. According to tradition, his son, Ghulam Qadir, was castrated and made to serve as page in the palace at Delhi, but a few years later, Ghulam Qadir was able to exact a terrible revenge.

Affairs in the capital were following a tortuous course, with the nobles intriguing against each other for the spoils of the decaying empire. One able administrator, Najaf Khan, succeeded for a time in organizing a small effective army to maintain order, but he eventually succumbed to the debilitating atmosphere.

Without any able or loyal followers, the emperor took a momentous step. In 1785 he invited the great Maratha chieftain

Mahadaji Sindhia of Gwalior to take charge of the Delhi administration. Appointed commander-in-chief and supreme regent (wakil-i-mutliq) of the empire, Sindhia tried to get the cooperation of Ghulam Qadir in dealing with the Sikhs, but Ghulam Qadir, waiting for a chance to repay the humiliation he and his family had suffered at the hands of Shah Alam, had no desire to strengthen the emperor's rule.

His opportunity came in 1787, when Sindhia was defeated by the Rajputs. Ghulam Qadir entered Delhi in September, 1787, and forced the emperor to appoint him mir bakhshi or paymaster, and regent. He was driven out of Delhi by the emperor's supporters, but entered the city again the following year, deposed Shah Alam, and blinded him.

A drunken ruffian, Ghulam Qadir behaved with gross brutality to the emperor and his family. Three servants and two water-carriers who tried to help the bleeding emperor were killed. According to one account, Ghulam would pull the beard of the old monarch, and say: "Serves you right. This is the return for your action at Ghausgarh." Servants were tortured and made to reveal the hidden treasures, and the entire palace was ransacked to find the buried wealth.

After ten horrible weeks during which the honor of the royal family and prestige of the Mughal empire reached its lowest ebb, Ghulam Qadir left with the booty for his stronghold. Sindhia's officers hunted him down and captured him in December, 1788. He was put to death with tortures which equalled his own fiendish cruelties.

When Delhi was retaken by the Marathas, the blind Shah Alam was enthroned again. While his action reconciled the people to Sindhia's rule, it meant that Delhi was being drawn into the great struggle then taking place between the Marathas and the British.

An account of that struggle and of British expansion is outside the scope of this chapter, for the British did not defeat Mughal India, but its successor states, both Muslim and Hindu. Conquest was cautiously achieved. Periods of rapid expansion alternated with long periods of consolidation. Military action was effectively aided by diplomatic activity. Local differences and jealousies were most skilfully exploited. The Company's forces were normally able to depend on the direct or indirect cooperation of the commander, or at least some of the major leaders, of the troops confronting them. At Plassey it was Mir Jafar; at Buxar, the differences between Shuja-ud-daula and Mir Qasim were fully exploited. In fact, British success owed as much to diplomatic skill and the demoralized state of Indian society as to valor and military organization.

The great period of expansion initiated during the governor-generalship (1798–1805) of Lord Wellesley saw Delhi and the Mughal emperor pass under British sway. But even as late as 1798 this absorption did not seem inevitable, for an attempt was made to create a confederacy of the Afghan king, the wazir of Oudh, and a number of Maratha chiefs, to strengthen the position of the emperor. Wellesley took the plan seriously enough to stir up trouble between the Persian and the Afghan courts, so that the Afghan ruler would not be able to give any attention to India.

More important for the fate of the Mughals was Wellesley's war with the Marathas in 1803. In a two-pronged attack, they were defeated in the Deccan and North India. Sindhia's defeat meant the capture of Delhi, and with this the Mughal empire, long a dependent of the Marathas, passed into British control. Yet after a century of decline, the Mughal emperor still remained a symbol of greatness that was not easily defaced. To many British, his continuance seemed absurd, at best an empty pageant. Yet as events were to show in 1857, even the last flickering shadow of Mughal greatness still appeared to be a possible center of power.

Causes of the Mughal Decline

Before turning to these last years of the Mughal empire, it may be useful to summarize what appear to have been certain general causes of Mughal decline, leaving aside such specific causes as external invasions and internal rebellions. One feature of Islamic power in India, as elsewhere, was the failure to make progress in certain vital fields. For example, even Akbar failed to see the possibilities in the introduction of printing. The scarcity of books resulted in comparative ignorance, low standards of education, and limitation of the subjects of study. Because of this, the governing classes were ignorant of the affairs of the outside world. The position becomes clear if we compare the books on India printed in Europe during the eighteenth century with the knowledge of the West current in India. The interest on the part of Europeans that led travelers like Bernier to make reports on their travels finds no parallel in Mughal India. So far from being concerned with Europe, the Mughals, after *Ain-i-Akbari,* made no real addition to their knowledge even of their own dominions.

The stagnation visible in the intellectual field was visible also in the military sphere. Babur had introduced gunpowder in India, but after him there was no advance in military equipment, although the organization and discipline of forces had been completely revolutionized in the West. The Portuguese had brought ships on which cannons were mounted, and had thus introduced a new element which made them masters of the Indian Ocean. What was a fortified wall round the country became a highway, and opened up the empire to those countries which had not remained stagnant. Mughal helplessness on the sea was obvious from the days of Akbar. Their ships could not sail to Mecca without a safe-conduct permit from the Portuguese. Sir Thomas Roe had warned Jahangir that if Prince Shah Jahan as governor of Gujarat turned the English out, "then he must expect we would do our justice upon the seas." The failure of the Mughals to develop a powerful navy and control the seas surrounding their dominions was a direct cause of their replacement by an European power having these advantages.

On land no real progress or large-scale training of local personnel in the use of artillery was made in Mughal India, and the best they could do was to hire foreigners for manning the artillery. The military weakness resulting from this was obvious, and was clearly visible to foreign observers. Bernier wrote in the early years of Aurangzeb's reign:" I could never see these soldiers, destitute of order, and marching with the irregularity of a herd of animals, without reflecting upon the ease with which five-and-twenty thousand of our veterans from the army in Flanders, commanded by Prince Condé or Marshal Turenne would overcome these armies, however numerous." With this condition of the Mughal army, the downfall of the empire was only a question of time.

Another factor which contributed to the fall of the Mughal empire was the moral decay of the ruling classes. This was partly due to the affluent standard of living maintained by monarchs like Shah Jahan and queens like Nur Jahan. Ostentatious luxury became the ambition of everyone who could afford it, and the puritanical

Aurangzeb's attempts to arrest the tide were without success. The evil had gone too far and was only driven underground, to reappear within ten years of the emperor's death, in the uncontrolled orgies of his grandson Jahandar Shah. Perhaps Aurangzeb's extreme asceticism and self-denial only intensified the reaction of the nobility. Many a Maratha hill fortress captured after long and dreary siege was lost because the Mughal commander, unwilling to spend the monsoon months in his lonely perch, came down to the plains, while the hardy Marathas, awaiting the opportunity, moved in.

The moral decline of the nobility showed itself in lack of discipline, laziness, evasion of duties, and even treacherous conduct. It also made them rapacious and heartless in dealing with the public. The extravagant standards that the Mughal bureaucrats tried to maintain were not possible without corruption, extortion, and the enrichment of the officers at the expense of the state and the people. These evils increased as Mughal authority weakened, but their seeds had been sown in earlier days and were a natural result of the efforts of the officers to maintain standards beyond their means.

These were the basic factors responsible for the downfall of the Mughal empire, but others were contributory. The fact that after the death of Aurangzeb no ruler of real vigor and resourcefulness came to the throne made recovery of the lost position almost impossible. Even Aurangzeb's long life was an asset of doubtful value in its last stages. He drove himself hard and resolutely, conscientiously performing his duties, but at the age of ninety he was subject to the laws governing all human machines. When he died, his son and successor Bahadur Shah was already an old man of sixty. He began well but was on the throne for barely six years, and with his death a disastrous chapter opened in Mughal annals.

Directly related to the troubles of this period was the absence of a well-defined law of succession to ensure the continuity of government. The result was that each son of a deceased king felt that he had an equal claim to the crown, and succession to the throne was invariably accompanied by bloody warfare. The disaster was compounded when the imperial princes, who were often viceroys governing vast territories, started making secret pacts with soldiers to ensure their support for the time when the fateful struggle would begin. Soon not only the imperial army but forces external to the empire—the East India Company, the Marathas, the Sikhs—were being used by claimants to the throne of Delhi, as well as to control of the provincial kingdoms. The results were fatal.

The Beginning of a New Era: 1803-1857

WE CONCLUDE our account of Muslim civilization in India with the exile of the last Mughal emperor from Delhi in 1858, and not with the British assumption of overlordship of Delhi in 1803, partly because even in 1803 large areas of the subcontinent were outside the control of the East India Company, and partly because the Company retained the legal fiction of Mughal sovereignty until 1857. At Delhi the Mughal ruler received all the courtesies of a king, and the Company paid him large sums of money, which were claimed on his behalf as the tribute paid by the Company by virtue of past arrangements and treaties. It was argued that "the Company was administering territories for him, as the Marathas had in constitutional theory done before the Company; that the Company's authority was derived from his farmans in so far as it was covered by the farmans, and was mere illegal usurpation in so far as it was not so covered." Against the background of actual military and political power these claims were mere pretensions, but legally and constitutionally the Delhi house had not been set aside from the position they had occupied when they granted the diwani to the Company in 1765. The Mughal ruler was designated shahinshah, and later padshah, in official correspondence. He continued to bestow titles of honor until 1828; coins continued to be issued in his name until 1835. It seemed in 1803 that the British representative was stepping into the shoes of Sindhia. Special arrangements were made for the administration of Delhi, where Muslim law was used in criminal cases. "Within the walls of the Red Fort the king retained his ruling powers. The inhabitants of the Fort bazar were his direct subjects, and the members of the imperial family who lived within enjoyed diplomatic immunity. The etiquette of the court was maintained, the sonorous titles and the language of the great Mughals continued, and the Resident attended the durbar in the Diwan-i-Khas regularly as a suitor. He dismounted like any other courtier ... and was conducted on foot ... to the imperial presence where he stood respectfully like the rest." Shah Alam died in 1806. His successor was Akbar II. With the consolidation of British power, a tendency grew to treat the Mughal emperor more and more as a pensioner of the East India Company, while he insisted on the privileges accorded at the time of the conquest of Delhi. The differences between Akbar Shah and the Company came to a head when a meeting between Lord Hastings the governor-general, and the emperor, could not be held because Akbar insisted that Hastings should appear as a subject and present the usual *nazr* or gift. He also refused to allow the governor-general a chair on the same level as his own at the time of the interview. Hastings refused a meeting on these terms; and soon after, the emperor's privileges were curtailed. The ruler of Oudh (hitherto called wazir) and the nizam of Hyderabad were encouraged to adopt royal titles. While the nizam declined to do so out of regard for the Mughal emperor, the ruler of Oudh accepted the suggestion. To present his case in London, Akbar Shah appointed the celebrated Bengali reformer Ram Mohan Roy, who was planning a visit to England, as the Mughal envoy to the Court of St. James, conferring on him the title of raja. Ram Mohan Roy submitted an ably drafted memorial on behalf of the Mughal ruler, but nothing came of his mission.

When Akbar II died in 1837, his successor, Bahadur Shah (r.1837–1858) refused to give up the claims put forward by his father. The East India Company gradually limited his powers and privileges, however, and when his heir-apparent died in 1856, the claims of the next surviving son were recognized on the condition that his title would only be prince or shahzada and not shah or king.

Whatever may have been the disputes between the emperor and the Company, there is no doubt that in some ways the position of the Mughal ruler improved with the British occupation of Delhi. There was peace and order, and the royal family was not exposed to those vicissitudes and uncertainties which it had suffered prior to the reoccupation of Delhi by Sindhia in 1788. Their financial position also improved, for income from the emperor's lands increased because of the greater general security. Even so, the emperor's income did not exceed 600,000 rupees a year, out of which he had to feed a horde of dependents. But the respect and the position which he enjoyed was out of all proportion to his material resources.

Cultural and Religious Vitality

The Mughals had learned the art of maintaining dignity in the most unpropitious circumstances, and the tawdry Mughal court became the cultural center of Muslim India. The court once again began to attract the most distinguished Muslim noblemen, ulama, and men of letters.

In particular the great Ghalib, who epitomised in his personality and works the splendor and humanity of Mughal culture, adorned his court, sang verses on the age-old themes of love and life, and recited eulogies which easily surpassed anything written by the court poets of Akbar and Jahangir. The influence of the court in the early years of the nineteenth century was felt throughout India, for Mughal manners and etiquette became the standard almost everywhere. As Percival Spear has pointed out, such an influence was of great importance in giving cohesion to Indian life. "The fall of the dynasty was a serious cultural loss, and inaugurated that period of nondescript manners and indefinite conduct from which India suffers today."

Second only to Delhi as a center of Islamic culture, and in many ways more cosmopolitan, was Lucknow, the capital of the rulers of Oudh. To some extent it was the heir of the older centers of Islamic culture in the Gangetic plain, Budaun and Jaunpur, but it also drew upon the great Hindu tradition that lived on in Benares and the surrounding region. It was also an asylum in the eighteenth century for refugees fleeing Delhi before the invasion of Nadir Shah, Ahmad Shah, and the Marathas. Furthermore, it was open to Western influences, and one of the interesting developments was the introduction of opera, a form of music quite unknown in India.

One important difference between Delhi and Lucknow was that the former was a religious as well as cultural center. This was not the case with Lucknow, for while it had learned ulama, their influence was scholastic and intellectual, not spiritual, with more attention paid to form than to content. This tendency reflected itself in all the arts of Lucknow. Lucknow poetry, for example, was rich in ornament and followed elaborate rules of prosody, but had little depth of thought or feeling. "Delhi was less careful about words and gave more attention to thought and subject." The emphasis at Lucknow on the formalities of court etiquette, purity of language, and appropriate enunciation added a distinct strand to Indo-Muslim civilization.

An interesting development of the period was the foundation of Delhi College in 1825. It was housed in the magnificent building of the madrassa founded in the eighteenth century by Nazim-ul-Mulk's son Ghazi-ud-din Khan I, and its development was greatly facilitated by the donation of 170,000 rupees in 1829 by a native of Delhi. It had European principals from the beginning, and marked a new experiment in education, with English as well as Oriental sections. The first head of the Arabic Department was a favorite pupil of Shah Abdul Aziz. An even more remarkable person was the second head, Maulana Mamluk Ali, who also had studied under members of Shah Waliullah's family. He headed the Arabic Department from about 1833 until his death in 1851. He found very little time for literary work, and devoted himself exclusively to teaching both at Delhi College and at his own residence. Among his private pupils were Sir Syed Ahmad Khan, the founder of Aligarh College. His nephew, Maulana Muhammad Qasim, who is generally regarded as the founder of the seminary at Deoband, studied with him for several years at Delhi, and for a brief period was enrolled as a student at Delhi College. This link between Delhi College and the two most important institutions of modern Muslim India led to the observation that, "After the Mutiny, Sir Syed Ahmad Khan took the English section of the Delhi College to Aligarh, and Maulana Muhammad Qasim took the Arabic section to Deoband." Of course this statement is correct only in a figurative and limited sense, but it may well explain many modern features of the seminary at Deoband, of which the founder was a nephew of Maulana Mamluk Ali, and his son was the first principal.

Of even more significance than the artistic and cultural life of the great Islamic cities were the vigorous spiritual movements of the time. The spiritual leader of Delhi, and indeed of all Islamic India, during the first half of the nineteenth century was Shah Abdul Aziz (1746–1823), the son and successor of Shah Waliullah. Shah Abdul Aziz was the most learned Islamic theologian in India, and his views on Muslim law were accepted by all parties among the Sunnis. Unlike most Muslims during this period, he recognized the value of learning English, and displayed no bitterness toward the conquerors. But he was a teacher and thinker rather than a leader, and the most vital Islamic movement of the period was headed by his disciple, Sayyid Ahmed Brelvi. While the spiritual basis of the new movement was found in Shah Waliullah's works, it was Sayyid Ahmed's organizing ability and knowledge of military affairs that gave it the impetus to overcome the apathy of many Muslims.

Sayyid Ahmed Brelvi had begun life as a soldier in the army of Nawab Amir Khan, the founder of Tonk state, but when the nawab came to terms with the British in 1806 he gave up military service and went to Delhi to study under Shah Abdul Aziz. His spiritual powers and organizing ability greatly impressed his teachers, and his reputation increased when Shah Abdul's nephew, Shah Ismail, and his son-in-law, Maulvi Abdul Hai, became Sayyid's disciples. Both of them were distinguished scholars and their example was followed by many others. In 1818, with the help of his two disciples, Sayyid Ahmed wrote *Sirat-i-Mustaqim*, which, apart from a mystical portion, is largely a summary of the reforms which Shah Waliullah had urged. About this time Sayyid Ahmed started to preach in public, and although he used simple words and images, soon made a great reputation for himself.

His activities were not confined to Delhi, and during a visit to Rampur some Afghan travelers complained to him about the Sikh persecution of Muslims in the Punjab. He expressed a desire to conduct a holy war against them, but he knew that war required elaborate preparations and, in any case, he wished to perform the Hajj before undertaking jihad. His journey to Calcutta on the way to Mecca was marked by enthusiastic demonstrations. At Patna so many people became his disciples that he appointed four caliphs, or spiritual viceregents, to look after them. At Calcutta the crowds flocked to him in such numbers that he could not follow the usual custom in making disciples by the laying on of hands, but had to stretch out his turban for people to touch.

At Mecca, Sayyid Ahmed must have gained fuller knowledge of the Wahhabis, the puritan sect that had been in control of the Holy Places some years earlier, and their teaching undoubtedly strengthened his resolve to carry on jihad against the Sikhs. He arrived in the Pathan area in December, 1826, just when the tribesmen had suffered grievously from raids by Sikh armies. Gathering the tribesmen, Sayyid Ahmed attacked the Sikh stronghold of Akora with such success that the Sikhs withdrew.

He carried the war into the plains, occupying Peshawar for two months, and won support from many of the tribal chieftains. But difficulties arose between his companions and the tribal chiefs. After the conquest of Peshawar Sayyid Ahmed wanted to introduce an Islamic system of government, but the tribal chiefs realized that this would work against their authority. His hold was further weakened by opposition to social reforms that he had introduced, and the hostility of the Sikhs and their allies, the Barakzais. In November, 1830, he was forced to relinquish Peshawar in favor of Sultan Muhammad, the old governor, on the promised payment of a fixed tribute. The biggest blow came when his deputies in Yusufzai villages were killed by the tribesmen themselves. Accompanied by a few faithful companions he left for Hazara, where after a few months of desultory warfare he was killed at Balakot by a Sikh contingent in May, 1831.

The Islamic Revival in Bengal

Although Sayyid Ahmed's military efforts ended in a disaster and many of his companions died on the battlefield, his meteoric career left a lasting impression in distant corners of the subcontinent. The scene of his activities on the Afghan frontier continued to attract *mujahids* (militant spiritual leaders), who gave considerable trouble to the Sikhs and later to the British. The effect of Sayyid Ahmed's activities in the eastern part of the country was even more far-reaching. During his leisurely trip to Calcutta and his long sojourn in that city, he had enrolled a number of disciples—many of them from distant areas in what is now East Pakistan—who continued his work. Some of them joined him in the jihad on the frontier, and many continued to send men and money to the mujahids, who kept up the struggle until the second half of the nineteenth century. But perhaps even more important was the extension of Shah Waliullah's reform movement in areas which had been cut off from Delhi for generations, and which, through these disciples, were now brought closer with the spiritual centers of Muslim India.

Islam had been spread in Bengal by the Sufi missionaries in the thirteenth and the fourteenth centuries, but a vigorous Hindu revival under the Vaishanavite leaders had infused new religious life into the Hindus. Assam and the neighboring hill areas were converted to Hinduism. Through its literary expression it also influenced Muslim society. The stream of Muslim missionaries to the area had dried up, and there was a general ignorance of Islam amongst the masses. A local popular religion grew up, thinly veiling Hindu beliefs and practices. Bengal Muslims who were schooled in their religion were steadfast in their observance of Islamic injunctions, but in distant villages, isolated by rivers and streams, there were serious obstacles to the spread of Islamic knowledge.

The nineteenth century saw a new movement of Islamic revival in Bengal. This was largely the work of local reformers and scholars, who took advantage of new conditions and the facilities of steamship travel to Arabia. The first of these was Haji Shariat Ullah, who was born of poor parents in the village of Daulatpur and received his early education at a religious seminary at Dacca or Faridpur. He went on pilgrimage to Mecca sometime around 1802, when he was about eighteen years old, and did not return until about 1820. While he was in Arabia he was influenced by Wahhabi doctrines, which he preached to the people of his native district on his return. He denounced the superstitions and corrupt beliefs which had been developed by long contact with the Hindus. He also opposed the prevalent procedure of the Sufi initiation, and replaced the expression *piri-muridi*, which suggested a complete submission, by the relationship between *ustad* (teacher) and *shagird* (pupil). Because of his insistence on *tauba*, or repentance for past sins, his followers called themselves *tawbar* Muslims. They were also known as "Faraizis" because of their insistence on the performance of *faraiz*, the obligations imposed by God and the Prophet. Haji Shariat Ullah was persecuted by zamindars who feared his emphasis on a common Islamic brotherhood, but he managed to continue his ministry until his death.

Even more influential was his son, Haji Muhammad Mohsin (more properly known as Dudhu Miyan), whose name became a household word in the districts of Faridpur, Pabna, Baqarganj, Dacca, and Noakhali. He was born about 1820, and visited Arabia at an early age. On his return he took up the leadership of the movement started by his father. He divided East Bengal into circles, and appointed a caliph, as spiritual leader, to look after his followers in each circle. Under him the movement became the spearhead of the resistance of the Muslim peasantry of East Bengal against Hindu landlords and European indigo planters. He especially denounced the custom of forcing Muslim peasants to contribute to the maintenance of Hindu shrines. He was harassed by lawsuits all his life and was repeatedly jailed. He died in 1860.

The doctrines preached by Haji Shariat Ullah and Dudhu Miyan for some forty years brought permanent changes in the spiritual life of Bengal, but the influence of their group gradually declined. Apart from the conflict with landlords, Dudhu Miyan's policy brought his group in conflict with other Muslims, especially as he used violence to get people to join his sect. The main religious dispute, however, centered around the observance of Friday prayers. To the ordinary believer, the ceremonial performance of the customary prayers was of great importance, but the Faraizis taught that the continuance of Friday prayers in India was unlawful. This was because the country was no longer dar-ul-Islam, or land of the faithful, but, because of conquest by the Christians, had become dar-ul-harb, land of infidels. The quarrel became particularly acrimonious because the Faraizis treated all Muslims who did not share their interpretation of the religious situation as kafirs, or infidels.

Aside from the Faraizis, the religious revivalists who had the greatest influence in East Bengal were four disciples of Sayyid Ahmed Brelvi. One of these was Maulvi Imam-ud-din, who was born in Hajipur in Bengal, but who was educated in Delhi under Shah Abdul Aziz, the son of Shah Waliullah. He became a disciple of Sayyid Ahmed Brelvi at Lucknow in 1824, and was with him at Calcutta during his triumphal journey to Arabia. At that time he had brought large numbers of people from his village to be initiated into the new movement by Sayyid Ahmed. He went to Arabia with Sayyid Ahmed, and later took part in the jihad on the frontier. After the disaster at Balakot, he returned to his home district, Noakhali, and converted many of its inhabitants to the doctrines of his master. Another of Sayyid Ahmed's disciples had a similar success in the Chittagong district. A third member of the group, Maulvi Inayat Ali of Patna, spent nearly ten years in central Bengal, building mosques and appointing qualified teachers. His great interest, however, was in the jihad which Sayyid Ahmed had started on the frontier. He died there in 1858.

The fourth of the great reformers was Maulvi Karamat Ali (d.1873), who devoted his life to the preaching of Islam in East Bengal. A superb organizer, for forty years he moved up and down the rivers with a flotilla of small boats, carrying the message of Islamic regeneration and reform from the Nagas of Assam to the inhabitants of the islands in the Bay of Bengal. His flotilla was often compared to a traveling college: one boat was for the residence of his family, another was reserved for the students and disciples accompanying him, while the third was for lectures and prayers. Maulvi Karamat Ali revitalized Islamic life in East Bengal, and it has been said that at the time of his death there was scarcely a village in Bengal that did not contain some of his disciples.

Maulvi Karamat Ali shared with the Faraizi leaders of East Bengal an abhorrence of all un-Islamic practices, but he violently disagreed with their position that because of the British conquest, the Friday prayers could no longer be observed. He argued that India had not become dar-ul-harb, but that even if it had, Muslims should still carry on all those observances which characterized dar-ul-Islam. This question of whether or not India had ceased to be dar-ul-Islam continued to be debated among Muslims, but the great majority of Bengal Muslims continued to celebrate Friday prayers. Only a very small group remained steadfast to the teaching of Haji Shariat Ullah that India was dar-ul-harb; they did not offer Friday prayers in the traditional manner until after the establishment of Pakistan in 1947.

The significance of this religious revival in Bengal in the nineteenth century has generally been overlooked, but there is no doubt that it gave new life to Islam. The emphasis on strict religious observances, the denunciation of participation in Hindu practices, and the call to an austere life, safeguarded the community in a time of political weakness. These particular "puritan" aspects of the reform movement have led it to be confused with the Wahhabi movement of Arabia, but there were important differences in spirit. The four great reformers derived their inspiration from Shah Waliullah, and they avoided the fanatic extremism usually associated with the true Wahhabis. They were more forward-looking, more concerned with spiritual improvement, than were the Arabian group. Above all, they were influenced by the mysticism of Indian Islam, and Shah Waliullah himself had adopted a conciliatory attitude towards the teachings of the Sufis. For the Wahhabis, on the other hand, the Sufis posed a threat to Islamic truth that could not be tolerated. What the Wahhabis and the disciples of Shah Waliullah shared in common was an emphasis on the ancient purity of the Islamic way of living, untainted by alien accretions.

The Indian Revolt, 1857–1858

The course of these religious movements, in common with almost every aspect of Indian life, was affected by the most spectacular event in the history of nineteenth-century India, the uprising of 1857. The causes of this outbreak have been a matter of endless dispute ever since. The range of opinion varied then, as it still does, from those who see it as a simple mutiny by disgruntled soldiers to those who see it as a nationalist war for an independent India. That the general cause was the distrust awakened by the rush of social change initiated by the British, and that this took the particular form of a fear that the changes presaged an attempt by the British to convert the people to Christianity, there can be little doubt. This fear was used by those who had been displaced from power by the British to rally support for one last desperate effort to regain what they had lost.

As far as Islamic civilization was concerned, the immediate result of the uprising was to cast suspicion on the Muslim community. As the rulers who had been overthrown, it was assumed that they would be the ringleaders in the war. Tangible proof of this was the assumption by Emperor Bahadur Shah of leadership of the revolt at Delhi. That his control was only nominal was plain enough, but his name still awakened echoes of past glory throughout India. Furthermore, in the great center of revolt, the Muslim kingdom of Oudh, the leaders were mainly Muslim, drawn from the ranks of the zamindars embittered by the recent British seizure of the state.

Evidence of the British feeling that the Muslims had a special responsibility for the uprising was shown when Delhi was recaptured. Accounts, some true and some false, of cruel massacres of British women and children by the mutineers had so enraged British officers that they forgot all considerations of justice and equity and indulged in an orgy of vengeance. The city was subjected to a punishment such as it had not undergone even in its dismal history during the eighteenth century. The massacre of Nadir Shah and the lootings by Marathas, Jats, and Afghans had continued for only a few days, but in 1857 the ordeal lasted for months. The entire population was driven out of the city, and in the absence of owners, the houses were broken into, their floors dug up, and contents removed or destroyed.

Next to suffer were the city buildings. The principal mosques were occupied by the British troops. One proposal was to sell the Grand Mosque of Shah Jahan. Another was to convert it into a barracks for the main guard of European troops. Muslims were not allowed to use it until five years later. Some parts of the Fatehpuri Masjid, the second largest in the city, remained in non-Muslim hands till 1875. The beautiful Zinat-ul-Masajid, built by Aurangzeb's daughter, was only restored to the Muslims by Lord Curzon at the beginning of the twentieth century. The royal palace and the fort suffered even more. The palace proper, the residence of the royal family, was razed and all the gardens and courts were completely destroyed. "Not one vestige of them now remains ... The whole of the haram courts of the palace were swept off the face of the earth to make way for a hideous British barrack, without those who carried out this fearful piece of vandalism, thinking it even worthwhile to make a plan of what they were destroying or preserving any record of the most splendid palace in the world." There was considerable damage to the public buildings also. The more important ones were retained, but the contents of the palace were looted, and even structural decorations were removed.

Perhaps an even greater loss was the destruction and dispersal of the royal library, where rare works had been accumulated since the days of Babur and Akbar. While it must have already been damaged during the depredations of the eighteenth century, it was still a great library at the time of the mutiny. The contents were looted and scattered to all corners of the earth, so that we find some leaves of one royal album at Patna, a few in Berlin, some more in the National Library of Paris, though the major portion found its way to the public and private libraries of England.

The Hindu population was allowed to return to the city in January, 1858, and Muslims were allowed a few months later, but the destruction of buildings continued for a long time. The large areas between the Jama Masjid and the fort, which are now covered by an extensive park, were originally the principal residential quarters of the Mughal nobility, and contained the large Akbarabadi Mosque, where Shah Waliullah's successors used to teach. All these buildings were razed and the entire area cleared, so that there should be a suitable field of fire beyond the walls of the fort to house the British garrison. In course of time peace and order returned. The civil authorities, many of whom were unhappy at what was going on, were at last able to assert themselves. Canning, the governor-general, was of a kindly disposition, and although the press cried for vengeance, gradually good sense prevailed, and by slow stages a return to civil administration was effected. Delhi recovered but it was now a small appendage of the Punjab. The grand edifices built by a succession of the Mughal monarchs remained as a reminder of what once had been, but they were an empty shell. The Delhi of the Mughals had perished for ever.

Out of the tragedy came at least one good result. The enforced dispersal of scholars meant that Lahore now replaced Delhi as the cultural center of Muslim India. Urdu was firmly rooted as the language of culture in the land of the five rivers. Similarly, although Delhi ceased to be a place of learning, those who had drunk at this fountainhead and had imbibed the spirit of Shah Waliullah and Shah Abdul Aziz established great centers of learning at Deoband and Aligarh, not far from the old capital.

Ghalib (1796–1869), the greatest of Urdu poets, saw the whole tragedy enacted before his eyes, but he was convinced that there were possibilities for new life in the destruction of the world he had loved. He had long forseen the breakup of the old system, before the mutiny he had written:

They gave me the glad tidings of the dawn in the dark night.
They extinguished the candle and showed me the rising sun.
The fire-temple got burnt; they gave me the breath of fire.
The idol-temple crumbled down and they gave me the lamentation of the temple-gong.
They plucked away the jewels from the banners of the kings of Ajam.
In its place they gave me the jewel-scattering pen.
They removed the pearl from the crown, and fastened it to wisdom.
Whatever they took away openly, they returned to me in secret.

The mutiny led to a careful reassessment of the administration and a reorientation of many policies. Developments in the political field paved the way for the later political struggle and the final independence. The control of the subcontinent by the East India

Company was transferred to the British government, which for the first time took direct responsibility for the administration of the area. This meant the replacement of an indirect rule by direct government administration. The old expansionist policy at the expense of the native administered territory was totally abandoned. No Indian state was later annexed, and Hyderabad, which was marked for an early annexation in the days of Dalhousie, escaped that fate. In religious matters the British had learned a bitter lesson, and henceforth they treated local religious sentiments with a respect that was not always visible in the first half of the nineteenth century.

In the political field a beginning was made which was to have farreaching consequences. Even before the embers of the great revolt had died out, and while martial law was yet in force, Sayyid Ahmed Khan, a sincere friend and fervent admirer of the British, whose loyalty had been tested in the great struggle itself, sat down to analyze the causes of the revolt. With his sturdy common sense and characteristic fearlessness he pointed out in a remarkable book that the basic cause of the revolt was the government's ignorance of the views of the vast population directly affected by its legislative and administrative measures. This criticism, coming from a friend, and reinfoıced by the observations of many Englishmen, led to remedial action. The Indian Councils Act of 1861 provided for the appointment of Indians to the governor-general's council for the first time. It marked the beginning of the association of the native population with the upper administrative councils of the subcontinent, an association which graduaily expanded under the pressure of public opinion, and ultimately led to the complete transfer of political control in 1947.

Seeds of Separatism

The twilight of the Mughals might seem, in view of the changes that followed, to have ended with a movement towards the progress and unity of the subcontinent. But in fact the seeds of separatism, which were to bear fruit in 1947, had already been sown. Some of the causes of this spirit of division between Muslim and Hindu can be traced to the changes taking place in the nineteenth century. The mutiny of 1857 was one answer to these changes; a more complex one was the growth of communalism. In the first half of the nineteenth century many innovations and reforms were introduced by the British. Some of these, such as the printing press, the telegraph, the railways, were the results of scientific progress in the West, which in course of time became available to other parts of the world. Other steps—the introduction of English education, suppression of sati—were the work of administrators impelled by a desire to bring about social change. The establishment of institutions of a kind unfamiliar to Indian society, such as the Asiatic Society with its work of editing and publishing the great works of both the Hindu and Muslim traditions, led to a new knowledge of the past. The role of this enterprise on the intellectual revival in the subcontinent cannot be overemphasized.

The general effect of these developments was healthy, forming a valued part of the heritage of India and Pakistan. All the new measures were not, however, so beneficial, and some of them have created stupendous problems. Even the literary and linguistic activity at Fort William College in Calcutta, which had an important share in the rise of the new Indian languages, did not prove an unmixed blessing. The bifurcation of the common spoken language of the Hindus and Muslims of northern India into two separate languages was partly the result of the attempts made at the college to create "literary" languages. Not only was the polite spoken language of northern India (Urdu-Hindustani) cultivated at that institution, but with the help of Lalluji Lal and other Sanskritists, practically a new language was created in the form of the modern Hindi. This was not the form of the language spoken by the Hindus or the evolution of any regional dialect, but a new, artificial language.

As Keay says in his History of Hindi Literature, modern Hindi, "was produced by taking Urdu and expelling from it words of Persian or Arabic origin, and substituting for them words of Sanskrit or Hindi origin." A somewhat similar process can be seen in the creation of modern Bengali. That in the eighteenth century Bengali was characterized by the presence of a large number of nonindigenous words is suggested by the comment made by Nathaniel Halhed in the preface to his Bengali grammar in 1778. "Those persons are thought to speak the compound idiom with most elegance," he wrote, "who mix the greatest number of Persian and Arabic nouns." This *do-bhashi*, or bilingual, form of Bengali fell into disrepute in the nineteenth century, and a highly Sanskritized vocabulary became the norm of excellence.

Other aspects of the language policy adopted by the East India Company had even more important consequences. In 1829 it was announced that it was "the wish and the admitted policy of the British Government to render its own language gradually and eventually the language of public business throughout the country," and in 1834, English replaced Persian in government offices. The reasons for this step can be understood, but the British claim of having given cultural consolidation to India would have had a firmer basis, if along with English an indigenous language had been given at least a secondary place throughout the country. This might have been Hindustani which, in its various forms, was understood throughout much of the subcontinent. Instead of one common language, an entire plethora of vernaculars was encouraged. Urdu, Hindi, Bengali, Gujarati, Sindhi—all seemed to get similar attention. Apart from ballads and simple verse, many of these had no literature, and the Mughals had refused to give them any official status. Now they were officially recognized. Prose works in them were systematically sponsored, and in course of time, a literature in each developed. Thus the cultural unity of the subcontinent of India became dependent on English, and the seeds of the present language problem of India and Pakistan were sown.

The British policy with regard to religious communities has also been a subject of criticism and controversy. The gradual evolution of a common legal system (outside the limited spheres of the personal law of the Hindus and the Muslims) and the impartial administration of justice on modern Western lines were perhaps the most substantial boon conferred on India by the British. In the administrative field, however, political considerations and historical factors intervened, and to many historians it has seemed that out of self-interest, the British sought to rule by dividing Hindus from Muslims. As already pointed out, the battle of Plassey was won by a combination of the officers of the East India Company and the Hindu merchant princes of Murshidabad, and for many years it seemed to be a sensible precaution to seek the support of the majority community, the Hindus, against the Muslims. This policy found a spokesman on the highest level in Lord Ellenborough, governor-general from 1842 to 1844, who wrote: "I cannot close my eyes to the belief that the [Muslim] race is fundamentally hostile to us and therefore our true policy is to conciliate the Hindus." The same idea had occurred to another British observer a few years earlier. It was desirable, he thought, that "the Hindoos should always be reminded ... that their previous rulers were as much strangers to their blood and to their religion as we are, and they were notoriously far more oppressive masters than we have ever shewn ourselves."

This same spirit was reflected in the preface to the great collection of Muslim histories made by Sir Henry Elliot, *The History of India as Told by Its Own Historians*. The intrinsic merit of the Muslim histories might be small, but, he argued, by showing Islamic rule in its true light, it would make "our native subjects more sensible of the immense advantages accruing to them under the mildness and equity of our rule." Those who "rant about patriotism and the degradation of their present position" would learn from reading the history of Islamic rule how in another time "their ridiculous fantasies would have been attended, not with silence and contempt, but with the severer discipline of molten lead and empalement." Elliot's work has been severely criticized by modern historians on the ground that the bias he displays in the preface prevented him making a selection that presents Islamic rulers in a true light. The work was more than a private scholarly enterprise: it received official support for publication, and became the source for most of the historical works produced on the Muslim period. While it would be difficult to document the effect of Elliot's work on communal relations in India, it is reasonable to suppose that the picture it gave to Indian students of Islamic India helped to strengthen the growing Muslim-Hindu antagonism of the nineteenth century.

Yet while some British policies led to a worsening of communal relations, it is only fair to note that they would not have had much effect if the soil had not been congenial. During the eighteenth and early nineteenth centuries, the relations between the Hindus and Muslims were generally peaceful, but it was because of the dominance of a third power, and not because of the integration of the two social groups. The two communities had coexisted—generally in harmony, often in friendship, occasionally in conflict—but had never coalesced. Indeed, as R. C. Majumdar, the Indian historian, has said, between Hindus and Muslims, "the social and religious differences were so acute and fundamental that they raised a Chinese wall between the two communities, and even seven hundred years of close residence (including two of common servitude) have failed to make the least crack in that solid and massive structure, far less demolish it." It was this dividing wall which led, in 1947, to the partitioning of the subcontinent.

Conclusion

Looking Back over the ten centuries of Muslim rule that we have briefly surveyed, it is possible to identify four main strands that have given Indo-Islamic culture its characteristic texture. The first of these is the Islamic religious inheritance, including those aspects specifically rooted in an Arabic tradition; the second was the Turkish origin of many of the rulers; the third was the pervasive influence of Persian culture; and finally there was the indigenous environment, both in India and in Afghanistan, into which Islam came. There has been a tendency to overlook this indigenous component, but its influence is deep-rooted and all-pervading. The predominantly non-Muslim environment in which Indo-Muslim culture developed and the heritage of an ancient civilization did not leave Islam untouched. Furthermore, the vast majority of the Muslims were either Hindu converts, which shows not only in numerous usages and practices carried over from the ancestral Hindu society, but also in unconscious reactions and mental attitudes. The vigorous Islamic revival of later centuries has tended to overshadow the indigenous element. While the Turkish rulers and aristocracy contributed much in the sphere of government, law, dress, and food, and the Persian element was prominent in literature, fine arts, mysticism, and philosophy, essentially the two basic components which gave the civilization its peculiar flavor were the Indian and the Islamic. It represents the creative efforts and reactions of a Muslim society in a predominantly non-Muslim area.

2

The Early European Settlements

Colonial India

Colonial India refers to areas of the Indian Subcontinent under the rule of European colonial powers.

The Portuguese sailor Vasco da Gama was the first European to arrive in India. Having arrived in Calicut he obtained from Samutiri Manavikraman Rajah permission to trade in the city.

Rivalry between European powers saw the entry of the Dutch, British, and French among others from the beginning of the 17th century. Following the decline of the Mughal Empire in the early 18th century, the fractured, debilitated kingdoms of the Indian subcontinent were gradually taken over by Europeans or indirectly controlled by puppet rulers. By the 19th century, the British had assumed direct and indirect control over most of India.

Overview

The Portuguese sailor Vasco da Gama was the first European to arrive in India. Having arrived in Calicut he obtained from Samutiri Manavikraman Rajah permission to trade in the city.

Pedro Álvares Cabral was commissioned in 1500 by king Manuel I of Portugal as ambassador to India and on the way to India he discovered Brazil.

The colonial era in India began in 1502, when the Portuguese established the first European trading centre at Kollam, Kerala. In 1505 the king of Portugal appoints Dom Francisco de Almeida as the first vice-Roy of India followed in 1509 by Dom Afonso de Albuquerque. In 1510 Afonso de Albuquerque established an important trading presence in Goa, by conquering the city, unitil then dominated by Muslims. Albuquerque inaugurated the policy of marrying Portuguese soldiers and sailors with local Indian girls, which had as consequence a great miscegenation in Goa and other Portuguese territories in Asia, reason why still nowadays Portuguese family names such as Silva, Sousa, Pereira, Noronha, etc. are so common in India.

Another feature of the Portuguese presence in India was the will to evangelize and promote Catholicism. In this the Jesuits played a fundamental role. Still nowadays the Jesuit Missionary Saint Francis Xavier id deeply revered among the Catholics of India.

In 1498 the Portuguese set foot in India, landing near the city of Calicut in the present-day state of Kerala in South India. The pursuit of trade and competition between European powers saw the entry of the British and French, among others, into India. After the decline of the Mughal Empire in the early 18th century, several fractured Indian kingdoms were eventually taken over by Europeans, who indirectly assumed control by subjugating rulers.

In 1661 Portugal was at war against Spain and needed support from England which led to the signing of the agreement of marriage between Princess Catherine of Portugal and Charles II of England with a most generous dowry that included the city of Bombay. This was the beginning of the British in India.

In 1757, Mir Jafar, the commander in chief of the army of the Nawab of Bengal, along with Jagat Seth, Maharaja Krishna Nath, Umi Chand and some others, secretly connived with the British, asking logistic support to overthrow the Nawab in return for trade grants. The British forces, whose sole duty until then was guarding their British East India Company property, were numerically inferior to the Bengali armed forces. At the Battle of Plassey on 23 June 1757, fought between the British under the command of Robert Clive and the Nawab, Mir Jafar's forces betrayed the Nawab and helped defeat him. Jafar was installed on the throne as a British subservient ruler. The battle transformed British perspective as they realized their strength and potential to conquer smaller Indian kingdoms, and marked the beginning of the imperial or colonial era. The British had direct or indirect control over all of present-day India by the early 19th century. In 1857, a local rebellion by an army of sepoys snowballed into the Rebellion of 1857. This resistance, although short-lived, was triggered by widespread resentment against certain discriminatory policies of the British. As a result of this, the British East India Company was abolished and India formally became a crown colony. The slow but momentous reform movement, perhaps influenced in India by contact with European ideas and institutions, developed gradually into the Indian Independence Movement. During the years of World War I, the hitherto bourgeois "home-rule" movement was transformed into a popular mass movement by Mahatma Gandhi, a pacifist. Apart from Gandhi, other revolutionaries such as Shaheed Bhagat Singh, Chandrashekar Azad and Subhash Chandra Bose, were not against use of violence to oppose the British rule. The independence movement attained its objective with the independence of Pakistan and India on 14 August and 15 August 1947 respectively.

Portuguese India

Portuguese India (Portuguese: *India Portuguesa* or *Estado da India*) was the aggregate of Portugal's colonial holdings in India.

The government started in 1505, six years after the discovery of sea route to India by Vasco da Gama, with the nomination of the first Viceroy Francisco de Almeida, then settled at Kochi. Until 1752, the name "India" included all Portuguese possessions in the Indian Ocean, from southern Africa to Southeast Asia, governed-either by a Viceroy or Governor-from its headquarters, established in Goa since 1510. In 1752 Mozambique got its own government and in 1844 the Portuguese Government of India stopped administering the territory of Macau, Solor and Timor, being then confined to Malabar.

At the time of British India's independence in 1947, Portuguese India included a number of enclaves on India's western coast, including Goa proper, as well as the coastal enclaves of Daman (Port: *Damão*) and Diu, and the enclaves of Dadra and Nagar Haveli, which lie inland from Daman. The territories of Portuguese India were sometimes referred to collectively as Goa. Portugal lost the last two enclaves in 1954, and finally the remaining three in December 1961, when they were occupied by India (although

Portugal only recognized the occupation after the Carnation Revolution in 1975).

Early History

Vasco da Gama (1498)

The first Portuguese encounter with India was on May 20, 1498 when Vasco da Gama landed in Calicut (Kozhikode) in the present-day Indian state of Kerala. Over the objections of Arab merchants, Gama secured an ambiguous letter of concession for trading rights from the Zamorin, Calicut's local ruler, but had to sail off without warning after the Zamorin insisted on his leaving behind all his goods as collateral. Gama kept his goods, but left behind a few Portuguese with orders to start a trading post.

Pedro Álvares Cabral (1500-01)

Pedro Álvares Cabral (ca. 1468 – ca. 1520; Portuguese pronunciation: (European) or (Brazilian)) was a Portuguese navigator and explorer. Cabral is generally regarded as the European discoverer of Brazil.

Early Life

Cabral is believed to have been born in Belmonte, in Portugal's Beira Baixa province. He was the third son of Fernão Cabral (c. 1427-c. 1492), the governor of Beira and Belmonte, and his wife Isabel de Gouveia de Queirós (c. 1433-c. 1483, a descendant of the first King of Portugal, Afonso I), and husband of Isabel de Castro, daughter of Fernão de Noronha (also descendant of King Afonso I). Cabral presumably had training in navigation and experience as a seaman, since King Manuel I of Portugal chose him to continue the work of Vasco da Gama.

Voyage

Cabral's task was to establish permanent commercial relations and to introduce Roman Catholicism wherever he went, using force of arms if necessary. Rich Florentine merchants contributed to equipping the ships, and priests volunteered to join the expedition. Among the captains of the fleet, which consisted of 13 ships and 1,500 men, were Bartolomeu Dias, Pêro Vaz de Caminha, Sancho de Tovar and Nicolau Coelho, who was the companion of Vasco da Gama. Vasco da Gama himself gave the directions necessary for the course of the voyage.

The fleet of thirteen ships left Lisbon on 9 March 1500, and following the course laid down, sought to avoid the calms off the coast of Gulf of Guinea. On leaving the Cape Verde Islands, where Luís Pires was forced by a storm to return to Lisbon, they sailed in a decidedly southwesterly direction. On 21 April a mountain was visible, to which the name of *Monte Pascoal* was given; on 22 April Cabral landed on the coast of Brazil, and on 25 April the entire fleet sailed into the harbor called *Porto Seguro*.

Cabral perceived that the new land lay east of the line of demarcation made by Pope Alexander VI, and at once sent Andre Gonçalves (according to other authorities Gaspar de Lemos) to Portugal with the important tidings. Believing the newly-discovered land to be an island he gave it the name of Island of the True Cross (or Island of Vera Cruz) and took possession of it by erecting a cross and holding a religious service. The service was celebrated by the Franciscan, Father Henrique de Coimbra, afterwards Bishop of Ceuta. The iron cross used in that service is now in Cathedral Treasure in Braga. It was taken back to Brazil for the inauguration of Brasilia in 1960.

Pedro Cabral resumed his voyage on 3 May 1500. By the end of the month the fleet approached the Cape of Good Hope, where it was struck by a storm in which four vessels, including that of Bartolomeu Dias, were lost. With the ships now reduced to one-half of the original number, Cabral reached Sofala on 16 July and Mozambique on 20 July.

In the latter place he received a cordial greeting. On 26 July he came to Kilwa where he was unable to make an agreement with the ruler. On 2 August, he reached Melinde; here he had a friendly welcome and obtained a pilot to take him to India. On 10 August, the ship commanded by Diogo Dias, separated by weather, discovered an island they named after St. Lawrence, later known as Madagascar.

Cabral continued to India to trade for pepper and other spices, establishing a factory at Calicut, where he arrived on 13 September 1500. In Cochin and Cannanore Cabral succeeded in making advantageous treaties. After a chain of bad luck, culminating in a two-day bombardment of the city, Cabral started on the return voyage on 16 January 1501. He arrived in Portugal with only 4 of 13 ships on 23 June 1501.

Legacy

Cabral died, largely forgotten, around 1520 and was buried in a monastery in Santarem, Portugal.

He has been honoured on a number of postage stamps, including one in a set of Brazilian stamps issued 1 January 1900 to mark the 400th anniversary of the discovery.

In Brazil, he is depicted on the 1 cent coin, and also on a special edition of the R$10 note.

Francisco De Almeida (1505-09)

Dom Francisco de Almeida, also known as "the Great Dom Francisco" (born c. 1450 in Lisbon; died March 1, 1510 at Table Bay, Cape of Good Hope), was a Portuguese nobleman, soldier and explorer. He distinguished himself as a counsellor to King John II of Portugal and later in the wars against the Moors and in the conquest of Granada in 1492. In 1503 he was appointed as the first governor and viceroy of the Portuguese State of India (*Estado da India*). Almeida is credited with establishing Portuguese hegemony in the Indian Ocean, with his victory at the naval Battle of Diu in 1509. Before Almeida or his son could return to Portugal, they lost their lives in surprise attacks in 1510 and 1508 respectively.

Exploits as Soldier

As was customary for men in his social circle, he joined the military at a young age. In 1476 he took part in the Battle of Toro. He then fought in conflicts in different parts of Morocco and in 1492 participated in the Christian conquest of Granada on the side of the Castilians.

Mission to the East

In 1503 King Manuel I of Portugal appointed Almeida, then in his mid 50s, as the first viceroy of Portuguese India (*Estado da India*). With an armada of 22 ships, including 14 carracks and 6 caravels, Almeida departed from Lisbon on March 25, 1505. The armada carried a crew of 1,000 and 1,500 soldiers. The flagship was the carrack São Rafael captained by Fernão Soares. The mission's primary aims were to bring the spice trade under Portuguese control, to construct forts along the east African and Indian coasts, to further Portuguese spice trade through alliances with local chieftains, besides constructing trading posts.

African Conquest

Almeida rounded the Cape of Good Hope and entered African coastal waters again at Sofala and the Island of Mozambique, whence they proceeded northwards to the coastal settlement of Kilwa. In July 1505 they employed 8 ships to conquer the ca 4,000 strong population of this harbour town. Because of the good harbour that the town provided, sufficient for anchoring ships up to 500 tons, the Portuguese decided to build a fort here. For this purpose Pêro Ferreira and a crew of 80 soldiers remained in the town.

In August 1505 the Portuguese arrived at Mombasa, a coastal port further north. The city with a population of about 10,000 was conquered in heavy combat against the troops of the local Arab sheik. The city was plundered and torched. The Portuguese were assisted in this attack by a Mombasa enemy, the Sultan of Melinde. The same month a caravel of Almeida's fleet captained by John (*João*) Homere captured Zanzibar island and claimed it for Portugal.

Viceroy in India

On 25 March 1505, Francisco de Almeida was appointed *Viceroy of India,* on the condition that he would set up four forts on the southwestern Indian coast: at Anjediva Island, Cannanore, Cochin and Quilon. Francisco de Almeida left Portugal with a fleet of 22 vessels with 1,500 men.

On 13 September, Francisco de Almeida reached Anjadip Island, where he immediately started the construction of Fort Anjediva. On 23 October, he started, with the permission of the friendly ruler Kôlattiri, the building of St. Angelo Fort in Cannanore, leaving Lorenzo de Brito in charge with 150 men and two ships.

Francisco de Almeida then reached Cochin in 31 October 1505, with only 8 vessels left. There he learnt that the Portuguese traders at Quilon had been killed. He decided to send his son Lorenzo with 6 ships, who destroyed 27 Calicut vessels in the harbour of Quilon. Almeida took up residence in Cochin. He strengthened the Portuguese fortifications of Fort Manuel on Cochin.

The Samorin of Calicut prepared a large fleet of 200 ships to oppose the Portuguese, but in March 1506 his son Lourenço de Almeida was victorious in a sea battle at the entrance to the harbour of Cannanore, the Battle of Cannanore (1506), an important setback for the fleet of the zamorin. Hereupon Lourenço de Almeida explored the coastal waters southwards to Colombo, modern Sri Lanka. In Cannanore however, a new ruler, hostile to the Portuguese and friendly with the samorin, attacked the Portuguese garrison, leading to the Siege of Cannanore (1507).

In 1507 Almeida's mission was strengthened by the arrival of Tristão da Cunha's squadron. Afonso de Albuquerque's squadron had however split from that of Cunha off east Africa and was independently conquering territories to the west.

In March 1508 a Portuguese squadron under command of Lourenço de Almeida was attacked by a combined Mameluk Egyptian and Gujarat Sultanate fleet at Chaul and Dabul respectively, lead by admirals Mirocem and Meliqueaz in the Battle of Chaul. Lourenço de Almeida lost his life after a fierce fight in this battle. Afonso de Albuquerque arrived at Cannanore at the close of 1508 and immediately made known an hitherto secret commission he had received from the King empowering him as governor to supersede Almeida at his term as viceroy. Almeida, determined to avenge the death of his son and free the Portuguese prisionners made at Chaul, refused to recognize Albuquerque's credentials immediately, and later arrested him.

In 1509, Almeida become the first Portuguese to set sail in Bombay. He sought Meliqueaz, to whom he had written a menacing letter, and the Mameluk Mirocem, fiercely investing at the naval Battle of Diu on February 3, 1509 commanding a fleet of 23 ships near the port of Diu. He inflicted a decisive defeat on a joint fleet from the Mamluk Burji Sultanate of Egypt, the Ottoman Empire, the Zamorin of Calicut and the Sultan of Gujarat, with technical naval support from the Republic of Venice and the Republic of Ragusa (Dubrovnik), that feared for its eastern trade links.

His victory was decisive: the Ottomans and Egyptians left the Indian Ocean, easing the Portuguese rule for over 100 years, into the 17th century when it was ended by the Dutch and English. Albuquerque was released after three months' confinement, on the arrival of the grand-marshal of Portugal with a large fleet, in November 1509.

Return and Death

Almeida sailed for Portugal in December 1509 and reached Table Bay near the Cape of Good Hope, where the Garcia, Belem and Santa Cruz dropped anchor late February, 1510, to replenish water. After friendly trade with the Khoikhoi some of the crew visited their nearby village where a dispute ensued. Almeida allowed his captains Pedro and Jorge Barreto to return to the village on the morning of March 1, 1510. The village's cattle herd was raided with the loss of one man, while Almeida awaited his men some distance from the beach. As the flagship's master Diogo d'Unhos moved the landing boats to the watering point, the Portuguese were left without a retreat. The Khoikhoi sensed the opportunity for an attack, during which Almeida and 64 of his men perished, including 11 of his captains. Almeida's body was recovered the same afternoon and buried on the shorefront of the current Cape Town.

Relatives and Subjects

Almeida was the son of the 1st Count of Abrantes and one of a number of highly distinguished siblings including two bishops, an ambassador to the Holy See and the Portuguese head of the Order of Malta. His son, Lourenço, was killed in battle, but he was survived by a daughter, Leonor, who married Rodrigo de Melo, Count of Tentugal, precursors of the Dukes of Cadaval.

There is also a community of Goan Christians, both in India and Pakistan, who carry the surname *Almeida* and are apparently his descendants through marriages/liaisons with native Indian women.

Ferdinand Magellan (*Fernão de Magalhães*) accompanied Almeida to the east, but was promoted to captain and only returned in 1512 after losing that commission.

Afonso De Albuquerque (1509-1515)

Afonso de Albuquerque was a Portuguese *fidalgo*, or nobleman, a naval general officer whose military and administrative activities as second governor of Portuguese India conquered and established the Portuguese colonial empire in the Indian ocean. He is generally considered a world conquest military genius, given his successful strategy: he attempted to close all the Indian ocean naval passages to the Atlantic, Red Sea, Persian Gulf, and to the Pacific, transforming it into a Portuguese *mare clausum* established over the Turkish power and their Muslim and Hindu allies. He was responsible for building numerous fortresses to defend key points that he was taking and established a net of diplomatic relations. Shortly before his death he was awarded viceroy and "Duke of Goa" by king Manuel I of Portugal, being the first Portuguese duke not from the royal family, and the first Portuguese title landed overseas. For some time he was known as *The Tirribil, The Great, The Caesar of the East, Lion of the Seas* and as *The Portuguese Mars*.

Early Life

Afonso de Albuquerque was born in 1453 in Alhandra, near Lisbon. He was the son of Gonçalo de Albuquerque, Lord of Vila Verde dos Francos and Dona Leonor de Menezes. Through his father, who held an important position at court, he was connected by remote illegitimate descent with the Portuguese royal family. He was educated in mathematics and Latin at the court of Afonso V of Portugal and served ten years in North Africa, where he acquired military experience. He was present the conquest of Arzila and Tangier in Morocco in 1471. On his return, he was appointed chief equerry (*estribeiro-mor*) to John II, whom in 1476 he accompanied in wars against Castile, like the Battle of Toro. He participated in the squadron sent in 1480 to rescue Ferdinand II of Aragon against the Turkish invasion of Italy that culminated in a Christian victory in 1481. In 1489 he returned to service in North Africa, in a expedition to defend the fortress of Graciosa, an island in the river Luco near the city of Larache. In 1490 was part of the guard of king John II, returning to Arzila in 1495.

First Expeditions to the East, 1503-1506

On April 6 of 1503, Afonso de Albuquerque set off on his first expedition to India with his cousin Francisco de Albuquerque, each commanding four ships, sailing along with Duarte Pacheco Pereira and Nicolau Coelho. They participated in several battles, having succeeded in establishing the king of Kochi securely on his throne, obtaining in return for this service a permission to build a Portuguese fort at Cochin, and establishing trade relations with Quilon, helping thus lay the foundation of his country's empire in the East.

Persian Gulf mission, 1506-1508

Albuquerque returned home in July 1504, and was well received by King Manuel I of Portugal who, after his participation in the design of a strategy for the Portuguese efforts in the east, entrusted him with the command of a squadron of five vessels in the fleet of sixteen sailing for India in early 1506 under Tristão da Cunha. He went as master chief of the "Coast of Arabia" sailing with Tristão da Cunha to reach Mozambique, to conquest Socotra and build a fortress there, hoping to close the trade in the Red Sea. He carried a secret mission ordered by the king: after fulfilling the first mission he should replace the Viceroy Francisco de Almeida, whose term ended two years later.

In Mozambique Channel they found captain João da Nova stranded while returning from India. They rescued him and the ship Frol de la mar, joining both to the fleet. After a series of successful attacks on Arab cities on east Africa coasts, they headed to Socotra island, hoping that it would be a base to stop the Red Sea commerce to the Indian sea. They occupied Suq, where they started a fortress. There their ways parted, Albuquerque sailing with a fleet of seven ships and five hundred men towards Ormuz in the Persian Gulf, one of the chief centres of commerce in the East. On this route they conquered the cities of Curiati (Kuryat), Muscat in July 1507 and Khor Fakkan, accepting the submission of the cities of Kalhat and Sohar. On September 25 they arrived at Ormuz and soon captured the city. Immediately Albuquerque began building the Fort of Our Lady of Victory later renamed Fort of Our Lady of the Conception. However, some of his officers revolted against the heavy works and climate, leaving for India. With the fleet reduced to only two ships and without supplies he was unable to maintain this position for long. Forced to abandon Ormuz in January 1508, he raided coastal villages to resupply the settlement of Socotra, returned to Ormuz and only then headed to India.

Arrested at Cannanore

Albuquerque arrived at Cannanore on the Malabar coast in December 1508, where he immediately revealed to the viceroy Dom Francisco de Almeida the secret commission he had received from the king, appointing him governor. The viceroy, then joined by the officers who had defeated Albuquerque in Ormuz, had a matching royal order, but refused to hand government, protesting that his term ended only in January and stating his intention to avenge his son's death by fighting in Diu, refusing Albuquerque's offer to fight it himself. Afonso de Albuquerque obeyed without confronting D. Francisco de Almeida-which could have lead to civil war-and moved to Kochi, pending on indications from the kingdom, supporting and housing his entourage himself. He was described by Fernão Lopes de Castanheda as patiently enduring an open opposition from the group that had gathered around D. Francisco de Almeida, with whom he kept formal contacts. Increasingly ostracized, he wrote to Diogo Lopes de Sequeira, who was arriving with a new fleet to India, but was ignored and Sequeira joined the Viceroy. At the same time Albuquerque refused approaches from opponents of the viceroy, who challenged him to take power.

On February 3, 1509 Almeida fought the naval Battle of Diu commanding a fleet of 23 ships against a joint fleet of Arabs, Mamluk Egyptians and Indian allies, taking it as personal revenge for the death of his son Lourenço de Almeida at the Battle of Chaul. His victory was decisive: Ottomans and Egyptians left the waters of the Indian Ocean, easing the Portuguese rule for over 100 years.

In August a petition from Albuquerque's former officers with the support of Diogo Lopes de Sequeira considered him unfit for governance, and he was sent in custody to St. Angelo Fort in Cannanore. There he remained isolated. In September 1509 Sequeira advanced the mission of establishing contact with the Sultan of Malacca but failed, leaving behind 19 Portuguese prisoners.

Governor of Portuguese India, 1509-1515

Albuquerque was released after three months' confinement in Cannanore, on the arrival of the grand-marshal of Portugal with a large fleet. He was the most important Portuguese noble ever to visit India and he brought an armada of fifteen ships and 3,000 men sent by the king to defend the rights of Albuquerque and take Calicut..

In October 1509 Albuquerque became the second Governor of the *State of India*, a position he would hold until his death. Almeida having returned home in 1510, he speedily showed the energy and determination of his character.

Albuquerque intended to dominate the Muslim world and control the spices' trading network. Initially king Manuel I and his council in Lisbon tried to distribute the power, creating three areas of jurisdiction in the Indian Ocean : in 1509 the nobleman Diogo Lopes de Sequeira was fitted with a fleet and sent to Southeast Asia, with the task of seeking an agreement with Sultan Mahmud Shah of Malacca, but failed and went back to the kingdom. To Jorge de Aguiar was given the area between the Cape of Good Hope and Gujarat, he was succeeded by Duarte de Lemos but left to Cochin and then for the kingdom, leaving his fleet to Albuquerque.

Conquest of Goa, 1510

In January 1510, fulfilling the orders from the kingdom, and knowing of the absence of Zamorin, Albuquerque advanced to Calicut (now Kozhikode). But he had to retreat after the Marshall D. Fernando Coutinho, against his warnings, ventured in the inner city fascinated by its richness, and suffered an ambush. To help him, Afonso de Albuquerque received a severe wound and had to retreat.

Soon after the failed attack on Calicut, Albuquerque hastened to form a powerful fleet of twenty-three ships and 1200 men. Contemporary reports state that he wanted to fight the egipcian Mamluk Sultanate fleet in the Red Sea or return to Hormuz. However, he had been reported by Timoji (a privateer in the service of the Hindu Vijayanagara Empire) that it would be easier to fight them in Goa, where they had sheltered after the Battle of Diu, and also of the illness of the Sultan Yusuf Adil Shah and war between the Deccan sultanates. So he invested by surprise in the capture of Goa to the Sultanate of Bijapur. He thus completed another mission, for Portugal wanted not to be seen as an eternal "guest" of Kochi and had been coveting Goa as the best trading port in the region.

A first assault took place in Goa from March 4 to May 20, 1510. After a first occupation, feeling unable to handle the city-given the poor condition of its fortifications, the cooling of Hindu population support and insubordination among his rank, after a severe attack of Ismail Adil Shah-Afonso de Albuquerque refused an agreement peace by the sultan and abandoned the city in August. His fleet was shattered and a palace revolt in Kochi hindered his recovery, so he headed to Fort Anjediva. When new ships arrived from the kingdom they were intended to Malacca, for nobleman Diogo Mendes de Vasconcelos, who had been given a rival command of the region. Only three months later, on November 25, Albuquerque reappeared in Goa with a fleet fully renovated, Diogo Mendes de Vasconcelos vexed by his side with the reinforcements of Malacca and about 300 Malabari reinforcements from Cannanore. In less than a day they took possession of Goa from Ismail Adil Shah and his Ottoman allies, who surrendered on 10 December. It is estimated that 6000 of the 9000 Muslim defenders of the city died, either on the fierce battle in the streets or drowned while trying to escape. Albuquerque regained the support of the Hindu population, although frustrating the initial expectations of Timoja, who aspired to become governor. Afonso de Albuquerque rewarded him by appointing him chief "Aguazil" of the city, an administrator and representative of the Hindu and Muslim people, as a knowing interpreter of the local customs. He then made an agreement to lower yearly dues.

In Goa Albuquerque started the first Portuguese mint in the East, after complaints from merchants and Timoja about the scarcity of currency, taking it as an opportunity to announce the territorial conquest. The new coin, based on the existing local coins, showed a cross on one side and the design of an armillary sphere (or "espera"), king Manuel's badge, on the other. Gold, silver and bronze coins were issued, respectively gold cruzados or *manueis, esperas* and *alf-esperas*, and "leais". More mints would follow in Malacca in 1511.

In spite of constant attacks, Goa became the centre of Portuguese India, with the conquest triggering the compliance of neighbouring kingdoms: the Sultan of Gujarat and the Zamorin of Calicut sent embassies, offering alliances and local grants to fortify.

Conquest of Malacca 1511-1512

In February 1511, through a friendly Javanese merchant called Ninchatu, Albuquerque received a letter from Rui de Araújo, one of the nineteen Portuguese arrested at Malacca since 1509. It urged moving forward with the largest possible fleet to demand their liberation, and gave details about the procedures. Albuquerque showed it to Diogo Mendes de Vasconcelos, as an argument to advance in a joint fleet. In April 1511, after fortifying Goa, he gathered a force of about 900 Portuguese, 200 Hindu mercenaries and about eighteen ships. He then set sail from Goa to Malacca, against the orders of the kingdom and under the protest of Diogo Mendes, who claimed the command of the expedition. Under his orders was Fernão de Magalhães, who had participated in the failed embassy of Diogo Lopes de Sequeira in 1509.

After a false start towards the Red Sea, they sailed to the Strait of Malacca. It was the richest city that the Portuguese tried to take, and the most important east point in the trade network where Malay traders met Gujarati, Chinese, Japanese, Javanese, Bengali, Persian and Arabic, among others, described by Tome Pires as of invaluable richness. Despite its wealth, it was mostly a wooden built city, with few masonry buildings. On the other hand it was defended by a powerful army of mercenaries and artillery, estimated at 20,000 men and more than 2000 pieces. Its greatest weakness being the unpopularity of the government of Sultan Mahmud Shah, who favoured Muslims producing dissatisfaction within other merchants.

Albuquerque made a bold approach to the city, his ships decorated with banners, firing cannon volleys. He declared himself lord of all the navigation, demanding the Sultan to release the prisoners, pay for the damage, and asking to build a fortified trading post. The Sultan eventually freed the prisoners, but wasn't impressed by the small Portuguese contingent. Albuquerque then burned some ships at the port and four coastal buildings, to test the response. The city being divided by the Malacca River, and connected by a bridge seen as a strategic point, on 25 July at dawn the Portuguese landed and fought in tough battle, facing poisoned arrows, taking the bridge in the evening. After waiting for the reaction of the sultan, they returned to the ships. As the sultan did not respond, they prepared a junk offered by Chinese merchants, filling it with men, artillery, sandbags. Commanded by António de Abreu it sailed the river at high tide onto the bridge, with success: the day after all had landed. Fighting fiercely, they broke down the barricades built in the meantime. Suddenly, the Sultan appeared, leading his army of war elephants to crush the invaders. Despite the surprise, one of the Portuguese, Fernão Gomes de Lemos, approached and spurred an animal with a spear, making him stand up and back. Other Portuguese emulated him and the front of elephants retreated in panic, overthrowing the army, and the sultan himself, wreaking havoc and dispersing it.. During a week Albuquerque rested his men and waited for the reaction of the Sultan. Merchants approached, asking for Portuguese protection. They were given flags to mark their premises, a sign that they would not be looted. On 24 August the Portuguese attacked again, but the Sultan had fled the city. Under firm orders they looted the city, respecting the flags, which still was a fabulous drawing.

Albuquerque remained in Malacca preparing its defences against any Malay counterattack, immediately building a fortress, distributing his men in shifts and using stones from the mosque and the cemetery. Despite the delays caused by heat and malaria, it was completed in November 1511, its surviving door known as "A Famosa" (the famous). He settled the Portuguese administration, re-appointing Rui de Araújo as factor, a post assigned previous to the 1509 arrest, and arresting and executing mercilessly a powerful Javanese merchant, Utimuta Raja, who maintained contacts with the exiled royal family.

Expeditions to the Kingdom of Siam and Moluccas

Most Muslim merchants having fled the city, at the same time Albuquerque invested in diplomatic efforts demonstrating a wide generosity with the merchants in Southeast Asia, like the Chinese, hoping that they echoed the good relations with the Portuguese. Trade and diplomatic missions were sent to continental kingdoms, like Sumatra, the Sumatran kings of Kampar and Indragiri sending emissaries to Albuquerque accepting the new power, as vassal states of Malacca. Knowing of Siamese ambitions over Malacca, Albuquerque immediately sent Duarte Fernandes in a diplomatic mission to the Kingdom of Siam (Thailand), travelling in a Chinese junk returning home. He was one of the former Portuguese arrested in Malacca, having gathered knowledge about the culture of the region. There he was the first European to arrive, establishing amicable relations between the kingdom of Portugal and the court of the King of Siam Ramathibodi II, returning with a Siamese envoy with gifts and letters to Albuquerque and the king of Portugal.

In November, after having secured Malacca and learning the location of the then secret "spice islands", Albuquerque sent an expedition of three ships sailing east to find them, led by trusted António de Abreu with the deputy commander Francisco Serrão. Malay pilots were recruited to guide them through Java, the Lesser

Sunda Islands and the Ambon Island to Banda Islands, where they arrived in early 1512. There they remained for about a month, buying and filling their ships with nutmeg and cloves. António de Abreu then sailed to Amboina whilst Serrão stepped forward to the Moluccas but was shipwrecked near Seram. Sultan Abu Lais of Ternate heard of their stranding, and, seeing a chance to ally himself with a powerful foreign nation, brought them to Ternate in 1512 were they were permitted to build a fort on the island, Fort São João Baptista de Ternate, built in 1522.

Shipwreck on the Flor De La Mar

In 1512 Albuquerque sailed from Malacca to the coast of Malabar on board of the old *Frol de la mar* carrack that had served to support the conquest of Malacca. Despite already being deemed unsafe, Afonso de Albuquerque used her to transport the treasure amassed in the conquest, given her large capacity : he wanted to give the court of King Manuel I a show of Malaccan treasures. There were also the offers from the Kingdom of Siam (Thailand) to the king of Portugal and all his own fortune. On the voyage a storm arose and the *Flor De La Mar* was wrecked, and he himself barely escaped with his life. In September of the same year he arrived at Goa, where he quickly suppressed a serious revolt headed by Hidalcão, and took such measures for the security and peace of the town that it became the most flourishing of the Portuguese settlements in India.

China Expeditions, 1513

In early 1513, Jorge Álvares— sailing in a mission under Albuquerque — was allowed to land at Lintin Island in the Pearl River Delta of southern China, and soon after Albuquerque sent Rafael Perestrello to southern China to seek out trade relations with the Ming Dynasty of China. In ships from Portuguese Malacca, Rafael sailed to Canton (Guangzhou) in 1513 and again from 1515–1516 to trade with Chinese merchants there. These ventures, along with those of Tome Pires and Fernão Pires de Andrade, were the first direct European diplomatic and commercial ties to China.

Return to the Red Sea and Ormuz 1513-1515

Albuquerque was, from the start, under orders from the kingdom to undertake an expedition to the Red Sea, in order to secure that channel of communication exclusively to Portugal. He accordingly laid siege to Aden in 1513, but was repulsed; and a voyage into the Red Sea, the first ever made by a European fleet, led to no substantial results. In order to destroy the power of Egypt, he is said to have entertained the idea of diverting the course of the Nile River and so rendering the whole country barren.

His last warlike undertaking was a second attack upon Ormuz in 1515. The island in the Persian Gulf yielded to him without resistance, and it remained in the possession of the Portuguese until 1622. Perhaps most tellingly, he intended to steal the body of the Prophet Muhammad, and hold it for ransom until all Muslims had left the Holy Land.

Last Years and Political Downfall

In 1514 Afonso de Albuquerque was devoted to the administration and diplomacy in Goa, concluding peace with Calicut and receiving embassies from Indian governors, strengthening the city and stimulating the marriage of Portuguese with Indians. At that time, Portuguese women were barred from travelling overseas due to superstition about women on ships, as well as the substantial danger of the sea route. In 1511, the Portuguese government encouraged their explorers to marry local women, under a policy set by Albuquerque. To promote settlement, the King of Portugal granted freeman status and exemption from Crown taxes to Portuguese men (known as *casados*, or "married men") who ventured overseas and married local women. With Albuquerque's encouragement, mixed marriages flourished.

In March 1514 King Manuel I of Portugal had sent to Pope Leo X a huge and exotic embassy led by Tristão da Cunha, who toured the streets of Rome in a extravagant procession of animals from the colonies and wealth from the Indies that struck Europe. His reputation reached its peak, creating the foundation of the Portuguese Empire in the East.

Dürer's Rhinoceros, woodcut, 1515.

In early 1514, Afonso de Albuquerque had sent ambassadors to Sultan Muzafar II, ruler of Cambay, to seek permission to build a fort on Diu. The mission returned without an agreement, but diplomatic gifts were exchanged, including a Indian rhinoceros. Albuquerque forward the gift, named *ganda*, and its Indian keeper, Ocem, to King Manuel I. In late 1515, the king sent it as a gift for

Pope Leo X, but it died in a shipwreck off the coast of Italy in early 1516. German painter Albrecht Dürer, based on a written description and brief sketch by an unknown artist, created then is famous Dürer's Rhinoceros in 1515. Dürer never saw the actual rhinoceros, which was the first living example seen in Europe since Roman times.

Political Downfall

Albuquerque's career had a painful and ignominious close. He had several enemies at the Portuguese court who lost no opportunity of stirring up the jealousy of King Manuel against him, insinuating that he intended to strike power in Portuguese India, and his own injudicious and arbitrary conduct on several occasions served their end only too well. On his return from Ormuz, at the entrance of the harbour of Goa, he met a vessel from Europe bearing dispatches announcing that he was superseded by his personal enemy Lopo Soares de Albergaria. The blow was too much for him and he died at sea on December 16, 1515.

Before his death he wrote a letter to the king in dignified and affecting terms, vindicating his conduct and claiming for his son the honours and rewards that were justly due to himself.

His body was buried in Goa according to his will, in the Church of Nossa Senhora da Serra (Our Lady of the Hill), built in 1513 thanking for his escape from a shipwreck off Kamaran island, in the Red Sea.. After 51 years, in 1566, he was moved to Nossa Senhora da Graça church in Lisbon, which was ruined and rebuilt after the 1755 earthquake. The king of Portugal was convinced too late of his fidelity, and endeavoured to atone for the ingratitude with which he had treated him by heaping honours upon his natural son Brás de Albuquerque (1500—1580). In 1572 Albuquerque's feats were inscribed in *The Lusiads,* the Portuguese main epic poem by Luís Vaz de Camões (Canto X, strophe 40 to 49). In 1576, Brás de Albuuqerque published a selection from his father's papers, which had been gathered in 1557, under the title *Commentarios do Grande Affonso d'Alboquerque.*

An exquisite and expensive variety of mango, that he used to bring on his journeys to India, has been named in his honour, and is today sold throughout the world as Alphonso mangoes.

Despite his fame, the city of Albuquerque in New Mexico is not named after him. It was named after a Spanish Viceroy of

Mexico named Don Francisco Fernández de la Cueva, who also held the title Duke of Alburquerque. There is, however, a town near the Spanish-Portuguese border named Alburquerque which may be the root of both names.

Portuguese in Kerala-1498 to 1660 Though the Portuguese were in Goa from 1530 till 1960, the Portuguese under Vasco da Gama first came to Calicut in 1498 and then shifted their base to Kochi and Kollam, where they ruled (or influenced the rule) and had their major presence for nearly 160 years changing the course of history in regard to politics, religion and trade in Kerala. From their base in Northern Kerala, they were able to defeat the Bijapur sultan. They finally shifted their capital to Goa in 1530.

In the 15th century, the Portuguese meddled in the church affairs of the Syrian Christians. The Udayamperoor Synod (1599) was the major attempt by the Portuguese Archbishop Menezes to latinize the syrian rite. Later in 1653, the Koonan Kurisu Sathyam (Coonan Cross Oath) led to the division of the local church into syrian catholics and syrian christians (jacobites).

The Dutch finally defeated the Portuguese in Kerala in the 1660 and pushed the Portuguese towards Goa,and the Daman, Diu colonies. Dutch influence in Kerala (Cochin and Kollam and Travancore) continued till 1741 when they were defeated by the Travancore King with the help of the British in the Battle of Colachel.

Portuguese on the Coromandel Coast. The Portuguese built the Pulicat fort in 1502, with the help of the Vijayanagar King. There were Portuguese settlements in and around Mylapore. The Luz Church in Mylapore, Madras (Chennai) was the first church that the Portuguese built in Madras in 1516. Later in 1522, the São Tome church was built on the grave of Saint Thomas.

Thus there are Portuguese footprints all over the western and eastern coasts of India, though Goa became the capital of Portuguese Goa from 1530 onwards until the liberation of Goa and its merger with the Indian Union in 1961.

After India's Independence

After India's independence from the British in 1947, Portugal refused to accede to India's request to relinquish control of its Indian possessions. On 24 July 1954 an organisation called "The United Front of Goans" took control of the enclave of Dadra. The remaining territory of Nagar Haveli was liberated by the Azad Gomantak Dal on 2 August 1954. The decision given by the International Court of Justice at The Hague, regarding access to Dadra and Nagar Haveli, was an impasse.

From 1954, peaceful Satyagrahis attempts from outside Goa at forcing the Portuguese to leave Goa were brutally suppressed. Many revolts were quelled by the use of force and leaders eliminated or jailed. As a result, India closed its consulate (which had operated in Panjim since 1947) and imposed an economic embargo against the territories of Portuguese Goa. The Indian Government adopted a "wait and watch" attitude from 1955 to 1961 with numerous representations to the Portuguese Salazar regime and attempts to highlight the issue before the international community.

Eventually, in December 1961, India militarily invaded Goa, Daman and Diu, where they were faced with insufficient Portuguese resistance. Portuguese armed forces had been instructed to either defeat the invaders or die. Only meager resistance was offered due to the Portuguese army's poor firepower and size (only 3,300 men), against a fully-armed Indian force of over 30,000 with full air and naval support.. The Governor of Portuguese India signed the Instrument of Surrender on 19 December 1961. The territories were annexed by India.

Portuguese and other European settlements in India.

Post-Annexation

Status of the New Territories

Dadra and Nagar Haveli existed as a de-facto independent entity from its liberation in 1954 until its merger with the Republic of India in 1961.

Following the annexation of Goa, Daman and Diu, the new territories became Union Territories within the Indian Union, now separately as Dadra and Nagar Haveli and Goa, Daman and Diu. Maj. Gen. K. P. Candeth was declared as military governor of Goa, Daman and Diu. Goa's first general elections were held in 1963.

In 1967 a referendum was conducted where voters decided whether to merge Goa into the neighbouring state of Maharashtra. The anti-merger faction won, but full statehood was not conferred immediately. On 30 May 1987 Goa became the 25th state of the

Indian Union. Daman and Diu was separated from Goa and continues to be administered as a Union territory.

The most drastic changes in Portuguese India after 1961 were the introduction of democratic elections, as well as the replacement of Portuguese with English as the general language of government and education. However the Indians allowed certain Portuguese institutions to continue unchanged. Amongst these were the land ownership system of the communidade where land was held by the community and was then leased out to individuals. The Indians left the Portuguese civil code unchanged in Goa, with the result that Goa today remains the only state in India with a common civil code that does not depend on religion.

Citizenship

The Citizenship Act of 1955 granted the government of India the authority to define citizenship in the Indian union. In exercise of its powers, the government passed the *Goa, Daman and Diu (Citizenship) Order, 1962* on 28 March 1962 conferring Indian citizenship on all persons born on or before 20 December 1961 in Goa, Daman and Diu.

Indo-Portuguese Relations

The Salazar regime in Portugal refused to recognize Indian sovereignty over the annexed territories, which continued to be represented in Portugal's National Assembly until 1974. Following the Carnation Revolution that year, the new government in Lisbon restored diplomatic relations with India, and recognized Indian sovereignty over Goa, Daman and Diu. Portugal continued to give the citizens of Portuguese India automatic citizenship. However, since 2006, this has been restricted to those born during Portuguese rule.

Postage Stamps and Postal History

Early postal history of the colony is obscure, but regular mail is known to have been exchanged with Lisbon from 1825 on. Portugal had a postal convention with Great Britain, so much mail was probably routed through Bombay and carried on British packets. Portuguese postmarks are known from 1854, when a post office was opened in Goa. An extraterritorial British post office in Damaun was open between 1854 and November, 1883. British Indian postage stamps were also available at the Portuguese post office at Goa from 1854 until 1877. A Portuguese post office opened at Diu in 1880.

The first postage stamps of Portuguese India were issued 1 October 1871 for local use. The design simply consisted of a denomination in the centre, with an oval band containing the inscriptions "SERVIÇO POSTAL" and "INDIA POST". In 1877, Portugal included India in its standard "crown" issue and from 1886 on, the pattern of regular stamp issues followed closely that of the other Portuguese colonies, the main exception being a series of surcharges in 1912 produced by perforating existing stamps vertically through the middle and overprinting a new value on each side.

The last regular issue was on 25 June 1960, for the 500th anniversary of the death of Prince Henry the Navigator. Stamps of India were first used 29 December 1961, although the old stamps were accepted until 5 January 1962. Portugal continued to issue stamps for the lost colony but none were offered for sale in the colony's post offices, and are thus not considered valid stamps.

Dual franking was tolerated from December 22nd 1961 until January 4th 1962. Colonial (Portuguese) postmarks were tolerated until May of 1962. Portuguese India stamps were available for sale up to December 28th, thus the period up to January 4th was an attempt to use up stocks in private hands. After January 4th, Portuguese India stamps were completely invalid or demonetised.

Outstanding stocks of charity tax stamps were overprinted for fiscal use, but not used. Portuguese India fiscals were overprinted in early 1962 in paisa and rupees and extensively used.

One of the prominent citizens from Panaji, Mr. Carvalho created several combination covers, using low face value definitives of Union of India and Portuguese India, on each of the days up to January 4th including Christmas Day 1961. Most were readdressed to his daughter in pen. Due to the absence of back-stamps or arrival CDSs, it's unlikely any of these went through the mail. Several unaddressed envelopes are to be found with similar combinations of Portuguese India and Union of India stamps in this time frame. The challenge being to obtain a postmark from each of the different days. Obtaining covers from late January to May 1962 with Portuguese India postmarks has proved to be quite difficult. These covers are scarce, but don't command high prices, which is good for the collector not for the speculator. Much more scarce are the Prisoner Of War (PoW) covers sent by Portuguese civilian internees from Goa to Portugal between late December 1961 and March 1962. These were free franked covers with appropriate markings and command a high premium.

Portuguese India philately started with combination covers (British India) and ended with combination covers (Sovereign India).

British

At the end of the 16th century, England and the Netherlands began to challenge Portugal's monopoly of trade with Asia, forming private joint-stock companies to finance the voyages—the English (later British) and Dutch East India Companies, chartered in 1600 and 1602 respectively. The primary aim of these companies was to tap into the lucrative spice trade, and they focused their efforts on the source, the Indonesian archipelago, and an important hub in the trade network, India. The close proximity of London and Amsterdam across the North Sea and intense rivalry between England and the Netherlands inevitably led to conflict between the two companies, with the Dutch gaining the upper hand in the Moluccas (previously a Portuguese stronghold) after the withdrawal of the English in 1622, and the English enjoying more success in India, at Surat, after the establishment of a factory in 1613.

Though England would ultimately eclipse the Netherlands as a colonial power, in the short term the Netherlands's more advanced financial system and the three Anglo-Dutch Wars of the 17th century left it with a stronger position in Asia. Hostilities ceased after the Glorious Revolution of 1688 when the Dutch William of Orange ascended the English throne, bringing peace between the Netherlands and England. A deal between the two nations left the spice trade of the Indonesian archipelago to the Netherlands and the textiles industry of India to England, but textiles soon overtook spices in terms of profitability, and by 1720, in terms of sales, the English company had overtaken the Dutch. The English East India Company shifted its focus from Surat—a hub of the spice trade network—to Fort St. George (later to become Madras), Bombay (ceded by the Portuguese to Charles II of England in 1661 as dowry for Catherine de Braganza) and Sutanuti (which would merge with two other villages to form Calcutta). British policy in Asia during the 19th century was chiefly concerned with protecting and expanding India, viewed as its most important colony and the key to the rest of Asia.

The East India Company drove the expansion of the British Empire in Asia. The Company's army had first joined forces with the Royal Navy during the Seven Years' War, and the two continued to cooperate in arenas outside India: the eviction of Napoleon from Egypt (1799), the capture of Java from the Netherlands (1811), the acquisition of Singapore (1819) and Malacca (1824) and the defeat of Burma (1826).

From its base in India, the Company had also been engaged in an increasingly profitable opium export trade to China since the 1730s. This trade, illegal since it was outlawed by the Qing dynasty in 1729, helped reverse the trade imbalances resulting from the British imports of tea, which saw large outflows of silver from Britain to China. In 1839, the confiscation by the Chinese authorities at Canton of 20,000 chests of opium led Britain to attack China in the First Opium War, and the seizure by Britain of the island of Hong Kong, at that time a minor settlement.

An 1876 political cartoon of Benjamin Disraeli (1804–1881) making Queen Victoria Empress of India. The caption was "New crowns for old ones!"

The end of the Company was precipitated by a mutiny of sepoys against their British commanders, due in part to the tensions caused by British attempts to westernise India. The rebellion took six months to suppress, with heavy loss of life on both sides. Afterwards the British government assumed direct control over India, ushering in the period known as the British Raj, where an appointed governor-general administered India and Queen Victoria was crowned the Empress of India. The East India Company was dissolved the following year, in 1858.

India suffered a series of serious crop failures in the late-19th century, leading to widespread famines in which at least 10 million people died. The East India Company had failed to implement any coordinated policy to deal with the famines during its period of rule. This changed during the Raj, in which commissions were set up after each famine to investigate the causes and implement new policies, which took until the early 1900s to have an effect.

Dutch

The Dutch East India Company established trading posts on different parts along the Indian coast. For some while, they controlled the Malabar southwest coast (Cranganore/Cranganor/ Kodungallor, Cochin de Cima/Pallipuram, Cochin, Cochin de Baixo/Santa Cruz, Quilon (Coylan), Cannanore, Kundapura, Kayankulam, Ponnani) and the Coromandel southeastern coast (Golkonda, Bimilipatnam, Jaggernaikpoeram/Kakinada, Palikol, Pulicat, Porto Novo/Parangippettai, Negapatnam) and Surat (1616-1795). They conquered Ceylon, nowadays Sri Lanka (1658-1796), from the Portuguese. The Dutch also established trading stations in Travancore and coastal Tamil Nadu as well as at Rajshahi in present-day Bangladesh, Pipely, Hugli-Chinsura, and Murshidabad in present-day West Bengal, Balasore (Baleshwar or Bellasoor) in Orissa, and Ava, Arakan, and Syriam in present-day Myanmar (Burma). Ceylon was lost at the Congress of Vienna in the aftermath of the Napoleonic Wars, where the Dutch having fallen subject to France, saw their colonies raided by Britain. The Dutch later became less involved in India, as they had the Dutch East Indies (now Indonesia) as their prized possession.

French

Following the Portuguese, British, and Dutch, the French also established trading bases in India. Their first establishment is in Pondicherry on the Coromandel Coast in southeastern India, in 1674. Subsequent French settlements are Chandernagore in Bengal, northeastern India in 1688, Yanam in Andhra Pradesh in 1723, Mahe in 1725, and Karaikal in 1739. The French were constantly in conflict with the Dutch, and later on mainly with the British in India. At the height of French power in the mid-18th century, the French occupied most of southern India and the area lying in today's northern Andhra Pradesh and Orissa. Between 1744 and 1761, the British and the French repeatedly attacked and conquered each others forts and towns, in southeastern India, and in Bengal in the northeast. After some initial French successes, the British decisively defeated the French in Bengal in the Battle of Plassey in 1757, and in the southeast in 1761 in the Battle of Wandiwash, after which the British East India Company was the supreme military and political power in Southern India as well as in Bengal. In the following decades it gradually increased the size of the territories under its control. The enclaves of Pondicherry, Karaikal, Yanam, Mahe and Chandernagore were returned to France in 1816, and were integrated with the Republic of India after its independence in 1947.

Danish

Denmark was a minor colonial power to set foot in India. It established trading outposts in Tranquebar, Tamil Nadu (1620), Serampore, West Bengal (1755) and the Nicobar Islands (1750s). At one time, the main Danish and Swedish East Asia companies together imported more tea to Europe than the British did. Their outposts lost economic and strategic importance, and Tranquebar, the last Danish outpost, was sold to the British in 1845.

French East India Company

The French East India Company (French: *La Compagnie française des Indes orientales* or *Compagnie française pour le commerce des Indes orientales*) was a commercial enterprise, founded in 1664 to compete with the British and Dutch East India companies.

Planned by Jean-Baptiste Colbert, it was chartered by King Louis XIV for the purpose of trading in the Eastern Hemisphere. It resulted from the fusion of three earlier companies, the 1660 Compagnie de Chine, the Compagnie d'Orient and Compagnie de Madagascar. The first Director General for the Company was François Caron, who had spent 30 years working for the Dutch East India Company, including more than 20 years in Japan.

History

The first state-sponsored French voyage to the Indies occurred in 1603, a voyage captained by Paulmier de Gonneville of Honfleur. French king Henry IV authorized the first *Compagnie des Indes Orientales,* granting the firm a 15-year monopoly of the Indies trade. This precursor to Colbert's later *Compagnie des Indes Orientales,* however, was not a joint-stock corporation, and was funded by the Crown.

The initial capital of the revamped *Compagnie des Indes Orientales* was 15 million livres, divided into shares of 1000 livres apiece. Louis XIV funded the first 3 million livres of investment, against which losses in the first 10 years were to be charged. The initial stock offering quickly sold out, as courtiers of Louis XIV recognized that it was in their interests to support the King's overseas initiative. The *Compagnie des Indes Orientales* was granted a 50-year monopoly on French trade in the Indian and Pacific Oceans, a region stretching from the Cape of Good Hope to the Straits of Magellan. The French monarch also granted the Company a concession in perpetuity for the island of Madagascar, as well as any other territories it could conquer.

The Company failed to found a successful colony on Madagascar, but was able to establish ports on the nearby islands of Bourbon and Ile-de-France (today's Reunion and Mauritius). By 1719, it had established itself in India, but the firm was near bankruptcy. In the same year the *Compagnie des Indes Orientales* was combined under the direction of John Law with other French trading companies to form the *Compagnie Perpetuelle des Indes)*. The reorganized corporation resumed its operating independence in 1723.

With the decline of the Mughal Empire, the French decided to intervene in Indian political affairs to protect their interests, notably by forging alliances with local rulers in south India. From 1741 the French under Joseph François Dupleix pursued an aggressive policy against both the Indians and the British until they ultimately were defeated by Robert Clive.

The Company was not able to maintain itself financially, and it was abolished in 1769, about 20 years before the French Revolution. King Louis XVI issued a 1770 edict that required the Company to transfer to the state all its properties, assets and rights, which were valued at 30 million livres. The King agreed to pay all of the Company's debts and obligations, though holders of Company stock and notes received only an estimated 15 percent of the face value of their investments by the end of corporate liquidation in 1790.

Several Indian trading ports, including Pondicherry and Chandernagore, remained under French control until 1954.

Dutch East India Company

The Dutch East India Company (*Vereenigde Oost-Indische Compagnie* or VOC in Dutch, literally "United East Indian Company") was a chartered company established in 1602, when the States-General of the Netherlands granted it a 21-year monopoly to carry out colonial activities in Asia. It was the first multinational corporation in the world and the first company to issue stock. It was also arguably the world's first megacorporation, possessing quasi-governmental powers, including the ability to wage war, negotiate treaties, coin money, and establish colonies.

The Dutch East India Company remained an important trading concern for almost two centuries, paying an 18% annual dividend for almost 200 years. In its declining years in the late 18th century it was referred to as *Vergaan Onder Corruptie* (referring to the acronym VOC) which translates as 'Perished By Corruption'. The VOC became bankrupt and was formally dissolved in 1800, its possessions and the debt being taken over by the government of the Dutch Batavian Republic. The VOC's territories became the Dutch East Indies and were expanded over the course of the 19th century to include the whole of the Indonesian archipelago, and in the 20th century would form Indonesia.

History

Background

During the 16th century, the spice trade was dominated by the Portuguese who used Lisbon as a staple port. Before the Dutch Revolt, Antwerp had played an important role as a distribution centre in northern Europe, but after 1591 the Portuguese used an international syndicate of the German Fuggers and Welsers, and Spanish and Italian firms that used Hamburg as its northern staple, to distribute their goods, thereby cutting out Dutch merchants. At the same time, the Portuguese trade system was so inefficient that it was unable to supply growing demand, in particular the demand for pepper. The demand for spices was relatively inelastic, and the lagging supply of pepper therefore caused a sharp rise in pepper prices at the time.

Likewise, as Portugal had been "united" with the Spanish crown, with which the Dutch Republic was at war, in 1580, the Portuguese Empire became an appropriate target for military incursions. These three factors formed motive for Dutch merchants to enter the intercontinental spice trade themselves at this time. Finally, a number of Dutchmen like Jan Huyghen van Linschoten and Cornelis de Houtman obtained first hand knowledge of the "secret" Portuguese trade routes and practices, thereby providing opportunity. The stage was thus set for Houtman's first voyage to

Banten, the chief port of Java, and back (1595–97), which generated a modest profit.

In 1596, a group of Dutch merchants decided to try again to circumvent the Portuguese monopoly. In 1596, a four-ship expedition led by Cornelis de Houtman was the first Dutch contact with Indonesia. The expedition reached Banten, the main pepper port of West Java, where they clashed with both the Portuguese and indigenous Indonesians. Houtman's expedition then sailed east along the north coast of Java, losing twelve crew to a Javanese attack at Sidayu and killing a local ruler in Madura. Half the crew were lost before the expedition made it back to the Netherlands the following year, but with enough spices to make a considerable profit.

In 1598, an increasing number of new fleets were sent out by competing merchant groups from around the Netherlands. Some fleets were lost, but most were successful, with some voyages producing high profits. In March 1599, a fleet of twenty-two ships under Jacob van Neck of five different companies was the first Dutch fleet to reach the 'Spice Islands' of Maluku. The ships returned to Europe in 1599 and 1600 and, although eight ships were lost, the expedition made a 400 percent profit. In 1600, the Dutch joined forces with the local Hituese (near Ambon) in an anti-Portuguese alliance, in return for which the Dutch were given the sole right to purchase spices from Hitu. Dutch control of Ambon was achieved in alliance with Hitu when in February 1605, they prepared to attack a Portuguese fort in Ambon but the Portuguese surrendered. In 1613, the Dutch expelled the Portuguese from their Solor fort, but a subsequent Portuguese attack led to a second change of hands; following this second reoccupation, the Dutch once again captured Solor, in 1636.

Formation

At the time, it was customary for a company to be set up only for the duration of a single voyage, and to be liquidated right after the return of the fleet. Investment in these expeditions was a very high-risk venture, not only because of the usual dangers of piracy, disease and shipwreck, but also because the interplay of inelastic demand and relatively elastic supply of spices could make prices tumble at just the wrong moment, thereby ruining prospects of profitability. To manage such risk the forming of a cartel to control supply would seem logical. This first occurred to the English, who bundled their forces into a monopoly enterprise, the East India Company in 1600, thereby threatening their Dutch competitors with ruin. In 1602, the Dutch government followed suit, sponsoring the creation of a single "United East Indies Company" that was also granted a monopoly over the Asian trade. The charter of the new company empowered it to build forts, maintain armies, and conclude treaties with Asian rulers. It provided for a venture that would continue for 21 years, with a financial accounting only at the end of each decade.

In 1603, the first permanent Dutch trading post in Indonesia was established in Banten, West Java and in 1611, another was established at Jayakarta (later 'Batavia' and then 'Jakarta'). In 1610, the VOC established the post of Governor General to enable firmer control of their affairs in Asia. To advise and control the risk of despotic Governors General, a Council of the Indies (*Raad van Indië*) was created. The Governor General effectively became the main administrator of the VOC's activities in Asia, although the *Heeren XVII* continued to officially have overall control.

VOC headquarters were in Ambon for the tenures of the first three Governors General (1610-1619), but it was not a satisfactory location. Although it was at the centre of the spice production areas, it was far from the Asian trade routes and other VOC areas of activity ranging from Africa to Japan. A location in the west of the archipelago was thus sought; the Straits of Malacca were strategic, but had become dangerous following the Portuguese conquest and the first permanent VOC settlement in Banten was controlled by a powerful local ruler and subject to stiff competition from Chinese and English traders.

In 1604, a second English East India Company voyage commanded by Sir Henry Middleton reached the islands of Ternate, Tidore, Ambon and Banda; in Banda, they encountered severe VOC hostility, which saw the beginning of Anglo-Dutch competition for access to spices. From 1611 to 1617, the English established trading posts at Sukadana (southwest Kalimantan), Makassar, Jayakarta and Jepara in Java, and Aceh, Pariaman and Jambi in Sumatra which threatened Dutch ambitions for a monopoly on East Indies trade. Diplomatic agreements in Europe in 1620 ushered in a period of cooperation between the Dutch and the English over the spice trade. This ended with a notorious, but disputed incident, known as the 'Amboyna massacre', where ten Englishmen were arrested, tried and beheaded for conspiracy against the Dutch government. Although this caused outrage in Europe and a diplomatic crisis, the English quietly withdrew from most of their Indonesian activities (except trading in Bantam) and focused on other Asian interests.

Growth

In 1619, Jan Pieterszoon Coen was appointed Governor-General of the VOC. He was a man of extraordinary vision, far beyond that of the cautious directors at home. He saw the possibility of the VOC becoming an Asian power, both political and economic. He was not afraid to use brute force to put the VOC on a firm footing. On 30 May 1619, Coen, backed by a force of nineteen ships, stormed Jayakarta driving out the Banten forces, and from the ashes, established Batavia as the VOC headquarters. To establish a monopoly for the clove trade, in the 1620s almost the entire native population of the Banda Islands, the source of nutmeg was deported, driven away, starved to death, or killed in an attempt to replace them with Dutch plantations, operated with slave labour. He hoped to settle large numbers of Dutch colonists in the East Indies, but this part of his policies never materialized, because the *Heren XVII* were wary at the time of large, open-ended financial commitments.

Another of Coen's ventures was more successful. A major problem in the European trade with Asia at the time was that the Europeans could offer few goods that Asian consumers wanted, except silver and gold. European traders therefore had to pay for spices with the precious metals, and this was in short supply in Europe, except for Spain and Portugal. The Dutch and English had to obtain it by creating a trade surplus with other European countries. Coen discovered the obvious solution for the problem: to start an intra-Asiatic trade system, whose profits could be used to finance the spice trade with Europe. In the long run this obviated the need for exports of precious metals from Europe, though at first it required the formation of a large trading-capital fund in the Indies. The VOC reinvested a large share of its profits to this end in the period up to 1630. The VOC traded throughout Asia. Ships coming into Batavia from the Netherlands carried supplies for VOC settlements in Asia. Silver and copper from Japan were used to trade with India and China for silk, cotton, porcelain, and textiles. These products were either traded within Asia for the coveted spices or brought back to Europe. The VOC was also instrumental in introducing European ideas and technology to Asia. The Company supported Christian missionaries and traded modern technology with China and Japan. A more peaceful VOC trade post on Dejima, an artificial island off the coast of Nagasaki, was for more than two hundred years the only place where Europeans were permitted to trade with Japan.

In 1640, the VOC obtained the port of Galle, Sri Lanka, from the Portuguese and broke the latter's monopoly of the cinnamon trade. In 1658, Gerard Hulft laid siege to Colombo, which was captured with the help of King Rajasinghe II of Kandy. By 1659, the Portuguese had been expelled from the coastal regions, which were then occupied by the VOC, securing for it the monopoly over cinnamon. To prevent the Portuguese or the English from ever recapturing Sri Lanka, the VOC went on to conquer the entire Malabar Coast upon the Portuguese, almost entirely driving them from the west coast of India. When news of a peace agreement between Portugal and the Netherlands reached Asia in 1663, Goa was the only remaining Portuguese city on the west coast.

In 1652, Jan van Riebeeck established an outpost at the Cape of Good Hope (the southwestern tip of Africa, currently in South Africa) to re-supply VOC ships on their journey to East Asia. This post later became a full-fledged colony, the Cape Colony, when more Dutch and other Europeans started to settle there.

VOC trading posts were also established in Persia (now Iran), Bengal (now Bangladesh, but then part of India), Malacca (Melaka, now in Malaysia), Siam (now Thailand), mainland China (Canton), Formosa (now Taiwan) and the Malabar Coast and Coromandel Coast in India. In 1662, however, Koxinga expelled the Dutch from Taiwan.

By 1669, the VOC was the richest private company the world had ever seen, with over 150 merchant ships, 40 warships, 50,000 employees, a private army of 10,000 soldiers, and a dividend payment of 40% on the original investment.

Reorientation

Around 1670, two events caused the growth of VOC trade to stall. In the first place, the highly profitable trade with Japan started to decline. The loss of the outpost on Formosa to Koxinga and related internal turmoil in China (where the Ming dynasty was being replaced with the Qing dynasty) brought an end to the silk trade after 1666. Though the VOC substituted Bengali for Chinese silk other forces affected the supply of Japanese silver and gold. The shogunate enacted a number of measures to limit the export of these precious metals, in the process limiting VOC opportunities for trade, and severely worsening the terms of trade. Therefore, Japan ceased to function as the lynchpin of the intra-Asiatic trade of the VOC by 1685.

Even more importantly, the Third Anglo-Dutch War temporarily interrupted VOC trade with Europe. This caused a spike in the price of pepper, which enticed the British East India Company (EIC) to aggressively enter this market in the years after 1672. Previously, one of the tenets of the VOC pricing policy was to slightly over-supply the pepper market, so as to depress prices below the level where interlopers were encouraged to enter the market (instead of striving for short-term profit maximization). The wisdom of such a policy was illustrated when a fierce price war with the EIC ensued, as that company flooded the market with new supplies from India. In this struggle for market share, the VOC (which had much larger financial resources) could wait out the EIC. Indeed by 1683, the latter came close to bankruptcy; its share price plummeted from 600 to 250; and its president Josiah Child was temporarily forced from office.

However, the writing was on the wall. Other companies, like the French East India Company and the Danish East India Company also started to make inroads on the Dutch system. The VOC therefore closed the heretofore flourishing open pepper emporium of Bantam by a treaty of 1684 with the Sultan. Also, on the Coromandel Coast, it moved its chief stronghold from Pulicat to Negapatnam, so as to secure a monopoly on the pepper trade at the detriment of the French and the Danes. However, the importance of these traditional commodities in the Asian-European trade was diminishing rapidly at the time. The military outlays that the VOC needed to make to enhance its monopoly were not justified by the increased profits of this declining trade.

Nevertheless, this lesson was slow to sink in and at first the VOC made the strategic decision to improve its military position on the Malabar Coast (hoping thereby to curtail English influence in the area, and end the drain on its resources from the cost of the Malabar garrisons) by using force to compel the Zamorin of Calicut to submit to Dutch domination. In 1710, the Zamorin was made to sign a treaty with the VOC undertaking to trade exclusively with the VOC and expel other European traders. For a brief time, this appeared to improve the Company's prospects. However, in 1715, with EIC encouragement, the Zamorin renounced the treaty. Though a Dutch army managed to suppress this insurrection temporarily, the Zamorin continued to trade with the English and the French, which led to an appreciable upsurge in English and French traffic. The VOC decided in 1721 that it was no longer worth the trouble to try and dominate the Malabar pepper and spice trade. A strategic decision was taken to scale down the Dutch military presence and in effect yield the area to EIC influence.

The 1741 Battle of Colachel by *Nairs* of Travancore under Raja Marthanda Varma was therefore a rearguard action. The Dutch commander Captain Eustachius De Lannoy was captured. Marthanda Varma agreed to spare the Dutch captain's life on condition that he joined his army and trained his soldiers on modern lines. This defeat in the Travancore-Dutch War is considered the earliest example of an organized Asian power overcoming European military technology and tactics; and it signalled the decline of Dutch power in India.

The attempt to continue as before as a low volume-high profit business enterprise with its core business in the spice trade had therefore failed. The Company had however already (reluctantly) followed the example of its European competitors in diversifying into other Asian commodities, like tea, coffee, cotton, textiles, and sugar. These commodities provided a lower profit margin and therefore required a larger sales volume to generate the same amount of revenue. This structural change in the commodity composition of the VOC's trade started in the early 1680s, after the temporary collapse of the EIC around 1683 offered an excellent opportunity to enter these markets. The actual cause for the change lies, however, in two structural features of this new era.

In the first place, there was a revolutionary change in the tastes affecting European demand for Asian textiles, and coffee and tea, around the turn of the 18th century. Secondly, a new era of an abundant supply of capital at low interest rates suddenly opened around this time. The second factor enabled the Company to easily finance its expansion in the new areas of commerce. Between the 1680s and 1720s, the VOC was therefore able to equip and man an appreciable expansion of its fleet, and acquire a large amount of precious metals to finance the purchase of large amounts of Asian commodities, for shipment to Europe. The overall effect was to approximately double the size of the company.

The tonnage of the returning ships rose by 125 percent in this period. However, the Company's revenues from the sale of goods landed in Europe rose by only 78 percent. This reflects the basic change in the VOC's circumstances that had occurred: it now operated in new markets for goods with an elastic demand, in which it had to compete on an equal footing with other suppliers. This made for low profit margins. Unfortunately, the business information systems of the time made this difficult to discern for the managers of the company, which may partly explain the mistakes they made from hindsight. This lack of information might have been counteracted (as in earlier times in the VOC's history) by the business acumen of the directors. Unfortunately by this time these were almost exclusively recruited from the political *regent* class, which had long since lost its close relationship with merchant circles.

Low profit margins in themselves don't explain the deterioration of revenues. To a large extent the costs of the operation of the VOC had a "fixed" character (military establishments; maintenance of the fleet and such). Profit levels might therefore have been maintained if the increase in the scale of trading operations that in fact took place, had resulted in economies of scale. However, though larger ships transported the growing volume of goods, labour productivity did not go up sufficiently to realize these. In general the Company's overhead rose in step with the growth in trade volume; declining gross margins translated directly into a decline in profitability of the invested capital. The era of expansion was one of "profitless growth".

Concretely: "[t]he long-term average annual profit in the VOC's 1630-70 'Golden Age' was 2.1 million guilders, of which just under half was distributed as dividends and the remainder reinvested. The long-term average annual profit in the 'Expansion Age' (1680-1730) was 2.0 million guilders, of which three-quarters was distributed as dividend and one-quarter reinvested. In the earlier period, profits averaged 18 percent of total revenues; in the latter period, 10 percent. The annual return of invested capital in the earlier period stood at approximately 6 percent; in the latter period, 3.4 percent."

Nevertheless, in the eyes of investors the VOC did not do too badly. The share price hovered consistently around the 400 mark from the mid-1680s (which, during a hiccup around the Glorious Revolution in 1688), and they reached an all-time high of around 642 in the 1720s. VOC shares then yielded a return of 3.5 percent, only slightly less than the yield on Dutch government bonds.

Decline

However, from there on the fortunes of the VOC started to decline. Five major problems, not all of equal weight, can be adduced to explain its decline in the next fifty years to 1780.

- There was a steady erosion of intra-Asiatic trade by changes in the Asiatic political and economic environment that the VOC could do little about. These factors gradually squeezed the company out of Persia, Surat, the Malabar Coast, and Bengal. The company had to confine its operations to the belt it physically controlled, from Ceylon through the Indonesian archipelago. The volume of this intra-Asiatic trade, and its profitability, therefore had to shrink.
- The way the company was organized in Asia (centralized on its hub in Batavia) that initially had offered advantages in gathering market information, began to cause disadvantages in the 18th century, because of the inefficiency of first shipping everything to this central point. This disadvantage was most keenly felt in the tea trade, where competitors like the EIC and the Ostend Company shipped directly from China to Europe.
- The "venality" of the VOC's personnel (in the sense of corruption and non-performance of duties), though a problem for all East-India Companies at the time, seems to have plagued the VOC on a larger scale than its competitors. To be sure, the company was not a "good employer". Salaries were low, and "private-account trading" was officially not allowed. Not surprisingly, it proliferated in the 18th century to the detriment of the company's performance. From about the 1790s onward,

the phrase *perished by corruption* (also abbreviated VOC in Dutch) came to summarize the company's future.

- A problem that the VOC shared with other companies was the high mortality and morbidity among its employees. This decimated the company's ranks and enervated many of the survivors.
- A self-inflicted wound was the VOC's dividend policy. The dividends distributed by the company had exceeded the surplus it garnered in *Europe* in every decade but one (1710-1720) from 1690 to 1760. However, in the period up to 1730 the directors shipped resources to Asia to build up the trading capital there. Consolidated bookkeeping therefore probably would have shown that total profits exceeded dividends. In addition, between 1700 and 1740 the company retired 5.4 million guilders of long-term debt. The company therefore was still on a secure financial footing in these years. This changed after 1730. While profits plummeted the *bewindhebbers* only slightly decreased dividends from the earlier level. Distributed dividends were therefore in excess of earnings in every decade but one (1760-1770). To accomplish this, the Asian capital stock had to be drawn down by 4 million guilders between 1730 and 1780, and the liquid capital available in Europe was reduced by 20 million guilders in the same period. The directors were therefore constrained to replenish the company's liquidity by resorting to short-term financing from anticipatory loans, backed by expected revenues from home-bound fleets.

Despite of all this, the VOC in 1780 remained an enormous operation. Its capital in the Republic, consisting of ships and goods in inventory, totalled 28 million guilders; its capital in Asia, consisting of the liquid trading fund and goods en route to Europe, totalled 46 million guilders. Total capital, net of outstanding debt, stood at 62 million guilders. The prospects of the company at this time therefore need not have been hopeless, had one of the many plans to reform it been taken successfully in hand. However, then the Fourth Anglo-Dutch War intervened. British attacks in Europe and Asia reduced the VOC fleet by half; removed valuable cargo from its control; and devastated its remaining power in Asia. The direct losses of the VOC can be calculated at 43 million guilders.

Loans to keep the company operating reduced its net assets to zero.

From 1720 on, the market for sugar from Indonesia declined as the competition from cheap sugar from Brazil increased. European markets became saturated. Dozens of Chinese sugar traders went bankrupt which led to massive unemployment, which in turn led to gangs of unemployed coolies. The Dutch government in Batavia did not adequately respond to these problems. In 1740, rumors of deportation of the gangs from the Batavia area led to widespread rioting. The Dutch military searched houses of Chinese in Batavia searching for weapons. When a house accidentally burnt down, military and impoverished citizens started slaughtering and pillaging the Chinese community. This Chinese Massacre was deemed sufficiently serious for the board of the VOC to start an official investigation into the Government of the Dutch East Indies for the first time in its history.

After the Fourth Anglo-Dutch War, the VOC was a financial wreck, and after vain attempts by the provincial States of Holland and Zeeland to reorganize it, was nationalised on 1 March 1796 by the new Batavian Republic. Its charter was renewed several times, but allowed to expire on 31 December 1800. Most of the possessions of the former VOC were subsequently occupied by Great Britain during the Napoleonic wars, but after the new United Kingdom of the Netherlands was created by the Congress of Vienna, some of these were restored to this successor state of the old Dutch Republic by the Anglo-Dutch Treaty of 1814.

Organization

The VOC had two types of shareholders: the *participanten,* who could be seen as non-managing partners, and the 76 *bewindhebbers* (later reduced to 60) who acted as managing partners. This was the usual setup for Dutch joint-stock companies at the time. The innovation in the case of the VOC was, that the liability of not just the *participanten,* but also of the *bewindhebbers* was limited to the paid-in capital (usually, *bewindhebbers* had unlimited liability). The VOC therefore was a limited-liability company. Also, the capital would be *permanent* during the lifetime of the company. As a consequence, investors that wished to liquidate their interest in the interim could only do this by selling their share to others on the Amsterdam Stock Exchange.

The VOC consisted of six Chambers (*Kamers*) in port cities: Amsterdam, Delft, Rotterdam, Enkhuizen, Middelburg and Hoorn. Delegates of these chambers convened as the *Heeren XVII* (the Lords Seventeen). They were selected from the *bewindhebber*-class of shareholders.

Of the *Heeren XVII*, eight delegates were from the Chamber of Amsterdam (one short of a majority on its own), four from the Chamber of Zeeland, and one from each of the smaller Chambers, while the seventeenth seat was alternatively from the Chamber of Zeeland or rotated among the five small Chambers. Amsterdam had thereby the decisive voice. The Zeelanders in particular had misgivings about this arrangement at the beginning. The fear was not unfounded, because in practice it meant Amsterdam stipulated what happened.

The six chambers raised the start-up capital of the Dutch East India Company:

Chamber	*Capital (Guilders)*
Amsterdam	3,679,915
Middelburg	1,300,405
Enkhuizen	540,000
Delft	469,400
Hoorn	266,868
Rotterdam	173,000
Total:	6,424,588

The raising of capital in Rotterdam did not go so smoothly. A considerable part originated from inhabitants of Dordrecht. Although it did not raise as much capital as Amsterdam or Zeeland, Enkhuizen had the largest input in the share capital of the VOC. Under the first 358 shareholders, there were many small entrepreneurs, who dared to take the risk. The minimum investment in the VOC was 3,000 guilders, which priced the Company's stock within the means of many merchants.

Among the early shareholders of the VOC, immigrants played an important role. Under the 1,143 tenderers were 39 Germans and no fewer than 301 Zuid-Nederlanders (roughly present Belgium and Luxemburg, then under Habsburg rule), of whom Isaac le Maire was the largest subscriber with *f*85,000. VOC's total capitalization was ten times that of its British rival. The logo of the VOC consisted of a large capital 'V' with an O on the left and a C on the right leg. The first letter of the hometown of the chamber conducting the operation was placed on top. The flag of the company was orange, white, blue with the company logo embroidered on it. The *Heeren XVII* (Lords Seventeen) met alternately 6 years in Amsterdam and 2 years in Middelburg. They defined the VOC's general policy and divided the tasks among the Chambers. The Chambers carried out all the necessary work, built their own ships and warehouses and traded the merchandise. The *Heeren XVII* sent the ships' masters off with extensive instructions on the route to be navigated, prevailing winds, currents, shoals and landmarks. The VOC also produced its own charts.

In the context of the Dutch-Portuguese War the company established its headquarters in Batavia, Java (now Jakarta, Indonesia). Other colonial outposts were also established in the East Indies, such as on the Spice Islands (Moluccas), which include the Banda Islands, where the VOC forcibly maintained a monopoly over nutmeg and mace. Methods used to maintain the monopoly included the violent suppression of the native population, not stopping short of extortion and mass murder. In addition, VOC representatives sometimes used the tactic of burning spice trees in order to force indigenous populations to grow other crops, thus artificially cutting the supply of spices like nutmeg and cloves.

French India

French India is a general name for the former French possessions in India. These included Pondichery (now Puducherry), Karikal and Yanaon (now Yanam) on the Coromandel Coast, Mahe on the Malabar coast, and Chandannagar in Bengal. In addition there were lodges (*loges*) located at Machilipatnam, Kozhikode and Surat, but they were merely nominal remnants of French factories.

The total area amounted to 203 square miles (526 km^2), of which 113 square miles (293 km^2) belonged to the territory of Pondichery. In 1901 the total population amounted to 273,185.

History

The first French expedition to India is believed to have taken place in the reign of Francois I, when two ships were fitted out by some merchants of Rouen to trade in eastern seas; they sailed from Le Havre and were never afterwards heard of. In 1604 a company was granted letters patent by Henry IV, but the project failed. Fresh letters patent were issued in 1615, and two ships went to India, only one returning.

From 1658, François Bernier (1625–1688), a French physician and traveler, became for 12 years the personal physician of the Mughal emperor Aurangzeb.

La Compagnie française des Indes orientales (French East India Company) was formed under the auspices of Cardinal Richelieu (1642) and reconstructed under Jean-Baptiste Colbert (1664), sending an expedition to Madagascar. In 1667 the French India Company sent out another expedition, under the command of François Caron (who was accompanied by a Persian named Marcara), which reached Surat in 1668 and established the first French factory in India. In 1669, Marcara succeeded in establishing another French factory at Masulipatam. In 1672, Saint Thomas was taken but the French were driven out by the Dutch. Chandernagore (present-day Chandannagar) was established in 1673, with the permission of Nawab Shaista Khan, the Mughal governor of Bengal. In 1674, the French acquired Valikondapuram from the Sultan of Bijapur and thus the foundation of Pondichery was laid. By 1720, the French lost their factories at Surat, Masulipatam and Bantam to the British.

On February 4, 1673, Bellanger, a French officer, took up residence in the Danish Lodge in Pondichery and the French Period of Pondichery began. In 1674 François Martin, the first Governor, started to build Pondichery and transformed it from a small fishing village into a flourishing port-town. The French were in constant conflict, in India, with the Dutch and the English. In 1693 the Dutch took over and fortified Pondichery considerably. The French regained the town in 1699 through the Treaty of Ryswick signed on September 20, 1697.

Between 1720 and 1741, the objectives of the French were purely commercial. The French occupied Yanam (about 840 kilometres or 520 miles northeast of Pondichery on Andhra Coast) in 1723, Mahe on Malabar Coast in 1725 and Karaikal (about 150 kilometres or 93 miles south of Pondichery) in 1739. After 1742 political motives began to overshadow the desire for commercial gain. All factories were fortified for the purpose of defence.

In the 18th century the town of Pondichery was laid out on a grid pattern and grew considerably. Able Governors like Pierre Christoph Le Noir (1726-1735) and Pierre Benoit Dumas (1735-1741) expanded the Pondichery area and made it a large and rich town. Soon after his arrival in 1741, the most famous French Governor of Pondichery and all French India, Joseph François Dupleix began to cherish the ambition of a French Empire in India but his superiors had less interest. French ambition clashed with the British interests in India and a period of military skirmishes and political intrigues began. Under the command of the Marquis de Bussy-Castelnau, Dupleix's army successfully controlled the area between Hyderabad and Cape Comorin. But then Robert Clive arrived in India in 1744, a dare-devil British officer who dashed the hopes of Dupleix to create a French Colonial India.

After a defeat and failed peace talks, Dupleix was recalled to France in 1754. In spite of a treaty between the British and French not to interfere in local politics, the intrigues continued. For example, in this period the French were also expanding their influence at the court of the Nawab of Bengal, and expanding their trade volume in Bengal. In 1756, the French encouraged the Nawab (Siraj ud-Daulah) to attack and conquer the British Fort William in Calcutta. This led to the Battle of Plassey in 1757 where the British decisively defeated the Nawab and his French allies, and extended British power over the entire province of Bengal.

Subsequently France sent Lally-Tollendal to regain the French losses and chase the British out of India. Lally arrived in Pondichery in 1758, had some initial success and razed Fort St. David in Cuddalore District to the ground in 1758, but strategic mistakes by Lally led to the loss of the Hyderabad region, the Battle of Wandiwash, and the siege of Pondicherry in 1760. In 1761 Pondichery was razed to the ground by the British in revenge and lay in ruins for four years. The French had lost their hold now in South India too.

In 1765 Pondichery was returned to France after a peace treaty with Britain in Europe. Governor Jean Law de Lauriston set to rebuild the town on the old foundations and after five months 200 European and 2000 Tamil houses had been erected. During the next 50 years Pondichery changed hands between France and Britain with the regularity of their wars and peace treaties.

In 1816, after the conclusion of the Napoleonic Wars, the five establishments of Pondichery, Chandranagore, Karaikal, Mahe and Yanam and the loges at Machilipattnam, Kozhikode and Surat were returned to France.

Pondichery had lost much of its former glory, and Chandernagore was eclipsed as a trading centre by the nearby British establishment of Calcutta (present-day Kolkata). Successive governors improved infrastructure, industry, law and education over the next 138 years.

By decree of the January 25, 1871, French India was provided with an elective general council (Conseil general) and elective local councils (Conseil local). The results of this measure were not very satisfactory, and the qualifications for and the classes of the franchise were modified. The governor resided at Pondichery, and was assisted by a council. There were two *Tribunals d'instance* (Tribunals of first instance) (at Pondichery and Karikal) one *Cour d'appel* (Court of Appeal) (at Pondichery) and five *Justices de paix* (Justice of the Peace). The agricultural produce consisted of rice, earth-nuts, tobacco, betel nuts and vegetables.

François Martin

François Martin (1634–1706) was the first Governor General of what is now Puducherry. He founded Pondicherry, the future capital of French India in 1674. He was Commissioner of French East India Company before holding this post and was preceded by François Baron and succeeded by Pierre Dulivier. There is a street named François Martin in Puducherry.

Pierre Dulivier

Pierre Dulivier was the Governor General of Pondicherry for two times. He was preceded by François Martin and succeeded by Guillaume Andre d'Hebert.

Guillaume Andre d'Hebert

Guillaume Andre d'Hebert was Governor General of Pondicherry for two times. He was preceded by Pierre Dulivier and succeeded by Pierre Andre Prevost de La Prevostiere.

Pierre Andre Prevost De La Prevostiere

Pierre Andre Prevost de La Prevostiere was Governor General of Pondicherry. At his time the main interests of the France was only commercial rather than political. So, no significant events occurred during his tenure. His Successor, Pierre Christoph Le Noir was a very able governor and actual development of Pondicherry started from him.

Pierre Christoph Le Noir

Pierre Christoph Le Noir was Governor General of Pondicherry twice (first time as acting governor). During his rule, Yanaon was added to the French Establishments of India as third colony in 1927. He expanded the Pondicherry area and made it a large and rich town. He even worked as Director for Compagnie perpetuelle des Indes from 8 August 1736 and 7 October 1738 to 26 February 1743.

Pierre Benoit Dumas

Pierre Benoit Dumas (1668–1745) was the French Governor General for Pondichery and Reunion. Predecessor of La Bourdonnais on the Isles and Dupleix in the Indies, Dumas hailed from Southern France. There is still a street in Pondicherry named after him.

The City of Reunion was established by him in 1730. It is he who launched the colonization of Reunion island decided by Desforges Boucher. 244 concessions were allotted during his 8 years of administration, between the Gully of Gol and the Gully of the Ramparts. Like Regnault, he wished to create a city around the immense concession (more than 10 km^2) which extended *du battant des lames au sommet des montagnes* on the future location Saint-Pierre. He even made Antoine of Bavaria draw a project of urban plan in a checkerboard and to this, he conceded 48 sites with the river initially on 26 August 1733.

He is also the man of the opening-up. He made Pierre Boisson and Abraham Muron to undertake the construction of a way connecting Saint-Denis to the commune of La Possession. This sinuous layout of 30 kilometers decided on 16 June 1730 was going to become the mountain road. On 3 August 1733 he charged Delisle and River to open the section Sainte-Marie-Saint-Benoit, and the road connecting Saint-Paul initially had the new concession of the River. Some time later, he became Governor General for the French Establishments in India.

Joseph François Dupleix

Joseph François Dupleix (1 January 1697 – 10 November 1763) was governor general of the French establishment in India, and was the rival of Robert Clive.

Biography

Dupleix was born in Landrecies, France. His father, François Dupleix, a wealthy farmer, wished to bring him up as a merchant, and, in order to distract him from his taste for science, sent him on a voyage to India in 1715 on one of the French East India Company's vessels. He made several voyages to the Americas and India, and in 1720 was named a member of the superior council at Pondicherry. He displayed great business aptitude, and, in addition to his official duties, made large ventures on his own account, and acquired a fortune. In 1730 he was made superintendent of French affairs in Chandernagore, the town prospered under his administration and grew into great importance. In 1741, he married Jeanne Albert, widow of one of the councilors of the company; Albert was known to the Hindus as Joanna Begum and proved of great help to her husband in his negotiations with the native princes.

His reputation procured him in 1742 the appointment of governor general of all French establishments in India. He succeeded Dumas as the French governor of Pondicherry. His ambition now was to acquire for France vast territories in India, and for this purpose he entered into relations with the native princes, and adopted a style of oriental splendour in his dress and surroundings. He built an army of native troops, called sepoys, who were trained as infantrymen. The British took the alarm. But the danger to their settlements and power was partly averted by the bitter mutual jealousy which existed between Dupleix and Bertrand François Mahe de La Bourdonnais, French governor of the Isle of Bourbon (today's La Reunion).

When the city of Madras capitulated to the French following the Battle of Madras in 1746, Dupleix opposed the restoration of the town to the British, thus violating the treaty signed by La

Bourdonnais. He then sent an expedition against Fort St. David (1747), which was defeated on its march by the Nawab of Arcot, ally of the British. Dupleix succeeded in winning over the Nawab, and again attempted the capture of Fort St. David, but did not succeed. A midnight attack on Cuddalore was repulsed at great loss to Dupleix.

In 1748 Pondicherry was besieged by the British, but in the course of the operations news arrived of the peace concluded between the French and the British at Aix-la-Chapelle. Dupleix next entered into negotiations whose object was the subjugation of southern India. He sent a large body of troops to the aid of the two claimants of the sovereignty of the Carnatic and the Deccan. The British sided with their rivals to check the designs of Dupleix.

From 1751, Dupleix tried to expand French influence in Burma by sending the envoy Sieur de Bruno, and helping militarily the Mons in their conflict with the Burmese.

The conflicts between the French and the British in India continued till 1754, when the French government, anxious to settle peace, sent a special commissioner to India with orders to supersede Dupleix and, if necessary, to arrest him. Dupleix was compelled to embark for France on 12 October 1754.

Jeanne Albert died in 1756.

Having invested his private fortune in the implementation of his public policies, Dupleix found himself ruined. The government refused to support him, and he died in obscurity and want on 10 November 1763.

Charles Godeheu

Charles Robert Godeheu de Zaimont was Acting Governor General of Pondicherry who is the Commissioner of French army during Dupleix's reign.

Important Incidents

In 1754, Charles Robert Godeheu gave up with the English the Indian territories, especially Madras which was conquered in 1746 by Dupleix and left French to maintain on Deccan region. Actually, from 1751 Dupleix's star began to wane. Robert Clive, a discontented young British factor who had left the countinghouse for the field, seized the fort of Arcot, political capital of Karnataka, with 210 men in August 1751. This daring stroke had the hoped-for effect of diverting half of Chanda Sahib's army to its recovery. Clive's successful 50-day defence permitted Mohamed Ali Khan Walajan to procure allies from Tanjore and the Marathas. The French were worsted, and they were eventually forced to surrender in June 1752. Dupleix never recovered from this blow; Dupleix was superseded in August 1754 by his director Godehou, who made an unfavourable settlement with the British. On 26 December 1754, he made a treaty with Thomas Saunders, the English East India Company's resident at Madras, that forbids to the British and French companies all political activity in India and the activity must be strictly commercial.

His intervention in French activity at that time made an unerasing scar on Dupleix's efforts and became death blow for future expansions of French Colonial Empire in India.

Georges Duval De Leyrit

Georges Duval de Leyrit was Governor General of Pondicherry between 1754 and 1758. He was preceded by Charles Godeheu and succeeded by as Arthur, comte de Lally-Tollendal.

3

British Invasion in India

British Invasion

Economic competition among the European nations led to the founding of commercial companies in England (the East India Company, founded in 1600) and in the Netherlands (Verenigde Oost-Indische Compagnie—the United East India Company, founded in 1602), whose primary aim was to capture the spice trade by breaking the Portuguese monopoly in Asia. Although the Dutch, with a large supply of capital and support from their government, preempted and ultimately excluded the British from the heartland of spices in the East Indies (modern-day Indonesia), both companies managed to establish trading "factories" (actually warehouses) along the Indian coast. The Dutch, for example, used various ports on the Coromandel Coast in South India, especially Pulicat (about twenty kilometers north of Madras), as major sources for slaves for their plantations in the East Indies and for cotton cloth as early as 1609. (The English, however, established their first factory at what today is known as Madras only in 1639.) Indian rulers enthusiastically accommodated the newcomers in hopes of pitting them against the Portuguese. In 1619 Jahangir granted them permission to trade in his territories at Surat (in Gujarat) on the west coast and Hughli (in West Bengal) in the east. These and other locations on the peninsula became centres of international trade in spices, cotton, sugar, raw silk, saltpeter, calico, and indigo.

English company agents became familiar with Indian customs and languages, including Persian, the unifying official language under the Mughals. In many ways, the English agents of that period lived like Indians, intermarried willingly, and a large number of them never returned to their home country. The knowledge of India thus acquired and the mutual ties forged with Indian trading groups gave the English a competitive edge over other Europeans. The French commercial interest—Compagnie des Indes Orientales (East India Company, founded in 1664)—came late, but the French also established themselves in India, emulating the precedents set by their competitors as they founded their enclave at Pondicherry (Puduchcheri) on the Coramandel Coast.

In 1717 the Mughal emperor, Farrukh-siyar (r. 1713-19), gave the British—who by then had already established themselves in the south and the west—a grant of thirty-eight villages near Calcutta, acknowledging their importance to the continuity of international trade in the Bengal economy. As did the Dutch and the French, the British brought silver bullion and copper to pay for transactions, helping the smooth functioning of the Mughal revenue system and increasing the benefits to local artisans and traders. The fortified warehouses of the British brought extraterritorial status, which enabled them to administer their own civil and criminal laws and offered numerous employment opportunities as well as asylum to foreigners and Indians. The British factories successfully competed with their rivals as their size and population grew. The original clusters of fishing villages (Madras and Calcutta) or series of islands (Bombay) became headquarters of the British administrative zones, or presidencies as they generally came to be known. The factories and their immediate environs, known as the White-town, represented the actual and symbolic pre-eminence of the British—in terms of their political power—as well as their cultural values and social practices; meanwhile, their Indian collaborators lived in the Black-town, separated from the factories by several kilometres.

The British company employed sepoys—European-trained and European-led Indian soldiers—to protect its trade, but local rulers sought their services to settle scores in regional power struggles. South India witnessed the first open confrontation between the British and the French, whose forces were led by Robert Clive and François Dupleix, respectively. Both companies desired to place their own candidate as the nawab, or ruler, of Arcot, the area around Madras. At the end of a protracted struggle between 1744 and 1763, when the Peace of Paris was signed, the British gained an upper hand over the French and installed their man in power, supporting him further with arms and lending large sums as well. The French and the British also backed different factions in the succession struggle for Mughal viceroyalty in Bengal, but Clive intervened successfully and defeated Nawab Siraj-ud-daula in the Battle of Plassey (Palashi, about 150 kilometres north of Calcutta) in 1757. Clive found help from a combination of vested interests that opposed the existing nawab: disgruntled soldiers, landholders, and influential merchants whose commercial profits were closely linked to British fortunes.

Later, Clive defeated the Mughal forces at Buxar (Baksar, west of Patna in Bihar) in 1765, and the Mughal emperor (Shah Alam, r. 1759-1806) conferred on the company administrative rights over Bengal, Bihar, and Orissa, a region of roughly 25 million people with an annual revenue of 40 million rupees. The imperial grant virtually established the company as a sovereign power, and Clive became the first British governor of Bengal.

Besides the presence of the Portuguese, Dutch, British, and French, there were two lesser but noteworthy colonial groups. Danish entrepreneurs established themselves at several ports on the Malabar and Coromandel coasts, in the vicinity of Calcutta and inland at Patna between 1695 and 1740. Austrian enterprises were set up in the 1720s on the vicinity of Surat in modern-day southeastern Gujarat. As with the other non-British enterprises, the Danish and Austrian enclaves were taken over by the British between 1765 and 1815.

French, English, and Clive 1744-67

In 1744 Raghuji's vizier Bhaskar Ram invaded Bengal through Orissa. Bengal *nawab* Alivardi lured Bhaskar and Maratha generals to the plain of Mankara, where they were treacherously massacred by the Afghan generals. When Alivardi broke his promise to make his general Ghulam Mustafa Khan governor of Bihar for having murdered Bhaskar, Mustafa Khan rebelled and assaulted Patna, inviting Raghuji to invade. In 1745 Mughal emperor Muhammad Shah promised to pay Shahu tribute for Bengal and Bihar. Raghuji invaded Bengal six times until he made a treaty with 'Alivardi Khan in 1751. The Marathas were to be given revenues from Orissa by Alivardi's deputy Mir Habib, and they promised not to invade Bengal anymore. Habib did not allow extortion and peculation, and he and his assistants were murdered by Maratha soldiers in

1752. Orissa became a Maratha province. The annual Maratha raids in the 1740s had plundered Bengal, devastated its inland economy, and caused many people to flee to the east, where some took refuge in the English settlement at Calcutta.

Joseph Dupleix had increased French trade in Bengal in the 1730s, surpassing the Dutch, and in 1742 he was appointed governor at Pondicherry. When a European war began in 1744 that opposed England against France, Dupleix proposed local neutrality agreements; but the English East India Company believed they could wipe out their French rivals. In 1745 Commodore Barnett captured French ships with Chinese goods in which Dupleix had an interest, and the latter called upon a French squadron that Governor La Bourdonnais was fitting out at Mauritius. After an indecisive battle, Captain Edward Peyton took the English ships back to Bengal. Dupleix goaded the French fleet into capturing Madras with a thousand men in 1746. Over Dupleix's objection, La Bourdonnais promised to give Madras back to the English for a ransom. When La Bourdonnais departed, Dupleix renounced the treaty and defended Madras from an attack led by Mahfuz Khan, son of Karnatak nawab Anwar-ud-din. Improved artillery and infantry armed with muskets and bayonets demonstrated European superiority over slow-firing Indian guns. The next year Dupleix tried to take Fort St. David, but the English (including young Clive) were able to defend it with the help of Nawab Anwar-ud-din's son Muhammad 'Ali and his 2,500 men. Capable Major Stringer Lawrence took command at Fort St. David in January 1748 and repelled Dupleix's third attempt. Admiral Boscawen's attempt to besiege the French at Pondicherry failed and lost more than a thousand men. In the 1748 treaty of Aix-la-Chapelle prisoners were exchanged, and England got Madras back in exchange for Cape Breton Island in North America.

Mughal vizier Safdar Jang did not like Nizam-ul Mulk's son Nasir Jang and urged his nephew Muzaffar Jang and Chanda Sahib to claim the Deccan; they invaded Karnatak with 14,000 cavalry and 15,000 infantry and were supported by 420 French soldiers from Pondicherry. In 1749 they defeated and killed Anwar-ud-din at Ambur, and his son Muhammad 'Ali fled to Trichinopoly. Nasir had 70,000 men on horses and 100,000 on foot with artillery and also hired Marathas; he was joined by Muhammad 'Ali and 300 English. They won the battle and captured Muzaffar because unpaid French officers refused to fight. However, Bussy's French troops captured the strong fortress at Jinji (Gingee). Nasir was shot dead during an attack on his camp ordered by France's Dupleix in December 1750. Dupleix recognized the freed Muzaffar as viceroy of the Deccan and Chanda Sahib as Karnatak nawab; but Muzaffar was killed the next month and was replaced by Salabat Jang, who had persuaded France's Bussy to support him. Bussy got Salabat Jang to give the French a lease in the Deccan.

While Dupleix negotiated, the new Madras governor Thomas Saunders sent a British force to defend Muhammad 'Ali. Dupleix countered by sending a French army under Jean Law. The English led by Robert Clive captured Arcot in 1751 and defended it against a force brought by Chanda Sahib. The French siege of Trichinopoly failed, and their ally Chanda Sahib surrendered to a Maratha commander. He turned him over to the confederate chiefs, who had Sahib beheaded to please Muhammad 'Ali. Law fled to the island of Srirangam but in June 1752 had to surrender 800 French soldiers, 2,000 sepoys, and 31 guns to Lawrence and Clive. The latter captured more forts, and by the end of 1752 Muhammad 'Ali possessed most of the Karnatak except Jinji.

Nizam-ul Mulk's oldest son Ghazi-ud-din was assigned the Deccan by the Mughal emperor in 1752 and had a Maratha escort. Bussy promised Maratha *peshwa* Balaji the Deccan province of Khandesh if he would support Salabat Jang, who was forced by the Marathas in November 1752 to give them much of Khandesh and Berar. In 1753 French Directors decided to recall Dupleix for having pursued territorial expansion. His replacement Robert Godeheu made a truce with the English, agreeing their companies would not interfere in Indian disputes. Soon after he arrived at Aurangabad, Ghazi-ud-din was poisoned by Nizam-ul Mulk's widow, the mother of Nizam 'Ali. Salabat Jang relied on Shah Nawaz Khan for financial administration of the Deccan, and in 1754 Nawaz made Raghuji Nagpur pay 500,000 rupees. Nawaz sent the Nizam army into Mysore and raised ten times that the next year; but the French were demanding 2,900,000 rupees a year for their troops. After Salabat Jang dismissed the French, Bussy seized Hyderabad. Nawaz was dismissed during an uprising, and Nizam 'Ali gained power. Marathas led by the Peshwa's son Vishvas Ras invaded and gained 2,500,000 rupees worth of Deccan territory in the treaty of January 1758. Bussy's manager Haidar Jang had

Nawaz Shah and Salabat Jang arrested; but Nizam 'Ali avoided that fate by murdering Haidar Jang. During a riot Nawaz was murdered in prison by a French officer. Bussy was recalled to Madras, and Nizam 'Ali returned to Hyderabad. Without French assistance, the Nizam army was easily defeated by the Marathas.

In 1756 war broke out again in Europe between France and England. Comte de Lally led the French attack that destroyed Fort St. David, but his invasion of Tanjore to get money failed. Lally besieged Madras in December 1758 but was defeated the next month trying to regain Arcot, as Bussy was captured. Eyre Coote arrived with a British fleet and defeated Lally in January 1760. Pondicherry was blockaded, and Lally surrendered a year later, ending French power in India. The 1763 treaty of Paris let them keep Pondicherry but without fortifications.

During the siege of Pondicherry, Muhammad 'Ali met all the expenses in order to receive the captured stores; but the Company took them and merely promised him credit. Muhammad 'Ali lived extravagantly in a palace outside of Madras and continually borrowed money at about 40% interest, enabling the English to acquire fortunes giving him loans. George Pigot demanded that Muhammad 'Ali pay five million rupees annually to the Company on his debt. He tried to get tribute from the fertile Tanjore, but Pigot arranged for this to go to the Company also. Nizam 'Ali offered the Company the Circars for military assistance against the Marathas. Together they planned an attack on Haidar 'Ali's fort at Bangalore; but the clever Mysore leader paid off the Marathas with 3,500,000 rupees and secretly plotted with Nizam 'Ali to attack the English. Muhammad 'Ali learned of it, and Col. Joseph Smith retreated in 1767. Near Trinomalee his army was attacked by the combined forces of Haidar and Nizam 'Ali but inflicted heavy casualties upon them. Haidar's son Tipu led a raid on the outskirts of Madras, frightening Council members.

When Nizam 'Ali learned another English force was coming from Bengal, he made a treaty with the English in 1768 and became known as their faithful ally. After failing to supply him before, now the Madras Council sent two deputies to make money supplying Smith's troops. Smith was recalled and replaced by the corrupt Col. Wood. Haidar 'Ali respected and avoided Col. Smith but was glad to attack Wood at every opportunity. By the end of 1768 the Madras Council recalled Wood and put him under arrest.

His charges were later dismissed because he was a relative of the powerful Company director Laurence Sulivan. Haidar asked to negotiate with Dupre, the most honest member of the Madras Council, and he agreed to a treaty in 1769 with the Company restoring all conquered territories under a mutual defence agreement.

Bengal nawab Alivardi died in 1756 and was succeeded by his grandson Siraj-ud-daula. Army commander Mir Jafar and the English conspired against him. When the Nawab ordered the English and French to dismantle their forts, the English refused. Siraj attacked Calcutta with a reported 50,000 men and captured Fort William in June 1756. English prisoners were confined in a small room called the "Black Hole" overnight. According to magistrate John Z. Holwell, of the 146 imprisoned he was one of only 23 who survived the suffocation; but many have questioned the accuracy of his account, and recent Indian studies found the number imprisoned was 64. Siraj was not blamed for the guards' incompetence. Clive arrived with an army that took over Calcutta and Hughli in January 1757; a treaty restored the East India Company's trading rights and factories. At war with France, the English attacked Chandernagar. Siraj complained but could do little except ask the French to leave Bengal. Clive accused the Nawab of violating the treaty and wrote he was asking for arbitration, but he occupied the fort at Katwa. When the Punjabi merchant Aminchand tried to blackmail Clive, threatening to warn Siraj, Clive fooled him with a forged agreement and never paid him. During the battle of Plassey in June 1757 Mir Jafar betrayed Siraj by going over to the winning English side. Clive joined Mir Jafar and his troops in Murshidabad. Siraj fled, was captured, and executed at the behest of Mir Jafar.

Clive presided over the installation of Mir Jafar as nawab, and for the first time the English were given land with zamindari rights. Mir Jafar promised to pay some twenty million rupees in compensation and gave Clive a present of 160,000 pounds. Later when he was criticized for accepting this, Clive replied that he was astonished at his own moderation, noting that Murshidabad was as populous and rich as London. Clive managed to get Mir Jafar recognized by the Mughal emperor, and Maratha *peshwa* Balaji kept getting the tribute agreed upon with Alivardi. The *dastaks* (passes) that Mir Jafar granted to Company servants exempted them from duties on private trade and gave them a competitive advantage over Indians. Some agents used the British name to extort even more money in the countryside.

The Calcutta Council elected Clive governor of Bengal in 1758. Clive sent Coote after the French led by Law, and the strict Coote had reluctant soldiers flogged. Facing a revolt in Bihar backed by the Awadh nawab, Mir Jafar asked Clive for help, because his mutinous army refused to march. Mughal prince 'Ali Gauhar, who later became Shah Alam II, invaded Bihar with 40,000 men. Clive pushed forward a battalion against him but then sent him 500 gold coins and persuaded him to withdraw. Clive stationed a garrison at Patna, and in gratitude Mir Jafar gave Clive a local tax district. Clive sent Francis Forde to help a raja who had taken over Vizagapatam. Forde's forces defeated the French, and Salabat Jang ceded territory to the English in May 1759. In July seven Dutch ships carrying soldiers tried to go up the Hughli to Chinsura. Mir Jafar ordered them to turn back but did nothing. Though England was not yet at war with Holland, Clive decided to enforce the Nawab's order after Hastings warned him the Nawab was conniving with the Dutch. Clive sent Forde with 300 Europeans, 800 sepoys, and four field guns that made the difference, killing and capturing 450 European soldiers near Badarah on the road to Chinsura. Six Dutch vessels surrendered to three larger English ships, and the other one fled. The Dutch had to admit they provoked the violence and pay a million rupees damages. The Dutch would not challenge the English in Bengal again.

Holwell replaced Clive as governor at Fort William for five months in 1760 and persuaded his successor Vansittart that Nawab Mir Jafar should be deposed. Vansittart secretly made a treaty with Mir Jafar's son-in-law Mir Qasim, making him *diwani* and giving him more authority than the Nawab. When Mir Jafar objected, the Governor and Mir Qasim besieged his palace in October 1760. After Mir Jafar abdicated, he was allowed to live in Calcutta. The new Nawab soon came into conflict with the English chief Ellis at Patna over duties on inland trade. Mir Qasim demanded that the Company's private trade be abolished, but Vansittart proposed paying nine percent duties on inland trade. Although Indian merchants paid forty percent, the Calcutta Council reduced the duty for company merchants to 2.5%, and it was only on salt. The Nawab's ordering that regulations be enforced provoked violence. He was also disliked for raising taxes more than they had been in the previous two centuries. Then in March 1763 he ordered a remission on all duties on inland trade for two years, hoping that letting Indians compete fairly would ruin English trade. Mir Qasim sent troops to Patna in June, but Ellis took over the factory city. Mir Qasim's forces captured Patna and killed the English envoy Amyatt, shocking the English who lost nearly 3,000 men. The Calcutta Council declared war on Mir Qasim. The English army of Bengal marched into Murshidabad and reinstated Mir Jafar. After Mir Qasim's army was defeated in June 1763, he killed his commander, some associates, and nearly two hundred English prisoners. Then he fled to Awadh.

In 1762 Shah Alam II and Shuja-ud-daula of Awadh had invaded Bundelkhand. The next year they marched toward Delhi hoping to unite Muslims; but the Sunni Afghans came into conflict with Shuja's Shi'a troops and departed. Shah Alam and Shuja gave refuge to Mir Qasim in Awadh. The Calcutta Council sent forces led by Major Carnac into Awadh. Negotiation with Shuja-ud-daula failed, because both he and Mir Jafar wanted Bihar. When Carnac refused to fight in the rainy season, he was replaced by Major Munro, who court martialed a few mutinous officers and executed them with cannons. When Mir Qasim ran out of money for Awadh's war, he was imprisoned. In October 1764 the English army of about 7,200 defeated Shuja's army of 30,000 at the battle of Buxar. Shah Alam surrendered and was allowed to govern only Allahabad and Korah for the next six years. In addition to these annual revenues of 2,800,000 rupees, he would receive tribute of 2,600,000 rupees from Bengal. As Subah of Bengal he bestowed on the Company the powerful office of Diwan. Shuja was defeated again the next year, but he promised to pay the Company five million rupees and was reinstated. These arrangements were made by Clive when he returned for a second term as governor in 1765.

The new Nawab was still head of revenue collection and the judiciary, but the army was controlled by the Company. Clive called this "dual government." Mir Jafar died and was succeeded by his grandson Najm-ud-daula. When Clive allowed the new Nawab an annual salary of 5,300,000 rupees, his character was revealed by his reply, "Thank God! I shall now have as many dancing girls as I please." Directors had ordered Clive to reform the system by limiting presents and checking the abuses of private trade. Presents over 4,000 rupees were forbidden, and those over 1,000 required official approval. Yet the Council had accepted presents totaling nearly 140,000 pounds from the new Nawab. Clive tried to increase salaries to reduce corruption, but the Directors balked at the cost and instituted commissions on revenues. He converted a gift from Mir Jafar into a fund for wounded and sick veterans. Clive reduced the corrupt allowances military officers had been receiving for years. Angry officers in the Monghyr brigade resigned their commissions, and the troops were near mutiny; but Clive used the sepoys (Indian troops) to force them to cooperate. Clive made the officers at Patna sign a three-year agreement with capital punishment for disobedience. He court martialed the "ringleaders" and deported them. Opposition to his reforms subsided, and Clive left India in February 1767. He predicted that the Company would make an annual profit of two million pounds and that the people of Bengal would be benefited, but the results of his efforts were quite different.

Marathas and Hastings 1767-84

Peshwa Madhav Rao and his uncle Raghunath met in 1767, but the latter lost a second civil war the next year and was imprisoned at Puna. Bombay sent Thomas Mostyn to Puna to keep the Marathas from joining Mysore's Haidar 'Ali and the Deccan's Nizam 'Ali, and the next year the English attacked Haidar's fleet on the west coast. Nizam made a treaty with Madras in 1768, but Haidar's victories the next year made Madras promise to defend him from Maratha attack, which they failed to do. Madhav Rao wanted to subjugate the Karnatak and in 1770 occupied several posts and two strong forts; he put Trimbak Rao in charge with a large army. In March 1771 Trimbak defeated Mysore's army, as Haidar fled to his capital in a disguise. Ill and out of money, the Peshwa told Trimbak Rao to make peace in 1772; Haidar 'Ali agreed to pay 3,100,000 rupees and surrendered some territory south of the Tungabhadra.

When the Marathas invaded Mysore, Haidar 'Ali asked for English assistance in accordance with their 1769 treaty; but Muhammad 'Ali was hostile to Haidar, and the Marathas asked for English help also. The Madras Council procrastinated, and Haidar resented this breach of the treaty. Madras governor Dupre wisely refrained from supporting Muhammad 'Ali's scheme to invade Tanjore, because it would provoke the Marathas. In late 1771 he approved a siege by General Joseph Smith, but Muhammad 'Ali changed his mind on being offered five million rupees by the Tanjore raja. Two years later the Madras Council, dominated by Paul Benfield, sent Smith to seize Tanjore for Muhammad 'Ali; but in 1775 the Company directors removed the Madras governor and ordered the Council to restore the raja. The Court of Proprietors appointed George Pigot governor, and he came into conflict with the Madras Council and Nawab Muhammad 'Ali. Pigot ordered Robert Fletcher arrested, but instead the Council put Pigot in prison, where he died in May 1777.

Peshwa Madhav Rao died of disease in November 1772 and was succeeded by his brother Narayan Rao. Raghunath Rao (Ragoba) organized a conspiracy and had his nephew murdered in August 1773, becoming *peshwa*. He made a treaty with Haidar 'Ali, trading territory for money. The late Peshwa's widow Ganga Bai gave birth to a son, and Nana Fadnavis led an effort to govern as regents for him. Raghunath appealed to Bombay and gained an English alliance in a 1775 treaty, ceding Salsette and Bassein. The Calcutta Council condemned the Bombay treaty and sent Col. Upton to Puna to annul it and make a new one with the regency that renounced Raghunath, who was promised a pension. The Bombay government rejected this and gave refuge to Raghunath. In 1777 Nana Fadnavis violated his treaty by granting the French a port on the west coast. Bombay reacted by sending a force toward Puna, but in January 1779 the British troops were defeated by a large Maratha army. In the convention at Wadgaon, Bombay had to relinquish all territory acquired since 1775. Bengal disavowed this, and an army led by Col. Goddard marched across India to take over Ahmadabad in February 1780 and Bassein in December.

Haidar 'Ali formed a triple alliance with the Deccan's Nizam 'Ali and the Marathas against the English, and they defeated the British advance on Puna. Haidar and his son Tipu trapped a British force of 3,800 led by Baillie, capturing all that had not been killed; about 200 Europeans were imprisoned for several years. Some of the prisoners were put to death, and others were converted to Islam. The Maratha-Mysore alliance took Arcot after a long siege, but Hastings and the Bengal council won Nizam back over by assuring him that his tribute would be paid and that Guntur would be restored to Basalat Jang. Another Bengal detachment led by Captain Popham helped the Rana of Gohad capture Gwalior in August 1780. Hastings sent more forces, and in 1781 Eyre Coote defeated Haidar at Porto Novo. General Camac also defeated Mahadji Sindia at Sipri. After these English victories, Sindia proposed a new treaty between Puna and the English, recognizing young Madhava Rao Narayan and giving Raghunath a pension. This treaty of Salbai was signed in May 1782 and ratified eight months later by Nana Fadnavis; it called for the Peshwa to make Haidar 'Ali relinquish his conquests and prisoners within six months of ratification. Haidar 'Ali was elderly and had died of cancer in December 1782; but his son Tipu continued the war. Bombay brigadier Mathews and his men captured Bednore and Mangalore in 1783 but surrendered to Tipu after he withdrew troops from the Karnatak. Lord Macartney at Madras recalled Col. Fullarton, and the 1784 treaty of Mangalore restored conquests and liberated prisoners.

The English East India Company's dividend was raised in 1766 from six to ten percent and to 12.5% the following year. The House of Commons appointed a committee to inquire into the Company's extraordinary money-making and reduced the dividend back to ten percent. Three Supervisors were sent out to reform the Company in September 1769, but the ship was lost at sea. Commodore John Lindsay had been made the King's Minister Plenipotentiary secretly after the Company's directors had opposed this.

The English used the dual Mughal revenue system in Bengal, but Clive's strict reforms provided little improvement. The English enriched themselves with bribes and by fixing prices. Crop failures led to a disastrous famine and pestilence in 1770 during which about ten million people died, a third of the Bengal and Bihar population. The English Company spent only 9,000 pounds on famine relief that helped about 400,000 people. Officials monopolized all grain and even forced ryots (peasants) to sell their seeds for the next harvest, compounding the misery. Revenues were still demanded and even increased, further decreasing cultivation. The justice system was corrupt, as judges were appointed by official favour, and not having salaries they depended on fines and perquisites. The Company's servants participated in inland trade without duties and drove most of the Indian merchants out of business. Verelst had failed even though he seemed to realize that acting as mere merchants, making immense revenues the only goal without protecting the people, was inhumane. He was replaced by Cartier in 1770. The Directors continued to pay the dividends even though the Company had to borrow from the Bank of England to do so.

In 1771 the Directors appointed the experienced Warren Hastings as governor of Bengal. Hastings wanted to cultivate peace and establish justice, reduce Company expenses, and limit remote wars. He had served in India since 1750 and spoke Bengali, Hindustani (Urdu), and some Persian, the official language of the Mughals. He believed that most Indians are gentle, kind, faithful in service, submissive to laws, and abhorred bloodshed. Hastings was secretly ordered to arrest the Nawab's chief minister Muhammad Reza Khan for fraud and embezzlement. However, the charges could not be proved, because the one accusing him was his ambitious assistant, the notorious Nandakumar, who had asked the English for a bribe to betray Siraj-ud-daula and the French when the English were planning to attack Chandernagore in 1757. Hastings took over the Nawab's authority but still used mostly Indian officials, believing their traditional corruption was not as bad as the greedy Englishmen. He paid thirty Company servants salaries in six Provincial Councils to oversee the Indian officials. He established criminal and civil courts of appeal in Calcutta and appointed Muslim and other law officers approved by the Nawab. Use of the *dastak* passes was abolished, and a uniform tariff of 2.5% was set on all internal trade.

The British Government loaned the Company 1.5 million pounds and ended their obligation to pay the Government 400,000 pounds annually. The Regulating Act of 1773 gave authority in Bengal to four councilors headed by the governor-general, who could break a tie. The other councilors, Philip Francis, General Clavering, and Colonel Monson, began investigating Hastings, who became governor-general in 1774. That year Clive committed suicide in England. When Awadh nawab Shuja-ud-daula died and was succeeded by his son Asaf-ud-daula, the Council insisted on a new treaty and gained concessions, causing his troops to mutiny for lack of pay and his zamindars to hold back revenue. Francis with a letter from Nandakumar accused Hastings of accepting 350,000 rupees in presents from the young Nawab's guardian

Mani Begum. Nandakumar was charged with forgery, which the British had made a capital crime, and after a trial Nandakumar was hanged. He was a Brahmin, and Indians were shocked by this extreme punishment. Monson died and was replaced by Richard Barwell. An attempt to remove Hastings and Barwell was blocked by the Court of Proprietors, who could not be bribed and did not want the King's friend Clavering to end the Company's power in India. Clavering died in August 1777, and the Directors extended Hastings' term past 1779.

News that France had declared war on England arrived in August 1778, and within a few months the English seized Chandernagore and Pondicherry. Hastings set up the Amini Commission to determine the real value of land by examining past revenues. Eyre Coote joined the Council in 1779. When Hastings believed that Francis had violated their agreement by blocking a military decision, their quarrel escalated to a duel in which Francis was wounded. Francis objected to Bengal being governed by foreign traders and wanted the British monarch to have authority. During the Mysore war Hastings asked Benares raja Chait Singh to contribute an extra 500,000 rupees and two thousand cavalry. After he provided only 200,000 rupees, Hastings had him arrested. Chait Singh's armed retainers freed him, killing most of the sepoys, who for some unknown reason had no ammunition. Severed heads of English officers were paraded in villages. The Company sent more troops and deposed Chait Singh, who fled with his treasure. They installed his young nephew and nearly doubled the annual revenue payment to 4,000,000 rupees. The treasure was eventually captured but was divided among the troops to Hastings' consternation. His treatment of Chait Singh later became the most serious charge in the famous Hastings impeachment trial.

Hastings replaced the provincial councils with a revenue administration and local Indian *diwans*, but this made it difficult to find positions for young Englishmen in India. Francis promoted investigation of Hastings in the House of Commons, and in 1782 Hastings was censored; but the Court of Proprietors rescinded the Directors' recall order. Lack of rain caused famine in northern India. Hastings visited Lucknow (Lakhnau), where the Awadh nawab lived in luxury in a palace tended by 4,000 gardeners. He managed to collect half the debt the opium-eating Asaf-ud-daula owed by sending troops to take it by force from the rich Begams.

Hastings lamented the encroaching spirit of the English that allowed and even protected licentious individuals. *Hicky's Gazette* began publishing sensational news, sarcasm, gossip, and scandals in 1780; but after it exposed Hastings' private life, he had Hicky arrested and deported. He welcomed orientalist William Jones and wrote an introduction to Wilkins' translation of the *Bhagavad-gita*. They founded the Asiatic Society of Bengal. After his council supporter Wheler died, Hastings handed his office over to Macpherson and left India in February 1785. His impeachment trial by Parliament began in 1788, but he was not acquitted on all charges until 1795. Even his detractor, the historian Macaulay, admitted that Hastings had been the most popular governor of India.

Marathas and Cornwallis Reforms 1784-1800

In England clause 34 of Pitt's India Act of 1784 enjoined the Company not to intervene in Indian politics, and Macpherson refused to join the Maratha alliance against Mysore unless the French were attacking them. To fight Tipu, Nana Fadnavis made an alliance with Nizam 'Ali and granted Garha-Mandla to Mudhoji Bhosle in exchange for 15,000 cavalry and 3,200,000 rupees; but he had to give Holkar a million rupees to pay his army. The Maratha army led by Hari Pant Fadke invaded Mysore in 1786. Tipu was in a strong position but feared British involvement and negotiated a treaty in March 1787, agreeing to pay six million rupees.

Lord Cornwallis was the Company's governor-general 1786-93 and was obligated to follow Pitt's India Act. Muhammad 'Ali was living in luxury in Madras, and the Company was paying his extravagant debts. Cornwallis made a treaty with him, promising to defend the whole Karnatak for a fee. Nizam 'Ali was supposed to give Guntur to the English when Basalat Jang died in 1782. Cornwallis finally got Guntur from Nizam 'Ali in 1788, and the next year he promised him two battalions of sepoys provided they were not used against the Company's allies, which did not include Mysore. Five months later Tipu attacked a line of defences in Travancore that had been originally built by the Portuguese, captured by the Dutch in 1662, and sold to the Travancore raja. Cornwallis considered this a violation and arranged a triple alliance against Mysore. The Company's Charles Malet formalized it with

Nana's Marathas at Puna, and John Kennaway did so with the Nizam at Hyderabad; each promised 10,000 cavalry. Tipu had a disciplined army of about 100,000, and they were much more mobile than the English, whose officers travelled with furniture.

Bombay governor Major-General Medows replaced the unprepared Madras governor Hollond and led 15,000 men, taking Coimbatore in July 1790. Tipu's large army forced Col. Floyd to retreat and ravaged the Karnatak; but outnumbered Col. Hartley defeated a Mysore army near Calicut on the west coast, and Bombay governor General Abercromby with a larger force landed and took over the Malabar province. Cornwallis joined Medows, and their combined army of 19,000 captured Bangalore in March 1791. Tipu retreated to his capital at Seringapatam while Cornwallis found his army bogged down by rain and starving bullocks; military stores and heavy guns had to be destroyed. Two Maratha armies brought supplies they sold, and eventually 28,000 bullocks were sent from the Karnatak. A Maratha army went off to plunder Bednor. Tipur still had 50,000 men but negotiated a surrender in March 1792. He ceded half his territory and promised to pay 33 million rupees; Cornwallis took two of his sons as hostages for two years until the indemnity was paid. The Nizam and the Peshwa split northern Mysore, and the English got Malabar with its spices for the Bombay presidency. The British restored the Karnataka to Muhammad 'Ali. Upon hearing news that England was at war with revolutionary France, Cornwallis took artillery to help Madras capture Pondicherry and then left for England in October 1793.

William Pitt's India Act of 1784 established a Board of Control that nullified the Company's Court of Proprietors but worked with the Directors to set policy. Pitt hoped this would guide politics in India with as little corrupt influence as possible. Both Macartney and Cornwallis refused to be governor-general unless they could control the council. Macpherson held the position for twenty months until Cornwallis was made commander-in-chief as well. Macpherson was criticized for making money for himself and his friends, but he managed to clear off military pay arrears. He offered the Nizam and the Marathas three battalions from Bombay to fight Tipu, but Cornwallis retracted that.

Pitt and Control Board chairman Henry Dundas wanted Cornwallis to institute reforms, and in his first three years peace allowed him to do so. Cornwallis suspended the Board of Trade and dismissed most of its members for irregularities. He stopped the selling of offices and enforced the ban on private trade by public servants by sending offenders home. He abolished sinecures and dismissed high officials, and he got the Company to reduce commissions and increase salaries so that honesty became practical. He did not trust Indians and confined them to inferior positions only. He cut back corruption in Awadh by reducing the seven million rupees paid for the troops to five million and stopped exempting Company servants from duties by making a commercial treaty with Awadh.

The British had been using the zamindari system in Bengal since 1765. Zamindars collected taxes in their districts, traditionally a third of the gross produce, keeping one-tenth of what they collected. Failure to pay the assessment was usually punished by fines, imprisonment, or flogging, not by confiscating. John Shore had been in charge of revenue for the last four years under Hastings, and his research was used for the ten-year settlement Cornwallis made in 1789. He persuaded Dundas to make the settlement permanent in 1793. Zamindars were considered landowners and still had to pay 90% of what they collected, and the cultivators were protected by the British collectors over them. Many of the new assessments were too high, and some zamindars had to sell to men with money in Calcutta. Personal connections between the zamindars and the peasants were often broken, and many landlords were absent. As improvements were made, the fixed settlement resulted in the zamindars becoming wealthy; but the peasants' status remained low, and they could be evicted for not paying their rent. The Board of Revenue was reorganized, reducing the districts from 35 to 23. Each collector had two European assistants, and his salary was increased from 1,200 rupees per month to 1,500 with a commission of one percent on revenue collected. This Permanent Settlement fixed land revenues; as time went on, some believed that the Bengal and Bihar governments suffered from inadequate revenues.

Cornwallis reformed civil law by instituting the English legal system for all but minor suits. By abolishing legal fees everyone could have access to the courts; but this resulted in a backlog, and it took many years to bring a case. Muslim law was modified to replace mutilation with fines and to abolish distinctions made between believers and infidels. In 1790 Cornwallis removed

Muhammad Reza Khan so that the governor-general and his council had supreme authority with the advice of a *qazi* (chief judge) and two muftis on Islamic law. Initial appeals were made to provincial courts at Calcutta, Murshidabad, Dacca, and Patna. Zamindars had to give up their private police forces. Being a district police chief *(darogha)* was one powerful position an Indian could fill. The complete revision of the legal system became known as the Cornwallis Code in May 1793. Perhaps most important was that he applied the rule of law to the governors as well as the governed. Cornwallis wrote,

The collectors of revenue and their officers, and indeed all the officers of Government, shall be amenable to the courts for acts done in their official capacities, and Government itself, in cases in which it may be a party with its subjects in matters of property shall submit its rights to be tried in these courts under the existing laws and regulations.

In regard to the debts of nawabs such as Muhammad 'Ali, the Board of Control overruled the Directors and declared all debts were due; they were influenced by Benfield and others in Parliament who benefited from this. Thus Madras continued to drain wealth from the Company at Bengal.

Slave trafficking in India was abolished by proclamation in 1789; but rural slavery of peasant serfs continued in much of India, and the households of landlords often had domestic slaves in areas where Islamic law still prevailed. In the early 19th century Buchanan reported that the price of adult slaves varied between fifteen and twenty rupees while children cost an average of one rupee for each year of their age. Many men sold their children into slavery for bread during famines.

John Shore succeeded Cornwallis in 1793. He was a devoted Christian but also promoted the study of Indian culture as the third president of the Asiatic Society. Resident Jonathan Duncan established a Sanskrit College at Benares in 1792 and began a campaign to end infanticide. Baptist missionary William Carey came to Calcutta in 1793, set up schools, and translated the Bible into Bengali. William Duane began publishing *Indian World* in 1794, but he was arrested and deported the next year. During this European war Madras forces attacked Dutch settlements in Sri Lanka and the Spice Islands. Shore declined to defend Nizam 'Ali in a conflict with the Maratha confederacy that formed after Mahadji

Sindia was succeeded by his nephew Daulat Rao Sindia. After a battle at Kharda with less than 200 casualties in March 1795, the Nizam's army dispersed; he ceded territory and agreed to pay the Marathas thirty million rupees. Nizam dismissed two battalions of the Company's sepoys but found he needed their aid when his son 'Ali Jah rebelled against him. Muhammad 'Ali died in 1795; but his son Umdut-ul-Umara would not modify the treaty, and the corruption continued. However, Alexander Read and Thomas Munro established a revenue administration in Madras that became the model for British India. After Peshwa Madhu Rao fell off a terrace and died in October 1795, the Marathas were divided over the succession of Raghunath's son Baji Rao II. The conflict enabled Nizam 'Ali to regain territory he lost at Kharda, but by December 1796 Baji Rao was recognized as the *peshwa* with Nana Fadnavis as chief minister. For a while Daulat Rao Sindia's father-in-law Sarza Rao Ghatge gained control at the Puna court and extorted wealth, arresting prominent persons. Mahadji's three widows protested but were defeated in 1798.

Company officers were upset about their poor pay and limited promotion opportunities compared to the King's officers; but Abercromby suggested modifying Shore's new regulations, and mutiny was averted. In 1797 Awadh nawab Asaf-ud-daula invited Shore to visit Lucknow. Shore hinted at a collective guilt when he commented on the succession struggle in Rohilkhand in which Ghulam Muhammad had killed the heir and then was defeated by his son.

No one can calculate the consequences of the violation of a moral principle; and there is some justice in your suspicion that the inveteracy of the Rohillas may be traced to the injustice of 1774.3

The Afghan Zaman Shah had recently invaded as far as Lahore, and Shore wanted concessions from the frightened Awadh nawab. Asaf-ud-daula agreed to pay more and replace a corrupt minister; when the threat faded, he declined to turn over the fortress of Allahabad. Asaf-ud-daula died six months later, and Shore replaced Vazir 'Ali, who was claiming to be the Nawab's son, with his brother Sa'adat 'Ali. The new Nawab then ceded Allahabad to the Company and raised the annual payment for its troops to 76 million rupees. Zaman Shah occupied Lahore again in 1798; but he returned to Afghanistan when he learned that his brother Shah

Mahmud had invited the Persian shah to invade. Shore objected to the aggressive methods of Madras governor Hobart and annulled a treaty he made with the intimidated Tanjore raja. Hobart wrote to Dundas threatening to resign if Shore was not replaced; but the Directors recalled Hobart for having coerced the Karnataka nawab.

Richard Wellesley was not quite 38 years old when he became governor-general at Calcutta in May 1798. He believed in British imperialism and thought that Shore had been a weak governor. Because of the European war he exaggerated the threat of the French in India. In June he learned that the French governor Malartic of Mauritius was raising volunteers to fight for Tipu Sultan against the English. Only a hundred recruits joined him, but Wellesley used it as an excuse to bully Tipu. His brother Arthur Wellesley advised him to be patient and let Tipu explain. Richard Wellesley goaded Madras into preparing for war and got Nizam 'Ali to dismiss his French officers and support the English Company. In February 1799 the combined army of the Company had 40,000 men with more than 100,000 camp followers. Tipu had only about 37,000 men and used his mobility and a scorched-earth strategy. After being defeated on March 27 by Company commander George Harris, Tipu retreated to Seringapatam. General Baird, who had suffered 44 months imprisonment in a Seringapatam dungeon, wanted revenge and led the attack that stormed and plundered the Mysore capital. Tipu was killed, and Arthur Wellesley had to use flogging and hanging to restore order. More than half of the two million pounds of booty was claimed by the officers as prize money, Harris getting 143,000. Richard Wellesley was offered 100,000, which he declined.

Governor-General Wellesley had 14,000 European troops but declared 31,000 were needed. The Company reluctantly agreed to 21,000, but the number only reached about 18,000. Wellesley installed a five-year-old Hindu prince in the small traditional kingdom of Mysore. By a treaty in 1800 Nizam 'Ali gave up the Mysore territories he had gained in both wars to the Company for protection and an end to his paying an annual subsidy. His many troops were disbanded and caused local disorders for several years. The Company gained control of Tanjore when the raja Serfogi they had installed accepted a 40,000-pound annual pension in October 1799. Five months later Wellesley ordered the Company to take over the port of Surat as its nawab was given a pension.

Wellesley believed that the English could govern better. After Muhammad 'Ali's son Umdat-ul-Umara died, the regents for his son rejected a pension agreement. So Wellesley offered one to Umdat-ul-Umara's nephew, and the Company took over the Karnataka in July 1801. The Directors approved the new treaty, because they believed the family of Muhammad 'Ali had forfeited its previous treaty rights by treasonable correspondence with Tipu.

More complicated machinations were used in regard to Awadh (Oudh). Vazir 'Ali resented having to live in Calcutta, escaped, and with several thousand armed men killed the Benares resident Cherry and other Englishmen in 1799. After Zaman Shah invaded from Afghanistan to Lahore again in the fall of 1798, Bombay governor Duncan and Wellesley sent envoys with gifts to urge the Persian shah to destabilize Afghanistan and oppose the French. In 1800 Zaman Shah was imprisoned and blinded by his half-brother Shah Mahmud. In 1799 Awadh's Sa'adat 'Ali had written to Wellesley that he would abdicate; but when he learned he could not choose his successor, he changed his mind. Wellesley ordered more troops into Awadh and told the Nawab he would have to pay for them. Sa'adat 'Ali objected that this violated the treaty; but in February 1800 he agreed to pay the Company and disband his own forces. The next year Wellesley demanded that the Awadh nawab cede at least half his territory to the Company, and the threat of force made him agree in November 1801. The ceded land of Rohilkhand and the Lower Doab bordering Bihar was most fertile. Sa'adat 'Ali was required to "act in conformity to the counsel of the officers of the Honourable Company." Wellesley named his brother Henry as president of the board of commissioners and lieutenant-governor of Awadh. This military and administrative control by the Company in exchange for subsidies in the name of a defensive alliance was called the "subsidiary alliance system."

In 1799 Richard Wellesley decreed that no newspaper could be published unless it had been previously inspected by the Government's Secretary, and the penalty for failure was deportation. He founded the College of Fort William in Calcutta to educate civil servants. The uninformed Directors objected, but they were overruled by Castlereagh on the Board of Control. In 1806 the Directors established Haileyburg College in England and reduced Fort William College to teaching Indian languages to Bengali civilians. Wellesley believed in free trade and arranged for 3,000 tons of shipping for private British traders so that they could compete with foreign merchants. Believing that the British could provide superior government, Wellesley made plans to improve drainage and roads in Calcutta and proposed experimental agriculture at Barrackpur. He encouraged missionaries, and the Bible was translated into Indian languages. He prohibited the sacrifice of children at Saugor Point by the Hughli River and tried to reduce the number of Hindu widows burned in *sati*.

Tukoji Holkar died in August 1797, and his sons fought over Malwa. Jaswant Rao Holkar emerged as regent and defended the Holkar House against the Maratha empire of Daulat Rao Sindia, who had 40,000 disciplined men under the French general Perron in his northern armies. The latter had Nana Fadnavis arrested on the last day of 1797, and Daulat's father-in-law Sarza Rao Ghatge terrorized Puna for three months to raise money. Nana was released in July 1798. That month the Company made a treaty with the Peshwa, who agreed to exclude the French from his army and pay the force from Bombay. This secret treaty was renewed annually three times. Meanwhile Lakhwa Dada led the war of Mahadji's widows against the tyranny of Daulat Rao Sindia that lasted four years. Young Peshwa Baji Rao II defeated the Kolhapur raja in 1799. Nana Fadnavis died in March 1800, and Daúlat Rao became the Peshwa's chief minister. The civil war in Daulat's family ended when Lakhwa Dada and the widows were driven out of Seondha in May 1801.

East India Company

East India Company, The British maritime organisation chartered by Queen Elizabeth I in 1600 AD with rights of monopoly trading in the eastern waters and later founding a colonial state in India. The opening of Trans-oceanic communication in the fifteenth and sixteenth centuries was closely accompanied by overseas colonial expansionism of the Maritime nations of Western Europe.

Origin and development The original name of the company, according to the Charter granted by the queen, was 'the Governor and company of Merchants of London trading into the East Indies'. For many years individual financiers fit out the voyages to the east. One of such voyages reached Surat in 1608, but without any transaction. The portuguese had driven them out of the area. The company got the right from the Mughal government to trade in Surat in 1612 when the Portuguese force could be met with force. In 1615 King James I sent Sir Thomas Roe as his ambassador to the court of Emperor jahangir. The gifts that Roe gave on behalf of the King and his personal manners pleased the emperor and he granted the company trading rights as pleaded by the ambassador. Thus the company began to set up trading stations what they called 'factories' in the western and eastern coasts of southern India. In 1639 the local chief of Wandiwash by a grant empowered the English company to build a fortress at Madras and govern it as their own territory. Fort St. George was built at Madras, which became the headquarters of the company's business in India.

The East India company set its foot in Bengal in 1633 when a factory was established at Hariharpur on the Mahanadi delta. On 2 February, the English obtained a *farman* from Emperor shahjahan permitting them to pursue trade and commerce in Bengal. The most important privilege was obtained from the Bengal governor shah shuja who permitted the English to have trade in Bengal without any customs duties in lieu of an annual lump sum of Rs. 3000 only. It was this unique privilege which would take the company to the political domination of Bengal in course of time. In the same year the English founded their factory at hughli. Another factory was opened at Kasimbazar in 1658. In 1668, a new factory was opened at Dhaka, the capital of Bengal. The process of factory settlement was completed by the founding of Calcutta by job charnock in 1690 and from that time onward began the processes of establishing political dominance of the company in Bengal.

The company saw to it that its claims on the *Subah* always rest on legal grounds. The company thus obtained a fresh *farman* from the emperor permitting it to trade in Bengal customs-free in lieu of an annual payment of Rs. 3,000. The rebellion of SHOBHA SINGH in 1696 offered the company an opportunity to obtain permission to fortify the Calcutta settlement and thus arrange its own defence. The *Subahdar* gave the permission without weighing its military significance. The next step was to extend the company's influence by purchasing the zamindari of Calcutta, Sutanuti and Govindapur, thus quietly laying the foundation of power. In 1998 a rival company was formed and it got parliamentary incorporation under the name of "General Society Trading to the East Indies". The establishment of fort william in Calcutta and turning it an independent Presidency in 1700 followed these events. The two rival 'East India Companies' were amalgamated in 1702 with a new charter and a new name-'The United company of Merchants of England Trading to the East Indies' though the popular name 'East India company' remained till the last days of the company.

From the beginning of the eighteenth century, the company was turning ever-increasing trade in Bengal. The number of ships coming to Bengal was increasing every year. This was also the time when Bengal had a great administrator in the person of Murshid Quli Khan. Under him the Bengal trade and commerce had witnessed remarkable development, particularly its foreign trade. The company tried to take advantage of the weakness of the centre after the death of Aurangzeb in 1707, but Murshid Quli was resolutely opposed to giving new advantages to the company while severely restricting the old privileges.

The company was particularly indignant about the harassment that its officials suffered at the *chowkis* or customhouses. The tendency of the officers to have their private trade made duty free in the name of the company's *dastak* led to frequent conflicts. Quite often company's boats were halted for proper check of their goods. Murshid Quli Khan never yielded to the demands of the company for more privileges. The Calcutta Council then sent an embassy under John Surman to Emperor Farrukhsiyar with lavish presents. The Surman Embassy was warmly received by the emperor who was pleased to issue a *farman*, popularly known as Farrukh Siyar's farman of 1717 (the date on the *farman* is December 30, 1716) which directed the Bengal *Subahdar* to give the following main privileges to the company:

- that in addition to the existing privileges the company was to be given zamindari right over the thirty eight *mouzas* adjoining the Calcutta settlement;
- that in case the goods belonging to the company and other English were stolen, attempts must be made to recover the goods failing which proper compensation must be given;
- that Madras rupees of Surat quality must pass in Bengal without any discount;
- that the original *sanad*s must not be demanded;

- that all persons who might be indebted or accountable to the company should be delivered up to the Chief of the Factory.
- that a *dastak* given by the chief of the factory should exempt the goods from being stopped or examined by the *chowkis*.
- that the *Subah* should allow the company to coin money at the Murshidabad Mint.

The company knew it very well that the *Subah*, as they knew him, would not be agreeable to abide by this charter of rights which was actually purchased from the needy emperor and which had undermined seriously the sovereign status of the kingdom. But they also knew that he had given them some legal basis of their extortionate trade and commerce in Bengal and fight for the realisation of the privileges on legal grounds. The *farman* did not enumerate the articles to be covered by *dastak*. So the nawab's *chowkis* and the company officials were in confusion and the situation resulted in frequent conflicts, sometimes skirmishes. While the company officials saw that the nawab himself gave many orders to arrest and confine the breakers of law, the company even threatened reprisal. But Murshid Quli Khan avoided the direct confrontation.

The death of Murshid Quli Khan in 1727 and subsequent capture of power by Shujahuddin Khan was an opportunity for the company to get their demands realised, especially the zamindari rights over thirty eight villages. Shujahuddin more or less followed the footstep of his predecessor and very cautiously followed a policy of keeping the continuation of export trade undisturbed and at the same time avoid any confrontation with the company. But on the trade item of salt, which was claimed to have been duty free by the company but not so by the nawab, the relation between the company and the *Subah* got embittered to the point of a war which was somehow avoided at the mediation of Fatehchand, the Jagat Sheth. The private trade under the cover of *dastak* was a major breach of trust between the company and the government. The private trade of company officials was widely carried under the privilege of *dastak*. The company would not allow the *chowkis* to examine the cargo of boats on the legal ground that the imperial *farman* of 1717 exempted them of such examination.

During Shujahuddin Khan's period (1727-1739) East India company's trade increased phenomenally in spite of very cold relation between the nawab and the English. With the expansion of trade and commerce grew the company's interest in Bengal. It became the company's policy to see a nawab at Murshidabad favourably disposed to it. Such a favourable disposition the company got, by default, during the regime of Alivardi Khan (1740-1756). Being constantly harassed by the Maratha raiders, Alivardi found it prudent not to create another front of harassment by taking strict measures against abuses and excesses of the East India company. But Maratha incursions withered away at the accession of sirajuddaula to the *masnad*. Sirajuddaulah directed the English three conditions to observe if they were inclined to continue trade and commerce in Bengal: (i) they must demolish the unauthorised fortification of Calcutta forthwith, (ii) they must stop abuses of *dastak* and (iii) they must abide by the law of the land. The Fort William Council disregarded the nawab's orders at which the exasperated nawab attacked Calcutta and the English quickly fled away downstream of the Hughli river. In celebrating the victory Sirajuddaulah renamed Calcutta as Alinagar after his grandfather. In his act against the English, Sirajuddaulah had moral support from the French.

It was the period of Seven Years War in Europe. To the British, the Alinagar action of Sirajuddaulah was interpreted as a double defeat-defeat with the native nawab and with the French who supported him. Soon reinforcement came from Madras under the command of Robert Clive. Clive recaptured Calcutta (January 2, 1757) and stormed the Mughal port of Hughli in reprisal. A dialogue was soon opened with the Murshidabad *Darbar* faction secretly opposed to the young nawab. Jagath Seth was its leader. There followed a secret treaty with the conspirators confirming all the privileges and compensations claimed by the English. Mir Jafar, the recently sacked *bakhshi* of the nawab, was chosen to be the next nawab of Bengal. According to the terms of the treaty a sham battle took place at Palashi on June 23, 1757. Most of the nawab's army remained firmly still at the instance of Mir Jafar and other conspirators. Sirajuddaulah was defeated and later slain by Mir Jafar's son, Miran.

Beginning of the end of the company The battle of palashi has been correctly interpreted in the eighteenth century European history as a British victory at one important front on the world theatre of battles fought overseas in the Seven Years' War by the two great rival powers-England and France. It was a defeat for Sirajuddaulah and for his ally France at the same time. The East India company's success in installing a puppet nawab on the Murshidabad masnad and ousting the French presence in Bengal had inaugurated informally the establishment of British political dominance in Bengal. In realising their goal the company proceeded step by step. The 24-Parganas were obtained from the new nawab as a gift to the company immediately after Palashi. In 1760, three large and resourceful districts of Bengal (Burdwan, Midnapur and Chittagong) were acquired. The diwani or revenue administration of Bengal, Bihar and Orissa was acquired in 1765. From 1765 to 1772, the company shared revenue of Bengal but took no responsibility in administering it. On behalf of the company, Syed Muhammad Reza Khan managed diwani administration. This was the period when the company and its servants plundered the country's resources wantonly. The consequence was the collapse of the economy and collapse of law and order of the country. The famine of 1769/70, which decimated one-third of the Bengal population, was the result of the great ravage.

The Bengal conquest by the company proved to be not only ruinous for Bengal, but also for the company itself. In a plundering mood the company and its servants became busier in enriching themselves. Consequently, ever since the Bengal conquest, the company, which used to declare hitherto attractive dividend every year, was running at a loss. The chronic losses forced the company at last to pray for a 'rescue loan' from government in 1771. The political considerations led parliament to grant a loan and at the same time interfere into the affairs of the company by enacting the regulating act, 1773.

Events towards the end of the company The Regulating Act of 1773 hinted at two parallel developments-gradual encroachment of government control on the company affairs and corresponding curtailment of power of the company until its complete abolition in 1858. The Regulating Act had defined how the affairs of the company including the governance of the new state had to be managed. Government reserved the right to interfere into the affairs of the company any time it felt necessary. It felt to interfere in 1784 by enacting a more elaborate law controlling the Indian affairs of the company. A permanent parliamentary committee called board of control was set up to oversee the affairs of the company. The members of the court of directors were barred from receiving gifts and presents from cadets whom they nominated to become members of the Civil Service in Bengal. A governor general, Cornwallis, was directly appointed by parliament with specific instructions to execute. Cornwallis, to the great disadvantage of the company, had formulated the mode of administration of the colonial state. Private trade and receiving gifts and presents on the part of officers were totally banned.

Under the pressure of the British private traders, the monopoly right of the company was greatly relaxed under the charter act of 1793. A definite amount of tonnage in the company's ships was kept reserved for the private traders. The Act redefined the company's status by declaring that the company's state in India belonged to the Crown and henceforth they would have to rule India on behalf of the Crown and the Board of Control was vested with the power of appointing the Governor General. Lord Wellesley, who turned the company's Bengal state into an Indian empire, was appointed by the Board of Control. The colonial state became such an unwieldy affair and the Free Trade pressure groups became so influential that parliament took several decisions affecting the interests of the company. The most crucial of them was the abolition of the monopoly right of the East India company by the Charter Act of 1813. India was thrown open to free trade. The company, as a commercial organisation, was now required to operate under the market forces.

Never used to compete within the Indian market, the East India company became a sick organisation commercially. Furthermore, the administrative branch to attract competent Britons to the commercial management of the company too pitiably overshadowed the commercial branch of the company. Under the circumstances, the company's commercial activities were abolished under the Charter Act of 1833. Only its China trade was retained.

Henceforth the company was purely an administrative body on behalf of the Crown. Its only privilege was to nominate cadets for the enrolment in the company's Covenanted Civil Service. This also was circumscribed by many limitations set by the Board of Control. Under the Charter Act of 1853, the company was shorn of the last vestige of its power and privilege; the Director's privilege to nominate cadets for company's Civil Service was abolished and the system of competitive examination for recruiting civilians on the basis of merit was introduced, instead. The East India company, the builder of the British empire in India and the largest corporate organisation in Britain for two hundred years, was thus left with its shell only. For all practical purposes, the company became an irrelevant and burdensome body. The sepoy revolt of 1857 came as an opportunity for parliament to get rid of this nominal body. By the Queen's Declaration of 1858, the East India company was formally abolished. [Sirajul Islam]

Sirajuddaula nawab of Bengal. After the battle of palashi (23 June 1757) in which Sirajuddaula was defeated and subsequently murdered, the British became the virtual masters of Bengal, reducing the later nawabs to mere puppets in their hands. Mirza Muhammad Sirajuddaula was the grandson of Nawab Alivardi Khan and son of Amina Begum and Zainuddin Ahmad Khan. He was born in 1733 and soon after his birth Alivardi Khan was appointed as the deputy governor of Bihar. So Sirajuddaula was regarded as a 'fortune child' in the family and his grandfather had special affection and favour for him. It is stated that Alivardi had given his heart to Sirajuddaula from the day of his birth and 'never kept him apart from himself'.

It may, however, be noted that Sirajuddaula was given the charge of the nawab's fleet at Dhaka while his younger brother Ikramuddaula commanded the army. Alivardi took young Siraj with him in his military campaigns against the Marathas in 1746. Alivardi Khan celebrated Sirajuddaula's marriage with great pomp and grandeur. In May 1752, the nawab declared Sirajuddaula as his successor. On this occasion the European trading companies in Bengal also greeted him. During the closing years of his reign, premature death of some family members shattered Alivardi both mentally and physically and the old nawab died on 10 April 1756 at the age of eighty. Immediately before his death the nawab advised Siraj to strive for the suppression of the enemies (of the province) and devote himself to secure the well-being of the subjects by removing all evils and disorders. He implored Siraj to nurture the goodwill of the people and follow his (Alivardi's) footsteps. Luke Scrafton relates that Sirajuddaula swore on the Quran at the deathbed of his grandfather that he would not touch any intoxicating liquor in future and that he kept the promise ever after. Siraj ruled for little over one year (April 1756 to June 1757) and the *Masnad* of Bengal was full of thorns for him. During his short lived-administration the young nawab faced enemies from within the family as well as from out-side.

Sirajuddaula's nomination to the nawabship caused jealousy and enmity of Ghaseti Begum (eldest sister of Siraj's mother), Raja Rajballabh, Mir Jafar Ali Khan and Shawkat Jang (Siraj's cousin). Ghaseti Begam possessed huge wealth, which was the source of her influence and strength. Apprehending serious opposition from her, Sirajuddaula seized her wealth from Motijheel Palace and placed her in confinement. The nawab also made certain changes in high government positions giving them to his own favourites. Mir Mardan was appointed *Bakshi* (Paymaster of the army) in place of Mir Jafar. Mohanlal was elevated to the post of *peshkar* of his *Dewan Khana* and he exercised great influence in the administration. Eventually Siraj suppressed Shaukat Jang, governor of Purnia, who was killed in a clash.

The accession of Sirajuddaula threatened the position of the dominant section of the ruling group in murshidabad, which was engaged in accumulation of wealth during the time of the earlier nawabs. With his assuming the reins of government, this group apprehended that he would be a danger to their continuous enjoyment of the sources of accumulation of wealth, as he was trying to raise another group to counterpoise the old one which usurped the power of the nawab to a great extent. Sirajuddaula's accession was a threat to the British also because he made it absolutely clear that unlike the previous nawabs he would not put up with the abuse of *dastaks* by the British and their illegal private trade. The threat came at a crucial time when the private trade of the Company's servants was facing a severe crisis.

Sirajuddaula had genuine grievances against the English east India company. First of all he suspected the company's design against his succession and expressed his annoyance to the British in no uncertain terms. His charges against the company were, first, that they strengthened the fortification around the fort william without his approval; second, that they grossly abused the trade privileges granted to them by the Mughal rulers by which the government incurred heavy loss of customs duties; and third, that they gave shelter to his officers like Krisnadas, son of Rajballav who appropriated government funds. The nawab also informed them of his intention to forgive them if they removed his complaints and agreed to trade upon the same terms and conditions as they did in the time of Murshid Quli Khan. But the company practically showed no respect to the nawab's demands. On the other hand, governor goger drake of the Calcutta Council insulted Naraigan Singh, nawab's special envoy to Fort William.

These events enraged the nawab and to retaliate he first captured the kasimbazar factory and then attacked Calcutta and drove the English out. This attack led to the so-called black hole incident. Following the Nawab's action at Calcutta and arrival of reinforcement from Madras the treaty of alinagar was signed between him and the English by which the nawab agreed to compensate the English their losses at Calcutta. But the English now became more arrogant. In fact re-establishment of the company's settlements in Bengal, after it's defeat at Calcutta, was possible only in two ways either to approach the nawab to forgive the company or to avenge the defeat by force. The English chose to avenge and in the garb of the peace treaty actual preparation for war began.

The English now turned to vigorous political and secret activities to destroy the French influence and to replace Sirajuddaula by a person entirely friendly to them. To this end the company successfully made a conspiracy against the nawab and enlisted the support of Mir Jafar, the Jagat Sheth and other disaffected courtiers. When everything was finalised the company's forces under Robert Clive and Charles Watson moved towards Murshidabad for a show down. The nawab met Clive at Palashi on 23 June 1757. The nawab was defeated in the battle that ensued and fled from the battlefield. On his way to Patna he was caught by a partisan of Mir Jafar and killed by an Iranian guard at the instance of Miran (son of Mir Jafar) on the night preceding 3 July 1757. In the mean time the company installed Mir Jafar as the new nawab of Bengal. Thus the English won the victory at Palashi not merely because of the strength of their forces but because of the strength of the conspiracy and the treason within Sirajuddaula's camp. The defeat of the nawab marked the beginning of the English ascendancy in Bengal and gradually the entire subcontinent surrendered its destiny to the East India Company.

Sirajuddaula was a victim of a conspiracy, engineered and encouraged by the British who roped in the disgruntled elements of the *darbar* in their 'project' of a coup. There is no denying that there was a simmering discontent in the nawab's court. But resentment against or dissatisfaction with the nawab might have created the necessary but not the sufficient condition for the hatching or the success of a conspiracy.

The Palashi conspiracy took the final shape only under the aegis of the British and without their active involvement, it would not have matured enough to bring about the downfall of the nawab. Thus, Sirajuddaula had to go both for the benefit of the British and the ruling clique at Murshidabad. And hence the Palashi revolution in which Sirajuddaula was deposed and Mir Jafar installed.

It may be true that as a nawab, he was a little arrogant and perhaps also short-tempered. In other words, he had his limitations. His main shortcomings were his lack of firm resolution, his vacillation and above all his bewilderment when faced with a critical situation. But one has to remember that he was still a young man in his early twenties, not yet fully mature and quite a little 'intoxicated' with his power and position. His greatest mistake was that, in his inexperience, he tried to deal with all his opponents at the same time, without having recourse to necessary precautions that they could not combine against him. His failure to do so and his irresolution till the last moment brought about his downfall.

Sirajuddaula's limitations and his public and private character should be judged considering the environment he worked in and the cause he fought for and gave his life. A marked change in his character was noticeable after he had become the nawab. Alivardi's last advice might have acted as a great influencing factor on him. The verdict of history is that whatever might have been his fault, Sirajuddaula neither betrayed his master nor sold his country. 'The name of Sirajuddaula stands higher in the scale of honour than does the name of Clive. He was the only one of the principal actors who did not attempt to deceive'. [Sushil Chaudhury and KM Mohsin]

The Battle of Palashi

Palashi, The battle of was fought between Nawab Sirajuddaula and the east India company on 23 June 1757. It lasted for about eight hours and the nawab was defeated by the company because of the treachery of his leading general Mir Jafar. Palashi's political consequences were far-reaching and devastating and hence, though a mere skirmish, it has been magnified into a battle. It laid the foundation of the British rule in Bengal. For the English East India Company, Bengal was the springboard from which the British expanded their territorial domain and subsequently built up the empire which gradually engulfed most parts of India and ultimately many parts of Asia as well.

The Background The battle had a long background that could be traced from the beginning of the East India Company's settlement in Bengal in early 1650s. The Mughal rulers of Bengal allowed the East India Company to settle in Bengal and trade free of duty on payment of an annual sum of three thousand taka. Within a few years of their settlement at Hughli and Kasimbazar the company's trade began to expand rapidly both physically and in terms of capital investment. But their intrusion into the internal trade of Bengal became a cause of conflict between Shaista Khan, the Mughal subahdar, and the English in the last quarter of the 17th century. After Shaista Khan had left Bengal the English were allowed to settle in Calcutta, purchase the zamindari rights over the three villages of Kalikata, Govindapur and Sutanuti. They established a fort at Calcutta and named it fort william.

The purchase of zamindari and the establishment of the Fort William proved highly profitable to the East India Company and the vested interest that was created in it led them to purchase more zamindari lands (38 villages) around Calcutta. Meanwhile the abuse of trade privileges progressively worsened their relations with the Bengal nawabs. The company's authority at Calcutta hardly paid any attention to the directives of the court of directors from London to stop this evil practice and the privileges of *dastak* was illegally extended from the import-export trade to cover also the internal trade. At the same time the servants of the company began to use the trade permit to cover their private trade.

The company in its attempt to secure more privileges approached the Mughal Emperor Farrukh Siyar, who by a *farman* (1717) granted it important privileges which included duty-free trade, establishment of a mint at Calcutta and right to purchase

38 villages on certain conditions. As other merchants had to pay duty at certain rates while the English and their partners traded duty-free, the local merchants were threatened to be eliminated from the internal trade.

Nawab Murshid Quli Khan obstructed the implementation of the *farman* as he realised that in spite of the growing import-export trade of the company, it would escape with the annual payment of a meagre three thousand taka and the privileges would also deprive the government of its legitimate revenues from the internal trade as well as from the mint duties.

With the accession of Sirajuddaula in April 1756, the conflict between the nawab and the English company became almost inevitable as the young nawab, for the first time, protested vehemently against the unlawful activities of the company in Bengal.

He had three main grievances against the British-the unauthorized fortifications of Fort William, illegal private trade and shameless abuse of *dastaks* by the company servants, and illegal shelter given to the nawab's erring subjects. The nawab asked the British to take measures to remove his grievances and sent several diplomatic missions to Calcutta for amicable settlement of the dispute. The nawab demanded the extradition of Krishna Das and asked the English to demolish the new fortifications and ordered to fill up the ditch, which surrounded the Calcutta Settlement. The English insulted nawab's special envoy, who carried his letter to Calcutta. When Narayan Sing reported how unceremoniously Roger drake, the English governor of Calcutta, had dismissed him, nawab's temper was inflamed. Drake is reported to have said, "the sooner he [the nawab] came to Calcutta the better and he [Drake] would make another nawab".

The nawab immediately ordered his forces to surround the Kasimbazar factory. The factory chief surrendered but the company's governor at Calcutta became obstinate. There upon, the nawab marched upon Calcutta and captured it. The re-establishment of the company in Bengal after their defeat was possible in one of the two ways either surrendering to the nawab or to apply force to avenge the defeat. The British in Bengal appealed for urgent reinforcements to Fort St. George (Madras) which decided to send an expeditionary force under Robert Clive and Admiral Charles Watson to Bengal. They recovered Calcutta in January 1757 and declared a manifesto of war against the nawab. At this Nawab Sirajuddaula was compelled to sign the alinagar treaty with the English.

The Conspiracy The tension of war continued as the English, disregarding the treaty, started hatching up a conspiracy with the disaffected courtiers of the nawab. There is no denial that a section of the influential members of the nawab's court at Murshidabad, who were dissatisfied with Sirajuddaula, was trying to hatch a conspiracy to oust the nawab. But the point to emphasise is that without the active involvement of the British, there would have been in all probability no Palashi 'revolution'. It was the British who were more anxious than the other conspirators to put their own scheme of overthrowing the nawab. The company servants and other merchant adventurers closely connected with the British trade in India-though not so much the Company Directors in London-did from time to time advocate, in no uncertain terms, the acquisition of territories in India. The private trades of the company servants was facing a severe crisis in the mid-18th century and in order to retrieve their private trade fortunes, they took recourse to 'sub-imperialism'.

In fact, the seeds of the Palashi conspiracy were sown in the 'Instructions' of the Fort George Council (13 October 1756) which recommended 'not mere retaking of Calcutta' and 'ample reparations', but urged 'to effect a junction with any powers in the province of Bengal that might be dissatisfied with the violence of the Nawab's government or that might have pretensions to the Nawabship'. The implication of the last portion of the recommendation is too obvious to be emphasised. Even Clive wrote before sailing from Madras that Sirajuddaula was a weak prince and that most of his courtiers were dissatisfied. It was on this resentment at the court of the nawab that the British played 'the nice important game', as Clive reflected later on, and precipitated the conspiracy leading to the Palashi coup.

Both Clive and Orme (who was the official historian of the English East India Company and was in Bengal in the early 1750s) were aware of Colonel Scott's plan, prepared in Calcutta in 1752, of the conquest of Bengal, which was then with the Fort George Council. Clive was greatly impressed by the wealth of Bengal on an earlier visit to Calcutta in the winter of 1749-50.

The British private trade was facing a severe crisis in the late 1740s and early 1750s because of the sudden spurt in the French private trade and Asian maritime trade under the Armenian merchant Khwaja Wajid as is borne out by the shipping lists in the Dutch records. So the destruction of the French, which would prevent a Franco-Bengali alliance, and the deposition of the nawab who was threatening to stop the illegal private trade and misuse of *dastaks*-both essential for rescuing the battered private trade fortunes of the British-became the main target of the company servants' sub-imperialism.

Despite the assertion of several historians that it was the Indian conspirators who got in touch with the British for cooperation in the proposed 'revolution', there can hardly be any doubt from a careful reading of the documents that it was the British who contacted the disgruntled elements in the court for their support in the British plan of the coup.

On 9 April 1757, Luke Scrafton wrote from Kasimbazar to Clive's confidant, John Walsh, 'For God's sake let us proceed on some fixed plan. How glorious it would be for the Company to have a Nawab devoted to them!'

He wrote to Walsh again on April 18 about the plan of setting up Yar Latif Khan as the new nawab. Meanwhile the Select Committee adopted on April 23 the *coup d'etat* as its official policy. On that very day Clive requested the committee to permit Scrafton to remain in Murshidabad as he 'had affairs of consequence to employ him in'.

William Watts and Scrafton were actively engaged in securing the support for the project at Murshidabad. Orme states that Clive, having received the information that Mir Jafar was not well disposed towards the nawab, advised Watts to cultivate his friendship. Watts and Scrafton communicated with umichand, the prominent Calcutta merchant, and established contact with principal *darbar* officials. Yar Latif confided to Umichand, who was deputed by Watts, his desire to become nawab and that he would be supported by the *diwan* Ray Durlabh Ram and the Jagat

Sheths, the powerful bankers. Watts jumped for the scheme immediately and communicated it to Clive, who approved it.

But another pretender soon appeared on the scene. Though Orme states that Mir Jafar conveyed his proposal through a Calcutta based Armenian merchant Khwaja Petruse, Watts himself however wrote to his father later on that it was he who 'applied' to Mir Jafar who 'with great willingness entered into *my scheme* of complying with and signing any reasonable article on condition of his being made Nabob by our assistance'. The Select Committee in Calcutta resolved unanimously to support the revolution in favour of Mir Jafar, while Watts was entrusted to negotiate the terms for the settlement with him.

But the conspiracy was still in an embryonic stage and Mir Jafar could not yet be taken for granted. So Clive wrote to Watts on May 2 to assure Mir Jafar 'to fear nothing', that the British were 'strong enough to drive' the nawab out of the country and that he (Clive) would stand by him (Mir Jafar) as long as there was a man left. Mir Jafar was in Murshidabad since May 30 but Watts failed to conclude the agreement with him. It was only on June 5 that Watts could get the red (false one to hoodwink Umichand's claim) and white agreements signed by Mir Jafar.

The battle The agreement notwithstanding, the Select Committee became extremely anxious to put its plan of 'revolution' into execution. On June 11, it deliberated whether it would be 'most proper' to march directly towards Murshidabad or wait for further advice and a plan of operation from Mir Jafar. It was resolved unanimously that the 'present conjuncture is the most favourable that can offer to carry the project for a revolution in favour of Mir Jaffier into execution' because any further delay might have led to the discovery of the conspiracy by the nawab with the consequent elimination of Mir Jafar in which case 'our whole scheme' would be '*overset*' and the British would be 'left to act against the united force of the country'. Accordingly Clive began his march towards Murshidabad on June 13.

On June 19 Clive reached Katwa, which was taken by Colonel Coote the previous day. Clive called a meeting of the War Council on June 21 when it was decided not to take 'an immediate action'. But later Clive changed his mind and decided to march the next day. At dawn on 22 June the British army under Clive set out for Palashi. However in the early afternoon of June 22 he received the long awaited communication from Mir Jafar and proceeded on his march towards Palashi, which he reached after midnight.

In the meantime the nawab had started from Murshidabad and encamped at Palashi to oppose the enemy. The war started at about 8 in the morning on 23 June 1757. Nawab's army under Mir Mardan, Mohanlal, Khwaja Abdul Hadi Khan, Naba Singh Hazari and a few others gave a brave fight while about two-thirds of the nawab's army under Mir Jafar, Yar Latif and Ray Durlabh Ram merely stood by and watched. Even after several hours of fighting, nothing decisive happened. Clive had not expected such a resistance and it is reported that Clive thought of returning to Calcutta in the darkness of night 'after giving the best fight during the day'. But around 3 in the afternoon a cannon ball struck Mir Mardan leading to his death.

Bewildered and baffled at Mir Mardan's death, Sirajuddaula called Mir Jafar and implored him to save his life and honour. Mir Jafar advised the nawab to suspend action for the day and start afresh the next morning, and soon passed on the message to Clive. With the nawab's commanders turning back, the British made a fresh onslaught and there followed a general rout. The battle was over by 5 in the afternoon and victorious Clive immediately proceeded towards Murshidabad. John Wood, a British soldier, who was present at Palashi, observed: 'such was this great and decisive battle by which a kingdom was conquered without there having been a general assault'.

The conspiracy and the subsequent Palashi 'revolution' was not only engineered and encouraged by the British but they tried their best till the last moment before the battle to persuade the Indian conspirators to stick to the British 'project'. The general notions that the conspiracy was 'Indian-born', that the British had no 'calculated plotting' behind it, that they had little or no role at all in the origin and/or development of the conspiracy, that it was the 'internal crisis' in Bengal which 'inevitably brought in the British' and that the British conquest of Bengal was almost 'accidental' are hardly tenable any more. The English won the victory at Palashi owing to the strength of their conspiracy leading to treason within Sirajuddaula's camp. The defeat of the nawab was political and not a military one.

Aftermath

The Battle of Plassey is considered as a starting point to the events that established the era of British dominion and conquest in India.

Mir Jafar Ali Khan (d. 1765) nawab of Bengal. He was an Arab by descent (son of Sayyed Ahmad Najafi) and had come to India as a penniless adventurer like his master Nawab Alivardi Khan, who gave him the hand of his half-sister (Shah Khanam) and raised him to the post of bakhshi, a position next only to the nawab himself.

Mir Jafar Ali Khan

But Mir Jafar's designs did not stop there. Nawab Sirajuddaula came to the throne in a house divided against itself and hostile factionalism grew in the army due to Mir Jafar's ambition. Soon after Alivardi's death Mir Jafar sent a secret letter to Purnia urging Shawkat Jang to invade Bengal, assuring him of his own support as well as the support of other disgruntled elements in the army and the court of Murshidabad.

His unbridled ambition made him plan for the dethronement of Sirajuddaula, and with that aim in view he started intrigues at the Delhi Imperial Court for a *farman* granting Shawkat Jang the three eastern *subahs*. But the conspiracy became known to Sirajuddaula, and he foiled it in time. Siraj reshuffled appointments, placing his own partisans in important posts.

Mir Jafar was replaced by Mir Madan as the *bakhshi*. When the English decided to overthrow Sirajuddaula and set up a friendly nawab on the throne, it became apparent at Calcutta that the great Hindu banker, Jagat Sheth; Rai Durlabh, the former *diwan*, and Mir Jafar had joined hands with the English to overthrow the nawab. Towards the end of April 1757 the English got promises of cooperation from these conspirators, and on 1 May 1757 the Calcutta Council agreed to a secret treaty with Mir Jafar, promising to place him on the throne on certain conditions. William Watts, the chief of the English factory at Kasimbazar, conducted and completed the conspiracy with remarkable diplomatic skill, secrecy and courage. On 5 June 1757 he visited Mir Jafar and obtained his oath of allegiance.

In the battle of Palashi, on receiving the news of Mir Madan's fall, Sirajuddula called Mir Jafar to his tent and begged his loyalty. Mir Jafar swore by the Holy Quran to fight the English; advised the nawab to withdraw the troops from the field and promised to fight with renewed vigour next morning. On coming out of the nawab's tent to his own troops in the field, he sent a letter to Robert Clive informing him of the nawab's helplessness and despair and urging the English to advance at once and seize the camp.

Mir Jafar's treacherous advice worked. The nawab suspended the engagement of his troops for the day and ordered the withdrawal. When the nawab's troops began to withdraw Clive launched an assault upon the retiring troops. The vast cavalry hordes of Mir Jafar, Durlabh Ram and Yar Latif were retiring further and further away without having fired a single shot during the whole day, while Clive's musketeers kept up a steady volley. Clive himself sprang forward to deliver the decisive blow. The nawab's army fled in confusion. The nawab himself was forced to flee, but soon after he was captured and put to death by one Muhammadi Beg under orders from Mir Jafar's son, Miran. On 29 June Clive met Mir Jafar at Sirajuddaula's Hirajhil Palace and there, in the presence of the rajas and other courtiers, he led Mir Jafar by the hand to the *masnad*, and saluted him as the nawab of Bengal, Bihar and Qrissa, upon which the courtiers congratulated him and paid him the usual homage.

As a reward the company was granted undisputed right to free trade in Bengal, Bihar and Orissa. It also received the zamindari of the 24 Parganas near Calcutta. Mir Jafar paid a sum of Rs. 17,700,000 as compensation to the company for Sirajuddaula's attack on Calcutta and the traders of the city. In addition, he paid large sums as 'gifts' to high officials of the company. Moreover, it was understood that British merchants and officials would no longer be asked to pay any taxes on their private trade. The company's officials wished to grasp all they could by using Mir Jafar as a 'golden sack' into which they could dip their hands at pleasure.

Mir Jafar soon discovered that it was impossible to meet all the demands of the company and its officials, who on their part, began to criticise the nawab for his incapacity in fulfilling their expectations. Therefore, in October 1760, the company forced Mir Jafar to abdicate in favour of his son-in-law, Mir Qasim. But soon the independent spirit of Mir Qasim led to his overthrow and the English restored Mir Jafar as nawab in 1763 and collected huge sums for the company and its high officials.

Mir Jafar's inglorious nawabship ended with his death in 1765. [Mohammad Shah]

Mir Qasim

Mir Qasim nawab of Bengal (1760-1763). He was put on the throne of Murshidabad by the east India company, replacing his father-in-law Mir Jafar, on 20 October 1760. Able and ambitious, Mir Qasim was determined to assert his independence at the earliest opportunity, and he embodied the Indian reaction to the English company's exploitations. But he had mortgaged his country's fortunes for the office: the three districts of Burdwan, Midnapur and Chittagong were assigned to the company for the maintenance of their troops; the outstanding debts of Mir Jafar were to be paid; and two hundred thousand pounds were paid in cash to the Calcutta Council.

Mir Qasim believed that since he had paid the company and its servants adequately for putting him on the throne, they should now leave him alone to govern Bengal. He realised that a full treasury and an efficient army were essential to maintain his independence. There were now two powers in Bengal, each determined to assert itself and each urgently requiring funds which it could only obtain at the other's expense. A clash was, therefore, inevitable and it was averted for three years, mainly due to the ability of the nawab and the divided Council at Calcutta.

By adroit diplomacy Mir Qasim both obtained his own investiture from Shah Alam II, the Mughal emperor, and induced him to leave Bihar. He was aware of the fact that in the last fifty years the English had developed much influence in the lower Gangetic region. He chalked out a strategy to hold the English in the lower deltaic region (where they were powerful because of their naval force) and not to allow them to spread their influence to the upper Gangetic region, where their presence was not yet felt owing to the distance from their gun boats. He next began to raise a force cf disciplined troops, and to secure himself from undue interference from Calcutta he transferred his capital from the riverine Murshidabad to the hilly district of Monghyr.

All these measures required money. He was able to increase the state revenue by resuming vast amount of lakheraj (rent-free) lands, by conducting a new survey of land and increasing the rate of land tax. He ousted those zamindars who were reluctant to pay enhanced revenue. As a result, state revenue increased remarkably. Thus, for the first time since Palashi, the nawab could pay his army and bureaucracy regularly. He then turned to the English and attempted to remove their corruption, which was harming his revenue administration. The English did not like this. They disliked the nawab's attempts to cheek the misuse of the imperial farman of 1717 by the company's servants, who demanded that their goods, whether destined for export or for internal markets, should be free of duties.

But actually the farman had exempted the company from all export and import duties on their foreign trade, but the private trade of the company's servants (particularly in salt and tobacco) was subject to the ordinary internal tolls. In 1757 Clive obtained from Mir Jafar the practical exemption of this private internal trade from duty without an express provision in the treaty. Naturally, the private trade of the company's servants grew apace while that of the Indian merchants dwindled. Indian merchants had to pay taxes from which the foreigners got complete exemption. Moreover, the company's servants illegally sold the dastaks or free passes to friendly Indian merchants who were thereby able to evade the internal customs duties. These abuses ruined the honest Indian traders through unfair competition and deprived the nawab of a very important source of revenue at the moment when he wished to increase it.

The Calcutta Council even revolted against a modest 9 percent duty on European traders' private goods as against a duty of 40 percent for the Indians, and refused to admit the right of the local faujdars or police officers to adjudge disputes. Though the duty was reduced from 9 percent to 2 1/2 percent on salt, the company rejected the right of the nawab's officers to interfere. Mir Qasim's attempt to enforce discipline through his faujdars was one of the immediate causes of the company's breach with him.

The nawab retaliated, decided to abolish customs duties on internal trade altogether, thus giving his own subjects a concession that the English had seized by force. But the alien merchants were no longer willing to tolerate equality between themselves and the Indians. They demanded the re-imposition of duties on Indian traders. Thus, there could be no compromise between the company's servants, who were determined to assert their supremacy in Bengal, and the nawab's resolve to be master in his own house, and therefore, war was now inevitable.

Mir Qasim was driven to a conflict in spite of the fact that he discharged the company's debt. Though he proved his ability by paying off the heavy arrears of his army, retrenching the expenses of his court and reducing the power of the zamindars, he was never given a fair chance. From the outset he was the object of suspicion and hostility of the majority of the members of the Calcutta Council. The conflict was precipitated at Patna where the Resident, Ellis, provoked the embittered nawab. A regular campaign ensued during the summer of 1763, during which the nawab's new army was defeated in pitched battles at Katwah, Murshidabad, Giria, Sooty, Udaynala, and Monghyr, and he fled to Patna; from there he went to Oudh.

Mir Qasim enlisted the support of Shujauddaula, the nawab wazir of Oudh, who was joined by the wandering Emperor Shah Alam II. Together they formed a confederacy with a view to recovering Bengal from the English. Fighting resumed in the autumn of 1764 and the campaign concluded with the resounding victory of the English at Buxar on 22 October. Shah Alam II joined the English camp and concluded peace with them. Shujauddaoula fled to Rohila Khand while

Oudh was overrun. Mir Qasim disappeared and died in obscurity near Delhi in 1777.

The short but decisive campaign of Mir Qusim is significant. It was a straight fight between two rival claimants for supremacy. Mir Qasim knew quite well that a final contest with the English was inevitable, and hence he equipped his army and husbanded his resources as best as he could. He was not inferior in capacity to an average Indian ruler of the day. His repeated defeats only demonstrated the inherent weaknesses of the army and the administrative machinery of Bengal. Yet the confederacy which he brought into being against the English shows his astute diplomacy, and its failure was again due to the inherent defects of the Indian army and state organisation. The engagements with Mir Qasim and the success at Buxar established the claims of the English as conquerors of Bengal in a much more real sense than did the battle of Palashi. [Mohammad Shah]

Battle of Buxar

The Battle of Buxar was fought in October 1764 between the forces under the command of the British East India Company, and the combined armies of Mir Kasim, the Nawab of Bengal; Shuja-ud-Daula, the Nawab of Awadh; and Shah Alam II, the Mughal Emperor. The battle fought at Buxar (currently in Bihar state, India), a town located on the bank of the Ganges river, was a decisive battle won by the forces of the British East India Company.

The Battle and Booty

British troops engaged in the fighting numbered 7,072 comprising 857 Europeans, 5,297 sepoys and 918 Indian cavalry. Estimates of the native forces vary from 40,000 to 60,000. Lack of coordination among the three disparate allies, each with a different axe to grind, was responsible for their decisive debacle.

British losses are said to have been 847 killed and wounded, while the three Indian allies accounted for 2,000 dead; many more were wounded. The victors captured 133 pieces of artillery and over 1 million rupees of cash.

Treaty of Allahabad

Suja-ud-Daula, the prime victim, signed the Treaty of Allahabad that secured Diwani Rights for the Company to administer the collection and management of the revenues of almost 100,000,000 acres (400,000 km) of real estate which currently form parts of the Indian states of West Bengal, Orissa, Bihar, Jharkhand, Uttar Pradesh, as well as of Bangladesh. He was also forced to pay a war indemnity of 5 million rupees. However, all his pre-war possessions were returned except for the districts of Karra and Allahabad.

Shah Alam II became a pensioner with a monthly stipend of 450,000 rupees towards upkeep of horses, sepoys, peons, burcandazes and household expenses. Mir Kasim, who was not a general, was quietly replaced. He also received a small share of the total land revenue, initially fixed at 2 million rupees.

The Battle of Buxar heralded the establishment of the rule of the East India Company in the eastern part of the Indian subcontinent. While the Battle of Plassey secured a foothold for the British East India Company in the rich province of Bengal, the Battle of Buxar is really the battle that made them the dominant force in India.

Shuja was restored to Awadh, with a subsidiary force and guarantee of defence, the emperor Shah Alam solaced with Allahabad and a tribute and the frontier drawn at the boundary of Bihar. In Bengal itself he took a decisive step.

In return for restoring Shah Alam to Allahabad he gave the imperial grant of the diwani or revenue authority in Bengal and Bihar to the Company. This had hitherto been enjoyed by the nawab, so that now there was a double government, the nawab retaining judicial and police functions, the Company exercising the revenue power. The Company was acclimatized, as it were, into the Indian scene by becoming the Mughal revenue agent for Bengal and Bihar. There was as yet no thought of direct administration, and the revenue was collected by a Company-appointed deputy-nawab, Muhammad Reza Khan.

But this arrangement made the Company the virtual ruler of Bengal since it already possessed decisive military power. All that was left to the nawab was the control of the judicial administration. But he was later persuaded to hand this over to the Company's deputy-nawab, so that its control was virtually complete.

In spite of all this the East India Company was again in the verge of bankruptcy which stirred them to a fresh effort at reform. On the one hand Warren Hastings was appointed with a mandate for reform, on the other an appeal was made to the State for a loan. The result was the beginnings of state control of the Company and the thirteen-year governorship of Warren Hastings. Hastings's first important work was that of an organizer. In the two and a half years before the Regulating Act came into force he put in order the whole Bengal administration. The Indian deputies who had collected the revenue on behalf of the Company were deposed and their places taken by a Board of Revenue in Calcutta and English collectors in the districts. This was the real beginning of British administration in India.

The Carnatic Wars

The Carnatic Wars (also spelled Karnatic Wars) were a series of military contests during the 18th century between the British, the French, the Marathas, for control of the coastal strip of eastern India from Nellore (north of Madras) southward (the Tamil country). In the 18th century the coastal Carnatca was a dependency of Hyderabad, within the Mughal Empire. There were three Carnatic Wars between 1744 and 1763. Though the name originates with the local name for the region (Karnataka), then-current spelling let to conflation of the name with *carne*, Spanish for "meat", leading at least one British general to jokingly term them the "Meat Wars."

First Carnatic War (1746-1748)

The roots of the First Carnatic War can be traced back to the death of Aurangzeb (1707). Several erstwhile Mughal colonies revolted, among them Carnat and Hyderabad. Carnat was ruled by Nawab Dost Ali, despite being under the legal purview of the Nizam of Hyderabad. Dost Ali's death sparked a power struggle in between his son-in-law Chanda Saheb and the Nizam's nominee, Anwar-ud-Din. The British enlisted the help of Anwar-ud-Din to oust Dupleix and the French from Madras.

The Governor of the French East India Company, Joseph François Dupleix, sought to establish a French colony in India. Immediately upon his arrival in India, he organized Indian recruits under French officers for the first time. The British and French went to war over the succession to the throne of Austria, as well as to expand their colonies in the Americas. Since Mughal power was on decline in India, it was also seen as a good opportunity by the trading companies of France and England to settle their trade rivalry in India. It is pertinent to note here, that the trading companies of both countries, that is Britain and France, were maintaining cordial relations among themselves in India whereas their parent countries were bitter enemies on the European continent. Dodwell writes, "Such were the friendly relations between the English and the French that the French sent their goods and merchandize from Pondicherry to Madras for safe custody."

After the British initially captured a few French ships, the French called for backup from as far afield as Mauritius, and on 21 September 1746, they captured the British city of Madras. Among the prisoners of war was Robert Clive. With the termination of the War of Austrian Succession in Europe, the First Carnatic War also came to an end. In the Treaty of Aix-La-Chapelle (1748), Madras was given back to the British, in return for the French fortress of Louisbourg in North America, which the British had captured.

Second Carnatic War (1749-1754)

After the death of the Nizam-ul-Mulk, the Nizam of Hyderabad, a civil war for succession broke out in the south between Mir Ahmad Ali Khan *Nasir Jung* (son of the Nizam-ul-Mulk) and Hidayat Muhi ud-Din Sa'adu'llah Khan *Muzaffar Jung* (grandson of the Nizam-ul-Mulk).

This opened a window of opportunity for Chanda Sahib, who wanted to become Nawab of Arcot. He joined the cause of Muzaffar Jung and began to conspire against the Nawab Anwaruddin Muhammed Khan in Arcot. The French allied with Chanda Sahib and Muzaffar Jung to bring them into power in their respective states. But soon the English intervened. To offset the French influence, they began supporting Nasir Jung and Muhammad Ali Khan Walajah (son of deposed Nawab Anwaruddin Muhammed Khan of Arcot). This resulted in the Second Carnatic War. Initially, the French succeeded in both states in defeating and murdering their opponents and placing their supporters on thrones in 1749. In 1751, however, Robert Clive led British troops to capture Arcot. Clive's success led to additional victories for the British and their Nizam and Arcot allies. The war ended with the Treaty of Pondicherry, signed in 1754. Muhammad Ali Khan Walajah was recognized as the Nawab of Arcot. The French leader Joseph François Dupleix was asked to return to France. The directors of the French East India Company were dissatisfied with Dupleix's political ambitions, which had led to immense financial loss. In 1754, Godheu replaced Dupleix.

Third Carnatic War (1757-1763)

The outbreak of the Seven Years' War in Europe resulted in renewed conflict between French and British forces in India. The Third Carnatic War spread beyond southern India and into Bengal where British forces captured the French settlement of Chandernagore (now Chandannagar) in 1757. However, the war was decided in the south, as British commander Sir Eyre Coote decisively defeated the French under the Comte de Lally at the Battle of Wandiwash in 1760. After Wandiwash, the French capital of Pondicherry fell to the British in 1761. The war concluded with the signing of the 1763 Treaty of Paris, which returned Chandernagore and Pondicherry to France, and allowed the French to have "factories" (trading posts) in India but forbade French traders from administrating them. The French agreed to support British client governments, thus ending French ambitions of an Indian empire and making the British the dominant foreign power in India.

4

Marathas and the English Company 1707-1800

Mughal Decline and Maratha Rise 1707-48

Aurangzeb's Intolerant Empire 1658-1707

Before he died on March 3, 1707, Aurangzeb wrote a will hoping that his Mughal empire would be divided between his three sons with Mu'azzam governing in Kabul, A'zam in Gujarat, and Muhammad Kam Baksh in Bijapur; but instead they followed his own example and fought. A'zam was supported by imperial vizier Asad Khan and immediately proclaimed himself and marched toward Agra. Mu'azzam was 1400 miles away; but he declared himself Bahadur Shah and in June arrived with his army at Agra, meeting his son Muhammad Azim, who had come from Bengal and secured the imperial treasure of 240,000,000 rupees. At Jajau, where Aurangzeb had defeated Dara Shukoh 49 years before, each side lost 10,000 men. Bahadur Shah won because A'zam Shah's army scattered; he and his two sons were killed.

In May 1707 A'zam let the detained Maratha prince Shahu leave. He was Shambhuji's son and challenged the leadership of the widow Tara Bai and Rajaram's son Shivaji II. *Diwan* Balaji Vishwanath supported Shahu in the battle at Khed. Tara Bai and her son fled to Karnataka and settled in Kolhapur. Shahu would remain *chhatrapati* (king) of the Marathas until he died in 1749, encouraging agriculture, low taxes, and religious toleration but letting his *peshwa* govern. In 1710 Chandrasen Jadhav led the Tara Bai faction in the Maratha civil war that ravaged the southern provinces, but they were defeated by Balaji Vishwanath, whom Shahu appointed *peshwa* in 1713.

Because of Maratha rebellions, Bahadur Shah had difficulty collecting taxes in the Deccan, and revenues from the northern provinces were also interrupted. Ajit Singh of Marwar, Jai Singh Kachhwaha of Amber, and Rana Amar Singh Sisodia of Mewar formed a confederacy in the Deccan to oppose Mughal rule. Bahadur Shah with his army occupied Amber in January 1708 and replaced Jai Singh with his more loyal brother Vijai Singh. Then his imperial troops seized the Marwar capital at Jodhpur, as Ajit Singh surrendered and was restored to his previous rank. A *qazi* and *mufti* were appointed to enforce Islamic law, and imperial officers were ordered to destroy temples, rebuild mosques, and collect the *Jiziya* tax on non-Muslims. Kam Baksh had also crowned himself but remained in the Deccan. So in May 1708 Bahadur Shah marched south with an army of 300,000, though Ajit Singh and Jai Singh escaped to Rajasthan. Kam Bakhsh alienated supporters by his cruel suspicions and confiscation of properties. Negotiations failed, and near Hyderabad the greatly outnumbered Kam Bakhsh and his two sons were also defeated and killed by Bahadur Shah's forces. Rana of Mewar helped Ajit Singh and Jai Singh regain their capitals, and together they besieged Ajmer.

Sikh Guru Gobind Singh supported Bahadur Shah and wanted him to punish Vazir Khan of Sirhind for having executed his two younger sons. After Gobind Singh was murdered by two agents sent by Vazir Khan in 1708, the Guru's loyal Banda Bahadur assembled angry Sikhs into an army and massacred Muslims in Punjab towns on their way to Sirhind, which they also plundered in 1710 after thousands of peasants overcame Vazir Khan's cavalry. Banda proclaimed himself the true *padishah* (sovereign) and issued Sikh coins. His army took over most of the Punjab, but thousands were killed on both sides in their failed attempt to take Lahore. A Mughal army besieged the Sikhs at Lohgarh, but Banda escaped to the Sarmar hills. He and the Sikhs came back to take Pathankot and Gurdaspur in November 1711, and by March 1712 they had recovered Sirhind and Lohgarh.

Emperor Bahadur Shah came to Lahore to suppress the Sikhs. He also stirred up protests of a hundred thousand Sunnis there, because he added the name 'Ali to the Friday prayers. While he was dying in early 1712, Bahadur Shah kept his four sons near him. His second son Azim-ush-Shan had acquired the largest fortune from Bengal and Bihar and thus had the largest army. However, Zulfiqar Khan had joined Bahadur's side and become viceroy of the Deccan. He formed a coalition of the other three princes with the plan that Rafi-ush Khan would rule at Kabul and Jahan Shah in the Deccan under the oldest Jahandar Shah in Sindh with Zulfiqar as vizier at Delhi. Thus the most powerful prince Azim-ush-Shan was defeated and fled, dying in quicksand. Then Zulfiqar Khan joined with Jahandar Shan to defeat and kill his other two brothers, enthroning him near Lahore on March 29, 1712.

Zulfiqar Khan had the power and made Daud Khan Panni viceroy of the Deccan as Jahandar's foster brother Kokaltash Khan was ignored. Zulfiqar Khan imprisoned and confiscated the property of dozens of nobles who had supported the dead brothers, and two emirs were publicly executed. He made concessions to the Rajputs and abolished the *Jiziya*. Ajit Singh and Jai Singh were promoted, and Shivaji II was given a noble rank. Emperor Jahandar Shah was criticized for drinking and favouring his low-born wife Lal Kunwar and her relatives with lavish expenses. He began intriguing with Kokaltash Khan. Collecting revenue was difficult and became more corrupt. Zulfiqar Khan and his officials ignored laws and were susceptible to bribes. Jahandar's troops remained unpaid, and inflation was rampant. Most of the revenue came from Bengal, where Azim-ush-shan's son Farrukh Siyar was supported by the Sayyid brothers Husain Ali and Abdullah Khan of the Baraha clan. They marched an army west and scattered a large army led by Jahandar's inexperienced son Azz-ud-din. Having no money to pay soldiers, Zulfiqar Khan passed out golden and silver vessels and jewels from the palace, raising 40,000 cavalry. In January 1713 the Turani contingents refused to fight, and Zulfiqar Khan fled toward Delhi.

Farrukh Siyar claimed the throne and named Abdullah Khan vizier and his brother Husain Ali chief military paymaster *(bakhshi)*. When Farrukh Siyar arrived, he had Zulfiqar Khan, Jahandar, Lal Kunwar, and several nobles executed. Three Timurid princes, including his own brother, were blinded and imprisoned. For the next six years the Mughal empire was torn by factions. Jai Singh agreed to govern Malwa, but Ajit Singh rejected Thatta (Sindh). Farrukh Siyar sent Husain Ali to bring Ajit Singh to court but secretly sent a message that Ajit Singh would be rewarded for killing Husain Ali. Instead, Ajit Singh made a treaty with Husain Ali, agreeing to govern Thatta. The Emperor entitled Nizam-ul Mulk and made him viceroy of the six Deccan provinces, which he reformed by using troops to keep away Maratha tax collectors and raiders. At court Farrukh Siyar diverted funds for troops to attack the Sayyid brothers. In 1714 Abdullah and Husain Ali joined their Baraha army in Delhi. After negotiations, Farrukh Siyar agreed to send Mir Jumla to govern Bihar; Husain Ali became governor of the Deccan; and Abdullah Khan stayed in Delhi as vizier. Nizam-ul Mulk would not help Farrukh Siyar against the Sayyids and lost his estates. Mughal precedent fell as Husain Ali gained the authority to appoint and dismiss all officials. The Emperor ordered Daud Khan Panni to kill Husain Ali; but his cavalry were outnumbered, and he was killed in the battle. Suspicion was so great that Abdullah was accompanied in the streets by at least 3,000 cavalry. Revenues were leased to the highest bidders, and Farrukh Siyar tried to revive the *Jiziya*, which provoked more Hindu opposition.

In 1714 Sirhind *faujdar* Zain ud-din Ahmad Khan attacked 7,000 Sikhs near Rupar and sent a hundred of their heads to Delhi. Yet Banda Bahadur led 14,000 Sikhs toward Sirhind. Farrukh Siyar sent Qamar-ud-din Khan with 20,000 troops from Delhi and ordered Kashmir governor Abdus Samad Khan to besiege the Sikh fortress at Gurudaspur in 1715. Banda retreated into a fortress that could only hold 1,250 men, while the other Sikhs fled or were killed. After eight months many had died of hunger; others near death were beheaded by the Mughals, who took some 200 prisoners. On the way to Delhi the imperial forces carried on their spears 2,000 Sikh heads with long hair, and Zakariya Khan captured more to make the number of prisoners 740. At Delhi in March 1716 a hundred Sikhs were beheaded each day for one week. Banda and his 26 officials were tortured for three months. Then Banda was brutally killed, and the others were beheaded. Before he died, Banda said that he was a scourge in the hands of God to punish the wicked; but he was now paying for his own crimes against the Almighty. Banda had practiced socialism by distributing all wealth among his followers and by abolishing the zamindari rent system. He tolerated all religions and had many followers who were poor Hindus and Muslims, though he was greatly hated by many Muslims for his raiding. He also opposed the use of all drugs including wine, tobacco, and bhang (marijuana). Farrukh Siyar ordered that every Sikh found must convert to Islam or be put to the sword, and this order was obeyed for a while in Sirhind, Lahore, and Jammu. During this persecution some Sikhs robbed, others shaved off their beards, and some by hiding or being peaceful escaped punishment.

Mir Jumla could not raise enough money in Bihar to pay his troops, who revolted and followed him back to Delhi. The angry Emperor took away his titles, but Abdullah Khan resolved the situation by getting Mir Jumla appointed as *qazi* (judge) of Lahore. Abdullah also granted the English trading rights. The Jats, who had raided both armies during the civil war, continued to rebel. The Emperor sent Jai Singh to besiege them at Thun in 1716; but vizier Abdullah Khan accepted a bribe and made a treaty with Jat leader Churaman. Husain Ali Khan was trying to control the Marathas in the Deccan but found that the Emperor's letters were encouraging their leaders to attack him. So in 1718 the Sayyid brothers made a treaty recognizing the Maharashtra territory of Shahu and the Marathas in exchange for ten million rupees tribute and 15,000 Maratha troops loyal to Husain Ali. Farrukh Siyar refused to ratify the agreement, but Husain Ali ignored this and other imperial orders.

Farrukh Siyar called on Ajit Singh from Gujarat, Nizam-ul Mulk from Moradabad, and Sarbuland Khan from Bihar, and they brought 70,000 troops to Delhi; but after delays they left or joined the vizier. Mir Jumla returned from Lahore but also sided with Abdullah. The Emperor had only Jai Singh and his 20,000 Rajputs. Husain Ali Khan marched north with 25,000 of his own forces and 10,000 Maratha horsemen under his pay, since Peshwa Balaji Vishwanath had agreed to a treaty with the Sayyids. In a complicated negotiation Farrukh Siyar and the Sayyids agreed to release each other's political prisoners and dismiss their forces in February 1719; but after an angry meeting in the palace, Farrukh Siyar retreated into his harem while Abdullah Khan took over the fort. After a bloody street battle in which 1500 Marathas were killed, the Sayyid brothers chose Bahadur Shah's grandson Rafi-ud-darjat as the new emperor. Farrukh Siyar was blinded immediately and strangled in prison two months later. Rafi-ud-darjat died in June of tuberculosis and was replaced by his older brother Rafi'-ud-daula as Shah Jahan II; but he was addicted to opium and also died of illness in September 1719. The powerful Sayyid brothers made Shah Jahan's 18-year-old son Emperor Muhammad Shah (r. 1719-48). They tried to conciliate the factions; but they were Indian Muslims and were resented by the Irani nobles from Persia and the Turani aristocrats from central Asia. Ajit Singh's widowed daughter, who had converted to Islam to marry Farrukh Siyar, was allowed to leave the harem and return to her home and religion. When the Sayyids tried to transfer Turani emir Nizam-ul Mulk from his appointment as governor of Malwa, he marched on Delhi, appealing to other nobles. Their army defeated the Sayyid-Maratha coalition in August 1720 at Shakarkhedla. After Husain Ali Khan was assassinated, Muhammad Shah joined the opposition that defeated and later executed Abdullah Khan. For deserting this Sayyid, Muhammad Khan Bangash was made the governor of Allahabad. Jai Singh of Amber and Girdhar Bahadur persuaded the new emperor to abolish the *Jiziya* tax. Nizam-ul Mulk went back to govern the Deccan and defeated resistance.

Various conflicts greatly weakened the Mughal empire, and many regions became independent. Awadh (Oudh) had fifteen governors in thirteen years before Muhammad Shah appointed Sa'adat Khan governor in 1722; after defeating and killing Mohan Singh in 1723, he acted independently. Muhammad Shah dismissed Ajit Singh from governing Gujarat and Ajmer; but after Ajit's murder by his son Bakht Singh in 1724, he recognized his son Abhay Singh, who governed Marwar until his death in 1748. Nizam-ul Mulk returned to Delhi as vizier in January 1722. He tried to remove the corruption from the court and reform the tax system; but his attempt to reimpose the *Jiziya* tax was opposed by the Hindu nobles. Disgusted with court squabbles, Nizam-ul Mulk left Delhi again in December 1723 to return to the Deccan. His enemies persuaded the Emperor to write secretly to urge Hyderabad governor Mubariz Khan to attack him; but Nizam-ul Mulk made an alliance with the Marathas, and in 1724 they defeated and killed Mubariz Khan at Sakharkhanda in Berar. The next year Nizam-ul Mulk took over Hyderabad. Thus he became essentially independent and was later recognized by the Mughal emperor. After Nizam-ul Mulk supported the claim of Shahu's Maratha rival Shambhuji, Peshwa Baji Rao I (r. 1720-40) avoided pitched battles and ravaged the country, starving the Nizam into accepting a 1728 treaty that recognized the six territories of Raja Shahu in the Deccan.

When Abdus Samad Khan was transferred to Multan in 1726, his son Zakariya Khan replaced him as Punjab governor and hunted down Sikhs until he suggested the Emperor give their leader a title in 1733. Kapur Singh was chosen nawab and was given a *jagir* (tax income) of 1,000,000 rupees. The army of the elder Sikhs was called Budha Dal, and the army of younger ones Taruna Dal. The Sikhs continued to rebel against the Mughal government, and the *jagir* was confiscated in 1735. After an imperial army of 7,000 attacked Amritsar, the Taruna Dal joined forces and defeated the Mughal army.

In 1729 Bundelkhand's Chhatrasal asked Peshwa Baji Rao for aid, and the Marathas defeated Muhammad Khan Bangash, taking more control after Chhatrasal died two years later. Shambhuji was defeated in 1730 and agreed to recognize Shahu's sovereignty for part of Konkan and Karnataka, and together in 1731 they defeated and killed Khande Rao's son Trimbak Rao in Gujarat. Abhay Singh tried to fight the Marathas but had to leave Gujarat in 1733. Despite his efforts and earlier ones by Nizam-ul Mulk and Sarbuland Khan, Gujarat was overrun by the Marathas and was lost to the Mughals by 1737. Baji Rao invaded Malwa in 1732. The Marathas captured Hindaun and Sambhar, and in 1735 the Emperor recognized Baji Rao as the governor of Malwa. After a revolution on the island of Janjira in 1733, the Maratha navy made the Sidi accept a treaty in 1736 with dual government. Under Baji Rao each Maratha *jagir* district was jointly held by two Maratha chiefs.

Murshid Quli Jafar Khan had been administering and collecting taxes in Bengal and Orissa since 1701. He was promoted in 1713 and governed until his death in 1727. In 1714 he crushed the last Hindu kingdom in Bengal. In his last fifteen years he sent an average of 10.5 million rupees annually to Delhi, accumulating six million rupees for himself. The new Bengal capital Murshidabad was named after him. In 1727 his son-in-law Shuja-ud-din Muhammad Khan, the deputy governor of Orissa, succeeded in Bengal and Orissa for the Mughal emperor. After his death in 1739 his son Sarfaraz Khan was defeated by Bihar deputy governor 'Alivardi Khan, and in 1740 Emperor Muhammad Shah had to recognize the virtually independent 'Alivardi Khan as governor of Bengal, Bihar, and Orissa.

Probably the most outstanding leader who remained loyal to the Mughal emperor was Jai Singh, who was appointed governor of Surat in 1721 and Agra the next year. Sent to suppress the Jats for having supported the Sayyid brothers, he captured their stronghold at Thun. Churaman committed suicide, and the Jats returned to their farms. Hoping to prevent their raiding, he gave the Jat chief Badan Singh the job of collecting duties on highways. Jai Singh served as an intermediary between Muhammad Shah and the Rajput rulers. He built up the new city of Jaipur and sponsored learning with research centres there and at Mathura, Banaras, and Ujjain, patronizing influential scholars and literature. He supported inter-caste dining and tried to stop female infanticide by trying to limit how much fathers spent on their daughters' marriages. Jai Singh of Amber governed Malwa 1729-37 except for 1730-32 when Muhammad Khan Bangash fought the Marathas. Jai Singh made peace with the Marathas by sharing with them the money Delhi sent for defending the province.

Sa'adat Khan complained that Jai Singh was ruining the empire. After negotiations in which Maratha *peshwa* Baji Rao asked for too many concessions the Mughal emperor would not grant, Baji Rao marched his army toward Delhi but refrained from attacking the capital. Muhammad Shah called on Nizam-ul Mulk, whose army of 35,000 was doubled when he was joined by Sa'adat Khan's troops and Rajput and Bundela forces. However, the Peshwa's army of 80,000 invaded Malwa and surrounded them at Bhopal. In January 1738 Nizam-ul Mulk signed another treaty in which more tribute and the rest of Malwa were granted to the Marathas. In 1737 the Marathas attacked the Portuguese on the west coast. Bassein capitulated in 1739 after each side suffered about 5,000 casualties. In the 1740 treaty the Portuguese ceded the northern province except for the port of Daman. In 1739 Sa'adat Khan was succeeded in Awadh by his son-in-law Safdar Jang, who declared complete independence. In December 1739 Baji Rao invaded the Deccan with 50,000 men; but Nasir Jang's army of 10,000 defeated them in a pitched battle, and the Marathas gave up their claims in the Deccan. Peshwa Baji Rao I died in 1740 and was succeeded by his son Balaji Rao. Because of the factions at court, Jai Singh remained neutral during the invasion by Nadir Shah's Persians; but after Delhi was plundered, the Mughal empire had little authority beyond Agra and Delhi.

In 1722 Afghan rebels led by Mir Mahmud defeated the Safavid dynasty of Persia and ruled there until they were defeated in 1729 by Nadir Quli Beg, who became the Persian shah in 1732. His army of 80,000 besieged Qandahar in 1737. Meeting little Mughal resistance, Nadir Shah moved on in 1738 to capture Ghazni and Kabul. After his envoy was killed at Jalalabad, he sacked the town. Nasir Khan tried to stop the Persians in the Khyber Pass with 20,000 Afghans; but Nadir Shah's veteran army forced them back. After occupying Peshawar, the Persians began plundering the country and crossed the Indus River. Lahore governor Zakariya Khan had no support from the Mughal emperor and surrendered in January 1739; after paying Nadir Shah two million rupees, he was reinstated.

Nadir Shah sent out 7,000 Kurdish cavalry as scouts from Sirhind. The Mughals assembled an army of about 75,000, but Mughal arrows were no match for Persian bullets. After Sa'adat Khan returned from fighting the pillaging Kurds, his baggage was plundered. He went to fight the Persians; but he was only supported by some 9,000 cavalry, and after being wounded he was captured. He advised Nadir Shah to negotiate with Nizam-ul Mulk, and they agreed on an indemnity of five million rupees with no territorial acquisitions. When Muhammad Shah promoted Nizam-ul Mulk to *Mir bakhshi* (military pay-master), Sa'adat Khan resented it and advised Nadir Shah he could get twenty million rupees and jewellery in Delhi. Nadir Shah took Nizam-ul Mulk and Muhammad Shah into custody and made them agree to escort the Persians into Delhi. When threatened with corporal punishment if they did not reveal the treasures, the two agreed to commit suicide; Sa'adat Khan took poison, but Nizam-ul Mulk did not and escorted Nadir Shah into Delhi.

Disturbances led to Persian casualties, and Nadir Shah sent troops to quell the riots; after a shot missed him but killed an officer, he ordered a massacre in Delhi. About 20,000 people were slaughtered, and several hundred women committed suicide to avoid being enslaved. Treasure estimated from thirty to seventy million rupees was taken from the capital, including the famous Peacock throne, Koh-i-nor diamond, and an illustrated Persian manuscript on Hindu music. The Mughals ceded all territory west of the Indus River, and Nadir's army also took away 300 elephants, 10,000 horses, and 10,000 camels. Before leaving, Nadir Shah advised Muhammad Shah on government and warned him that Nizam-ul Mulk was too ambitious. On their long march through the Punjab the Persians' loot was often plundered by Jat peasants and Sikhs.

After Nadir Shah's invasion, Jai Singh tried to govern Malwa; but he ceded it to the Marathas in 1741. That year Maratha *peshwa* Balaji helped Nizam-ul Mulk to suppress a rebellion by his second son Nasir Jang in the Karnataka. Nizam-ul Mulk took his son prisoner but reinstated him two years later. After the rebellion, Nizam-ul Mulk used his army of 280,000 to pacify Karnataka. He maintained good relations with the Europeans trading on the Coromandel coast.

Like his father Baji Rao I, Balaji Rao (r. 1740-61) was only about twenty years old when he became the *peshwa* for Maratha *chhatrapati* Shahu. Disputes over the thrones in the Rajput states at Jaipur, Jodhpur, Kota, and Bundi called upon the Marathas to intervene in 1740 and help destroy Mughal authority in Rajputana. Yet in the confusion conflicts festered between Marathas. In 1741 Balaji led the Maratha campaigns in Bihar and Bengal. When he drove Raghuji Bhonsle's Maratha forces out of Bihar in 1743, Shahu ordered them to stay in separate regions. Balaji was given Malwa, Agra, Ajmer, Allahabad, and most of Bihar, while Raghuji was assigned Bengal, Orissa, Awadh, and part of Bihar. Karnataka nawab Dost Ali tried to expand his realm. His son Safdar Ali and son-in-law Chanda Sahib took over Trichinopoly and Madura; but the Marathas defeated them at Tanjore. In 1741 Marathas from the north killed Dost Ali, took over Trichinopoly, and captured Chanda Sahib, imprisoning him for seven years. Safdar Ali succeeded his father but in late 1742 was murdered by his cousin Martaza Ali, who was replaced by Anwar-ud-din Khan the next year.

After Persian Nadir Shah took over Afghanistan and invaded India in 1739, 'Ali Muhammad Rohilla (r. 1721-48) gathered a cavalry of about 40,000 Afghans and expanded his territory to include Muradabad, Kumaun, and Bijnor. In 1745 he dismantled fortifications at Bangarh to accept a Mughal position; but he declared his independence before he died in 1748. Two of his sons were still hostages and had been moved to Abdali's Qandahar, and so he was succeeded by his third son, the dissolute Sadullah. Vizier Safdar Jang got Bangash chief Qaim Khan to attack the Afghans, but he was shot dead in the losing battle.

Dal Khalsa Sikhs were organized into eleven major communities, each called a *misl,* which means equal or alike. The largest group was the Bhangi who liked that drug (cannabis). In 1745 Zakariya Khan was succeeded by his son Yahiya Khan, who continued the persecution. Lahore *diwan* Lakhpat Rai was sympathetic with the Sikhs until his brother was killed; then he vowed to exterminate them. In his 1746 campaign his forces killed about 7,000 Sikhs and took 3,000 prisoners, executing them in Lahore. The next year Shah Nawaz Khan defeated his brother Yahiya in a civil war and put Lakhpat in prison. Shah Nawaz chose the Sikh Kaura Mal as his *diwan;* but when the Mughals considered him a usurper, he appealed to Afghanistan's Ahmad Shah Abdali.

Afghan Invasions, Sikhs, and Marathas 1748-67

After Nadir Shah was assassinated in 1747, Ahmad Shah Durrani of the Abdali clan proclaimed himself king in Afghanistan, taking control of Qandahar, Kabul, and Peshawar. Ahmad Shah Abdali invaded India with 12,000 veterans, but after seizing Lahore in January 1748 he was defeated in March near Sirhind by Mughal prince Ahmad Shah and Muin-ul-mulk (Mir Mannu), who was named governor. That year the Sikhs ousted the Mughals from Amritsar and built the fort Ram Rauni. The aging Kapur Singh resigned, and Jassa Singh Ahluwalia became the Sikh commander. Muin-ul-mulk besieged the Sikhs for three months until Ahmad Shah Abdali invaded again in December 1748. When Abdali was recognized as ruling territory west of the Indus, he agreed to depart. Shah Nawaz Khan was appointed governor of Multan and challenged Muin-ul-mulk with an army of 15,000. Kaura Mal mediated an alliance, and the Sikhs were granted a *jagir* (tax district) of twelve villages. Ahmad Shah Abdali returned to Lahore in 1751 and demanded tribute from Muin-ul-mulk. Sikhs were on his side, but the Afghans defeated them and conquered the Punjab and Kashmir, forcing Mughal emperor Ahmad Shah to cede territory up to Sirhind. After Madho Singh invaded Jaipur to collect money for the Marathas, the Rajputs rebelled and massacred his troops in January 1751. That year other Marathas drove the Rohillas into the hills and sacked their entire country, taking over half the Bangash territory in the Doab.

In 1752 Ahmad Shah Abdali sent Abdullah Khan Ishaq Aqasi with 15,000 Afghans into Kashmir, where Abul Qasim Khan had recently replaced the war hero Abu Barakat Khan; but Abul Qasim had ruled so tyrannically that appeals were made to Abdali. The Afghans defeated the Kashmiris in fifteen days as their commander defected. Ishaq Aqasi ruthlessly extorted money and appointed his deputy Khwaja Abdullah Khan; but he was assassinated after four months. The secretary Sukhjewanmal (r. 1753-62) became *raja* (king) and was the first Hindu to rule Kashmir for four hundred years and the only one under the Pathan domination of Abdali and his successors that lasted until 1819. Ishaq Aqasi came back with 30,000 men, but Kashmiris defending themselves defeated them. Sukhjewanmal alienated Muslims by banning cow-slaughter, and he provoked Abdali by recognizing Mughal emperor Alamgir II; but he governed for nine years. In 1766 Abdali sent Khurram Khan to replace a tyrannical governor of Kashmir.

Nizam-ul Mulk and Emperor Muhammad Shah both died in 1748. Ahmad Shah (r. 1748-54) was 22 years old when he succeeded his father as the last Mughal emperor with any real power; but having been brought up in a harem, he lacked education and experience. He appointed the Irani Safdar Jang vizier but listened mostly to the illiterate eunuch Javid Khan, who took control. Nobles were revolted by his corruption and usually kept their revenues; pay for imperial employees fell behind by 14 months and more. Zamindars usurped lands, and the Marathas took over more territory. Safdar Jang as a Shi'a had much opposition at court; after an assassination attempt, he moved his tents outside of Delhi. From late 1749 to 1752 he spent much time away trying to subdue Rohilkhand. The chief *bakshi* Salabat Khan came back from his Rajput expedition in 1750 with 18,000 troops demanding pay. Dismissed and imprisoned by Javid, Salabat sold all his property to pay what he could and lived in poverty like a dervish. Javid made the Turanis Ghazi-ud-din chief *bakshi* and Intizam-ud-daula in charge of Ajmer.

After making an alliance with the Jat leader Suraj Mal, Safdar Jang was wounded in the neck while fighting against Ahmad Khan's Bangash, who then besieged Allahabad and invaded Safdar's province of Awadh in 1751. Safdar Jang dismissed his Maratha allies and went back to Awadh; its governor Naval Rai had been killed fighting the Bangash Afghans. After recovering, Safdar paid Marathas and Jats to join him invading Rohilkand. When Emperor Ahmad Shah asked his vizier to bring Marathas to fight off the next Afghan invasion, he made a treaty in which Ahmad Khan Bangas promised to pay the debt Safdar Jang owed to the Marathas. Safdar Jang made a defensive treaty with Peshwa Balaji, offering the Marathas one-fourth of imperial revenues in the Punjab, Sindh, Aurangabad, and Gujarat. Safdar Jang arrived with 50,000 Marathas in April 1752; the Marathas foraged around Delhi until Javid Khan paid them to leave. When Javid would not let Safdar Jang punish Balaram (Balu) Jat for having plundered Sikandrabad, Safdar had Turkish soldiers murder Javid. Safdar antagonized nobles by taking over their tax revenues, and he made the mistake of appointing young Imad-ul-mulk as chief *bakshi*. Imad won over the Emperor, plotted with the queen mother, and got Safdar Jang dismissed. Salabat Khan urged Safdar to fight a civil war that lasted six months. Rohillas led by Najib Khan made the difference; Suraj Mal mediated a peace, and Safdar Jang went back to Awadh in November 1753.

Pay for the imperial army of 80,000 was seven months in arrears, and salaries of Mughal officials and servants were 32 months behind. The Emperor paid paymaster Imad-ul-mulk 1,500,000 rupees, but he kept the money for himself. Imad then sent Aqibat Mahmud to arrest the Emperor and vizier while the palace and crown lands were plundered. Imad's allied Marathas attacked the imperial camp with 20,000 troops. As soon as Ahmad Shah made Imad vizier in June 1754, he was replaced and imprisoned; Alamgir II was proclaimed emperor. Raghunath demanded money for the Marathas from the Delhi government, but they could not pay; starving soldiers rioted in the streets and plundered the wealthy. Jats and Gujars usurped imperial lands south of Delhi.

Shahu died in 1749 and was succeeded by Tara Bai's grandson Ram Raja on the Maratha throne, but Peshwa Balaji defeated Tara Bai and Damaji Gaikwar, arresting the young monarch and keeping him a prisoner in the palace. In 1753 the Marathas tried to collect tribute from the Rajputana states but were defeated by the Jats the next year. They marched toward Delhi and helped Imad-ul-Mulk (Ghazi-ud-din the younger) in a six-month civil war to depose the Mughal emperor Ahmad Shah Bahadur, install 'Alamgir II, and become his vizier. Imad-ul-Mulk was also aided by Najib Khan and the Rohillas, and he got the Sunnis to turn against Shi'a Safdar Jang by calling him a heretic. The Marathas under Balaji Baji Rao hired mercenaries, adopted western warfare methods, and allowed chiefs to use predatory warfare that ravaged Hindus as well as Muslims. The Marathas made a strategic error when they joined with the British to destroy the navy of Tulaji Angria in 1756, and the next year they exacted tribute south of the Krishna River, invading Bednore and Mysore. Malhar Rao Holkar and Raghunath Rao (Ragoba) led campaigns in the north and won over the Jats and the Doab. Since 1753 Peshwa Balaji had been campaigning in Karnataka to collect tribute and establish Maratha authority. In 1760 Marathas led by Sadashiv Rao Bhau invaded Udgir and defeated the Nizam forces by taking Burhanpur, Daulatabad, Ahmadnagar, and Bijapur.

In the Punjab Muin-ul-mulk went back to trying to suppress the Sikhs in 1753, but he died in November. After his infant sons were appointed and one died, his widow Mughlam Begum took power in May 1754. The new emperor Alamgir II appointed Momin Khan governor of Lahore. Nobles, resenting Mughlam's eunuchs and paramours, revolted. She seized their leader and had him beat to death, but Khwajah Mirza Jan took over Lahore and put her in prison. She appealed to the Afghan Abdali, who sent a force led by Khwajah Ubadullah Khan; he restored her for three months before confining her and ruling himself. He plundered his subjects and was replaced a few months later by Momin Khan and Adina Beg in 1756. Mughlam Begum called on Abdali again, and Ubadullah Khan took control. During this confusion Abdali was also invited back by Emperor Alamgir and Rohilla chief Najib Khan.

So Abdali entered India again, harassed by marauding Sikhs; but this time the Afghans plundered Delhi in January 1757. Punjab, Kashmir, Sindh, and Sirhind were ceded to him; but after raiding the Jat country south of Delhi, Abdali departed, leaving Najib Khan in Delhi and his son Timur Shah as viceroy at Lahore with his general Jahan Khan as vizier. Sikhs rebelled, but Jahan Khan defeated them at Amritsar and desecrated their shrine. The Marathas ousted Najib and made a treaty with Imad-ul-Mulk in June 1757 that doubled their share to half of all the revenues they collected in Mughal dominions. Marathas led by Raghunath Rao invaded Rajputana and plundered old Delhi in August, making peace with the Rohillas the next month. Then 50,000 Maratha troops entered the Punjab in 1758, driving the Afghans out of

Sirhind and Lahore. They appointed Adina Beg Khan their viceroy; but after they left, his death brought chaos to the Punjab. The Sikhs offered zamindars protection *(rakhi)* for one-fifth of the rent. The Afghan army attacked them at Kartarpur and Amritsar, but the Sikhs joined with Adina Beg in an army of 25,000 to defeat the Afghans near Mahilpur in December 1757. Sikhs allied with the Marathas and plundered Sirhind and Lahore. Raghunath's army left Lahore in May 1758; Adina Beg tried to suppress the Sikhs, but he died in September.

The Marathas appointed Dattaji Sindia, and in August 1759 he sent Sabaji Sindia to push back the Afghan invasion of Jahan Khan, who came back two months later, forcing Sabaji to retreat from Lahore so that Dattaji could aid the *peshwa* in getting money from Bengal. Dattaji's attempt to build a bridge across the Ganges was sabotaged by Najib-ud-daula, who invited Abdali's invasion and secretly organized Mughal nobles. In 1758 Imad had expelled crown prince Ali Gauhar from Delhi, and he took refuge in Awadh with Shuja ud-daula. In November 1759, Imad-ul-Mulk sent men who murdered Emperor Alamgir II and former vizier Intizam. Shah Jahan II was proclaimed emperor. The next month Ali Gauhar crowned himself Emperor Shah Alam II and appointed Shuja ud-daula his vizier; but his invasion of Bihar failed.

The assassination of Alamgir II motivated Abdali to advance toward Delhi. Dattaji tried to stop him but was killed in January 1760. The Afghans plundered old Delhi, and Abdali campaigned against Jats and Marathas. Two months later near Sikandarbad the Afghan general Jahan Khan routed the Marathas led by Malhar Rao. The Marathas fled from the invading Afghans, who would not agree on a peace treaty because of Peshwa Balaji's exorbitant demands. The ailing Peshwa gave command to the Udgir victor Sadashiv Rao instead of Raghunath Rao. In contrast to Shivaji's forces a century before, this Maratha army was accompanied by retinues, wives, and luxurious tents. The Marathas captured Delhi in August 1760; but they lost the support of Suraj Mal and his Jats when they plundered palaces, tombs, and shrines that the Persians and Afghans had respected. In October, Sadashiv Rao imprisoned the puppet Shah Jahan III. While the Marathas were taking and plundering the fort at Kunjpura from 10,000 Rohillas, Abdali's Afghan army crossed the Jumna River to cut off Maratha supply lines. In December, 20,000 foraging camp followers were slaughtered. The climactic battle between the Marathas and the Afghans took place at Panipat in January 1761. Half of the 60,000 on the Afghan side were Rohillas, Bangash, and Mughals. The Maratha army had 45,000 men, but hundreds were dying every day of hunger and disease. The starving Maratha army left their defences to fight a desperate battle. The victorious Afghans enslaved women and children, taking 50,000 horses, 200,000 cattle, 500 elephants, plus money and jewellery. Only one-fourth of the Maratha army returned to the Deccan. Peshwa Balaji retreated to Puna, where he died in June 1761. The Maratha confederation was shattered as local chiefs regained control-Mahadji Sindia in Gwalior, Raghuji Bhonsle in Nagpur and Berar, Malhar Rao Holkar in Malwa, and Damaji Gaikwar in Gujarat. Abdali named 'Alamgir II's son 'Ali Gauhar emperor in Delhi as Shah 'Alam with Imad as vizier and Najib-ud-daula as Mir Bakshi (military commander). The Afghan troops were two years behind in their pay and insisted that Abdali leave India before the hot summer, and they refused to go to Mathura, where hundreds had died of cholera four years before. His retreating army was followed and plundered by the Sikhs, who were reported to have freed about 2200 Hindu women.

After the Marathas' disaster at Panipat, Nizam 'Ali invaded Maharashtra with about 60,000 troops, but he lost allies by destroying Hindu temples at Toka and was defeated near Puna in January 1762. In a treaty the new Peshwa gave back half of what his father had gained in the Deccan. Nizam 'Ali took over the government at Bihar, put Salabat Jang in prison, and ruled the Mughal Deccan for the next forty-one years. In the south Haidar 'Ali rose to power in Mysore by defeating his rival Khande Rao in 1761. Balaji Rao died in June 1761, and his 17-year-old son Madhav Rao became *peṣhwa,* his uncle Raghunath Rao (Ragoba) acting as regent. Conflict led to a civil war, and in November 1762 the Peshwa yielded to Raghunath, who had to surrender the Daulatabad fort to Nizam 'Ali. After plundering each other's territories in 1763, the Peshwa defeated Nizam 'Ali's army and gained land. That year Haidar 'Ali conquered Bidnur and Sunda. The Marathas led by the Peshwa defeated Haidar the next year, occupying Haveri and Dharwar and making peace in 1765. The Marathas formed an alliance with Nizam 'Ali so they could fight Haidar and take more territory in another treaty in 1767. That year Nizam 'Ali and British troops led by Joseph Smith invaded Mysore, but Nizam went over to Haidar's side. Sikhs took over the Punjab, and about a third of the 30,000 Sikhs who fought to stop Abdali's sixth invasion of India were killed in February 1762. Four months later Abdali's Afghans attacked them at Amritsar, and in October many of the 60,000 gathered were massacred. Abdali also annexed Kashmir before returning to Afghanistan at the end of 1762. In January 1764 Jassa Singh Ahluwalia led 40,000 Sikhs of the Dal Khalsa in an attack on Sirhind that killed Zain Khan, and the next month they took over Lahore and plundered the upper Doab. They gathered at Amritsar and minted coins of pure silver, but they lost Lahore when Abdali invaded again in October 1764.

Suraj Mal and the Jats retained strong forces by not participating in the Panipat debacle, and in June 1761 they captured the Agra fort by bribery. Najib-ud-daula had to collect the tribute from India for the Afghan king, and he suppressed rebellion in Hansi-Hussar. After Suraj Mal attacked Baluch zamindars, Najib moved against the Jats; Suraj Mal was shot dead in December 1763 and was succeeded by his rebellious son, Jawahir Singh. He won the loyalty of the Jat army of 30,000 by paying their salaries that were two years behind, and he hired 20,000 Marathas under Malhar Rao Holkar. Najib did not invade the Jat kingdom, because he had to respond to the Sikh invasion of the upper Doab, enabling Jawahir Singh to recover the middle Doab. In January 1765 the Jats bombarded Delhi as Jawahir paid 15,000 Sikh allies to attack the city; but the Rohillas defended Delhi. Najib negotiated a peace as Sikhs, learning that Abdali was approaching Lahore, left. Frustrated Jawahir turned against his own officers and extorted money from rich Jats to pay for his losses; Balaram and another Jat grandee felt so disgraced that they cut their own throats in prison. Najib showed his power to tax by massacring his villages of Buana and Bhiwani in 1765. The growing power of the Sikhs was manifested when an army of 120,000 gathered at Amritsar in the spring of 1767. The next year Najib retired with riches only surpassed in India by the Jat king. He passed his office to his deputy Zabita Khan. Sikhs abandoned Lahore again in 1767 to the Afghans on Abdali's eighth invasion. In 1769 Ahmad Shah Abdali got as far as Peshawar but retreated, because his unpaid soldiers mutinied; he died three years later.

Shah Waliullah (1703-62) was born in Delhi and became an influential Islamic theologian. He memorized the *Qur'an* as a child and in 1732 went on a pilgrimage to Mecca, where he studied with eminent theologians. He believed in independent thinking and tried to harmonize Islamic law with mysticism and the four traditional schools of jurisprudence. He translated the *Qur'an* into Persian and wrote a commentary, and two of his sons translated it into Hindivi. In social morality he argued that justice is the highest principle and that it manifests in personal behaviour as courtesy, in finances as economy, in community as civil liberty, in politics as order, and as the social good of fellowship. He believed that society is corrupted when the pursuit of wealth and the satisfaction of desires for luxury and dissipation became the primary goals in life. Then the rich find ways to oppress the peasants, traders, and artisans; the economy becomes perverted by luxury goods while the lower classes are impoverished. His remedy was to abolish the entire system and establish justice and harmony. However, his method of bringing about these reforms was to turn to powerful Muslim leaders such as Najib-ud-daula, Nizam-ul Mulk, and Ahmad Shah Abdali. Waliullah's son Shah Abdul Aziz (d. 1823) educated thousands of Muslims over sixty years at his Madrasa-i-Rahimiya in Delhi.

British Conquest of Marathas 1800-18

Sikhs and North India 1767-1800

In the north Marathas led by Malhar Rao Holkar and Mahadji Sindia gradually fought back from the devastation of the Panipat disaster. After Ahmad Shah Abdali went back to Afghanistan, in December 1767 the Bhangi Sikhs crossed the Jamuna and invaded the Doab. They defeated Najib-ud-daula in March 1768 and again in December. Jawahir Singh was assassinated in June, and his brother Ratan Singh hired the Europeans Rene Madec and Walter Reinhard. When Ratan Singh was murdered by his Brahmin priest in 1769, Jat commander Dan Shah became regent for Ratan's son Kesari Singh; civil war weakened the Jats. The Peshwa sent more troops, and 30,000 Marathas ravaged Jat territory in 1770. The Sikhs plundered Panipat and reached Delhi in January 1770, followed by Najib's son Zabita Khan. Negotiations failed, and Zabita Khan retired to his Rohilla estate, enabling the Sikhs to enter the Doab. A Jat army pursued the Sikhs and defeated them in February. Hari Singh Bhangi died and was succeeded by Jhanda Singh, who made the Jammu and the Pathans of Kasur pay tribute.

Jhanda also captured the citadel at Multan. Learning that Zabita Khan had succeeded his father Najib, the Sikhs plundered Panipat again.

Zabita Khan was defeated by the Marathas as Mahadji Sindia and Visaji Krishna occupied Delhi. They invited Shah 'Alam II to come from Allahabad. The Marathas defeated the Rohillas and captured Zabita Khan, causing other Rohilla chiefs to make a treaty with Awadh's Shuja-ud-daula in 1772. The Marathas controlled Emperor Shah 'Alam II and made him grant them Kora and Allahabad; Zabita Khan joined their side, and they wanted him appointed Mir Bakhshi. Emperor Shah Alam objected, but the Marathas defeated his imperial forces. Sirhind governor Mughal Ali Khan crossed the Jamuna but was attacked and defeated by Sikhs, who invaded the Doab again a year later. In 1773 the English and Awadh defended Rohilkhand from a Maratha attack, and in a treaty Awadh nawab Shuja received Kora and Allahabad in exchange for paying five million rupees for a British garrison. In 1774 Shuja-ud-daula and the English invaded Rohilkhand, driving out 20,000 Rohillas and annexing most of that province to Awadh. In Delhi the Persian adventurer Mirza Najaf Khan commanded the Mughal army for the Emperor from 1772 until he died in 1782, repelling the Sikhs, suppressing the Jats, recovering Agra, and holding off the Marathas.

In the Punjab the Sikhs could usually govern themselves and had much less violence, though in 1774 Jai Singh Kanhaya got Jhanda Singh assassinated and joined with Jassa Singh Ahluwalia to expel the carpenter Jassa Singh. When Afghanistan's Ahmad Shah Abdali died in 1772, his son Timur Shah was governing Herat. He rushed to Qandahar and was elected by the Durrani chiefs. Shah Vali Khan had tried to raise an army and was executed for treason. For two years Timur Shah was busy suppressing disorders in his kingdom, but his army crossed the Indus in January 1775 and defeated some Sikhs. Realizing he needed more men, he withdrew to Peshawar, where Faizullah Khan organized an assassination plot; but Timur hid in the tower until his guards were aroused and caused Faizullah to flee. In fury Timur ordered a massacre of about a third of the 6,000 men in Peshawar. He promised to forgive Faizullah; but when he surrendered, he was beheaded. Timur Shah invaded India again in 1779 and tried to get Multan back with diplomacy, but the Sikhs shot his envoy dead. Timur sent 18,000 men under Zangi Khan Durrani, and they killed several thousand Sikhs in the battle of Rohtas. After losing 2,000 more casualties at Shujabad, 7,000 Sikhs retreated into the fort at Multan; but they surrendered and were allowed to depart in February 1780. Timur Shah had forts built but returned to Afghanistan before the hot weather. In October 1780 Timur Shah invaded Bahawalpur; but when 20,000 Sikh horsemen attacked Multan, he asked for peace.

In 1774 the Sikhs ravaged the Doab, approached Delhi, and were bought off by the Emperor, who offered them the district of Shahbazpur for the service of 10,000 horsemen. In 1775 Zabita Khan incited the Sikhs to plunder imperial lands; but in July he was defeated by Najaf Khan, and the Sikhs went home. In March 1776 Zabita Khan and his Rohillas attacked and killed Mughal commander Abul Qasim, and in May the Sikhs led by Gajpat Singh defeated and killed Mulla Rahimdad Khan, gaining seven villages. Zabita Khan and the Sikhs went to Delhi the next month and were pardoned by the Emperor; but in the fall about 60,000 Sikhs plundered Delhi's neighbours. Zabita Khan and the Sikhs fought Najaf Khan's imperial army in 1777. When Zabita Khan was defeated, he fled to the Sikhs and converted to their religion. In 1778 they raided the Doab and stayed in Delhi for a month. The next year Abdul Ahad led the imperial army but had to retreat in October. The Sikhs did not attempt to win political power in the region but were intent on gaining plunder.

The Emperor's grand-nephew Mirza Shafi led several campaigns against the Sikhs and even recruited dissident Sikhs into his army. He imprisoned Gajpat Singh and three other Sikh chiefs and in 1781 took Sadhaura from the Sikhs. Despite the conflicts among the Sikhs, the Mughals were not able to defeat them because Najaf Khan could not provide Shafi's army with enough supplies. Najaf Khan tried to get Zabita Khan to help Shafi but could not pay his troops. The Sikhs used guerrilla warfare and ravaged the Doab. In June 1781 Zabita Khan mediated an agreement giving the Sikhs the right to collect taxes *(rakhi)* in the upper Doab, and the Sikhs promised to stop raiding imperial territory. Yet the Sikhs continued to ravage imperial lands. A week before he died in April 1782, Najaf Khan sent Shafi with 10,000 troops against the Sikhs. Najaf's slaves Afrasiyab Khan and Najaf Quli Khan struggled for power with Shafi Khan and Mughal officer

Muhammad Beg Hamdani, but the Maratha chief Mahadji Sindia took power in Delhi. Lack of rain caused a devastating famine that destroyed about a third of the population in 1783. Many Sikhs moved from the Setluj territory to the upper Ganga Doab.

After raiding as far as the Ganges, Baghel Singh and Jassa Singh Ahluwalia led the Sikh army of 60,000 that plundered Delhi in March 1783. Reinhard's widow Begam Samru was invited to negotiate, and it was agreed that Baghel Singh would remain in the capital with 4,000 troops to keep order. Shafi was Mughal regent and with Afrasiyab tried to suppress the revolt of Hamdani, who assassinated Shafi in September. Afrasiyab became regent until he was murdered by Shafi's brother Zain-ul-Abidin Khan in November 1784. During this period of weakness Mahadji Sindia met with Emperor Shah Alam and represented the Marathas' Peshwa. In December 1784 the Sikhs plundered the suburbs of Delhi, alarming the English. Early in 1785 about 30,000 Sikhs, led by Baghel Singh, Gurdit Singh, and Jassa Singh Ramgarhia, crossed the Jamuna and ravaged the upper Doab. A subsidiary British force led by Awadh *diwan* Raja Jagan Nath skirmished with the Sikhs. Najaf Quli invited the Sikhs to approach Delhi, and they did so collecting tribute. Mahadji Sindia sent Ambaji Ingle to win over the Sikhs, and in March they agreed on a provisional treaty. The Sikh chiefs tried to form an alliance with the English by making a false accusation against Sindia but then concluded a treaty with him in May in which they would receive a million rupees income for 5,000 cavalry. The Sikhs quickly broke the treaty by collecting extra revenue in the Doab, and Dhar Rao Sindia led 10,000 troops to expel them. He was joined by Gajpat Singh and demanded money from Ghulam Qadir, who had succeeded his father Zabita Khan in January.

Jai Singh Kanhaya was paramount in the Punjab until about 1785 when Mahan Singh and Jassa Singh Ramgarhia defeated the Kanhayas. Mahan Singh was the most powerful Sikh in the Punjab until he died in 1792. In 1783 Murtaza Khan and Zaman Khan complained to Timur Shah that their brother Azad Khan had expelled them from Kashmir. The Afghan king gave them 30,000 troops, and at the Kishanganga River they killed 2,000 Kashmiris; but Azad Khan's cousin Pahalwan Khan rallied their troops and defeated the imperial army. At Srinagar the Afghan army was defeated again. Angered Timur Shah sent a larger force from

Peshawar. Azad Khan fled, was imprisoned, and killed himself. On learning that Shah Murad of Balkh was preparing to invade Afghanistan, Timur Shah returned to Kabul in May 1786. On Timur Shah's fifth campaign into India he led an army of 120,000 and massacred the inhabitants of Bahawalpur in January 1789. He demanded four million rupees and 3,000 camel loads of water bags from the raja of Jodhpur; but Rae Dhanje promised Mahadji Sindia he would starve the Afghans in Kachh Bhuj. So Timur Shah went into Sindh and collected six million rupees in tribute. News of disturbances by Shah Murad of Turan persuaded Timur to retreat again. For the next three years rumors abounded that Timur Shah was planning to capture Delhi, but he died at Kabul in 1793 and was succeeded by his son Shah Zaman.

The Sikhs continued their raiding, and in 1787 they plundered the territory of Ghulam Qadir and others. Ghulam Qadir joined forces with Ambaji for a while. Meanwhile Mahadji Sindia was defeating the Rajputs of Jaipur; Hamdani was killed, and the *raja* promised to pay 6,300,000 rupees. When Ambaji joined Sindia in Jaipur, Ghulam Qadir got Sikhs to join him in challenging the Marathas. In September 1785 Ghulam Qadir took power in Delhi while his ally Isma'il Beg occupied Agra. Begam Samru's battalions reached Delhi three days later. The Emperor named Ghulam regent, and he secured the fortress of Aligarh and took control of the Doab. Emperor Shah Alam II demanded tribute from Najaf Quli Khan; but the imperial forces were slaughtered by the Sikhs, and Begam Samru mediated a reconciliation. The Sikhs plundered the territory of Ghulam Qadir while he was fighting the Marathas and Jats near Bharatpur. Ghulam returned to Delhi in July 1788. His Rohillas stripped and raped princesses and ladies, letting many die of starvation while they searched for treasures, which his wife later estimated at 250 million rupees. When Shah Alam could not disclose more secrets, Ghulam Qadir blinded him. The Marathas attacked Delhi; Ghulam fled and was captured in December. Sindia had his body mutilated before putting him to death.

Mahadji Sindia put 'Ali Bahadur in charge, tried to conciliate Tukoji Holkar by giving him a million rupees worth of land, and went to Mathura in 1788. He granted the Sikhs feudal tenures in 1789, allowing a thousand Sikhs to collect taxes with Maratha officers; but the Sikhs plundered the Doab again in 1790. They captured the British commander Robert Stuart and held him at

Thanesar for nearly ten months in 1791 before the English agreed to pay Bhanga Singh a ransom of six million rupees that was transferred by Begam Samru. Mahadji Sindia got Comte de Boigne to train his troops with European discipline, and by 1792 Sindia established Maratha supremacy over the Rajputs and Jats; but he had conflicts with 'Ali Bahadur and Holkar. In 1793 De Boigne's infantry attacked Holkar's troops near Ajmer. Mahadji Sindia died of illness in 1794; he was succeeded by his nephew's son Daulat Rao Sindia, who was only 14 and inept. He appointed the Shenvi Brahmin Lakhba Dada to govern northern India, which was ravaged so badly that land was hardly cultivated. The artillery of Begam's regiment forced the Sikhs to retreat to their own territory in 1794. An attempt to collect revenue in Karnal provoked a war with the Sikhs in 1795, and they invaded the upper Doab. The Sikhs were also torn apart by civil war, though Rae Singh Bhangi persuaded Gurdit Singh to leave the Maratha camp. Maratha chief Nana Rao entered Thanesar and was enticed to march toward Patiala to secure money; but fierce fighting by the Sikhs persuaded him to return to Delhi. In 1796 the Sikhs massacred and plundered pilgrims at Hardwar.

Afghanistan's Shah Zaman invaded India in 1794, plundering and burning Jhelum. He demanded revenue payments from chiefs of Bhakar, Multan, Sindh, and Kashmir before returning to Peshawar, where he blinded his rebellious brother Humayun. Shah Zaman invaded again and captured Rohtas in November 1795; but an insurrection by Mahmud at Herat and an invasion by Persian shah Agha Muhammad Khan Qajar forced his quick return. He left Ahmad Khan Shahanchibashi in Rohtas and Bahadur Khan with 12,000 cavalry to conquer Gujrat, but the latter was defeated and killed by Sikhs led by Sahib Singh. Ranjit Singh got to Rohtas before Sahib and claimed it as Shahanchibashi fled to Peshawar.

In 1796 Shah Zaman tried to negotiate a safe passage through the Punjab. Some Sikhs agreed, but Ranjit Singh promised a battle. Shah Zaman divided his army under seven commanders with 12,000 men each. Ranjit Singh forced Pind Dadan Khan's men back at the Jhelum River. Shah Zaman ordered his men at Rohtas not to seize property or wrong people and to pay for grass and fuel. Sher Muhammad Khan Vazir entered Lahore on the last day of 1796, and Shahanchibashi proclaimed security of life and property in Kotwal. Shah Zaman even ordered the noses cut off of any Durranis who oppressed the people. When houses and shops were not illuminated, Shah Zaman ordered Hindus to pay a poll tax; but Muslims were exempted. Sikhs gathered 50,000 men at Amritsar and defeated the Afghan army on January 12, 1797, and 35,000 were reported killed in this battle. Shah Zaman retreated to Lahore, repaired the fort, and manufactured arms. The Taruna Dal Sikhs were defending their homeland, but the Budha Dal and Phulkian Sikhs across the Setluj River did not participate. Once again Shah Zaman returned to quell disturbances by his brother Mahmud at Herat. Before they left, troops collected 2,200,000 rupees from Lahore. Sindh governor Shahanchibashi was killed by Sikhs fighting to recover their territory, and the Durranis fled.

Shah Zaman still had his own governors in Kashmir, Peshawar, Derajaṭ, Multan, and Sindh. On his fourth invasion he left Peshawar in October 1798 and defeated Sikhs at Attock. The Afghan shah appointed Wafadar Khan chief commander, but this was resented by vizier Sher Muhammad Khan, whose letters warning Sikh chiefs were found. The Sikhs were not united either and withdrew as the Afghan army advanced. Ranjit Singh gathered some men at Amritsar, and Shah Zaman sent 10,000 troops that battled 2,500 Sikhs, killing 500 on each side. As Shah Zaman entered Lahore, various bands of Sikhs cut off supplies from the Durrani army. Some Sikhs even surrendered to Shah Zaman by coming at night. When 4,000 Sikhs gathered by the Beas River, the Shah sent 24,000 troops, causing the Sikhs to disperse. Shah Zaman tried to negotiate, and early in 1799 some settlements were made. Meanwhile Bombay governor Duncan had sent Mehdi Ali Khan to urge the Persian Shah to invade Khurasan, while Mahmud was incited to revolt again. Zaman Shah decided to return to Kabul, and Ranjit Singh persuaded the Sikhs not to molest the retreating army. This was the last Afghan invasion of India.

The Irish George Thomas fell in love with Begam Samru and then married the slave girl Marie. In 1789 he had prevented the Emperor from being taken prisoner by helping to defeat Najaf Quli's attack on the imperial army. After Le Vaisseau married Begam, his intrigues caused Thomas to revolt in 1792. Thomas surrendered and was released. He served the Maratha chief Apa Khande Rao, and in 1795 he expelled Sikh raiders. When Begam Samru was imprisoned by Zafaryab Khan at Sardhana, Thomas defeated and imprisoned Zafaryab, restoring Begam to her position. When Comte de Boigne left India in 1796, he was succeeded by French general Perron. In 1798 Thomas led a Maratha attack on rebellious Sikhs in a bloody battle that killed 1500, but a peace treaty allowed the Sikhs to evacuate the place. Almas Beg let Thomas use Hansi as his headquarters, and for a while he governed and collected taxes from 253 villages. When Sikhs raided his territory, he pursued them to Patiala. The Sikhs fought in alliance with Shambu Nath against Ashraf Beg, who was aided by Perron. Using local Muslims, Perron invaded Karnal and signed a peace treaty with the Sikhs at Thanesar in March 1799 before being joined by Begam's four battalions. Perron led the Marathas, and he ordered Louis Bourquien with his 2,000 men to join 6,000 Sikhs against 5,000 men led by Thomas at Georgegarh in 1801. Each side lost 2,000 in battle, and then Thomas was besieged. Reduced to 700 men and lacking supplies, Thomas surrendered and was allowed to go to British territory.

Ranjit Singh was born November 13, 1780. His father died in 1792, and five years later he became chief of the Sikh *misl* Sukarchakia. At that time between the Indus and Setluj rivers were 27 Hindu states, 25 Muslim states, and 16 Sikh states. Ranjit Singh made political alliances by marrying a Kanahya princess in 1796 and a Nakai princess in 1798. The next year the citizens of Lahore invited Ranjit Singh to occupy their city, and Shah Zaman authorized him to govern it for the Afghans, enabling Ranjit Singh to take over Lahore with little resistance. In 1800 Governor-general Wellesley sent Yusaf Ali to persuade Ranjit Singh not to form an alliance with Shah Zaman. However, Shah Zaman was deposed and blinded by his brother Mahmud, who was overthrown by Shah Shuja in 1803.

Mysore and its Resistance to British Expansion

The Anglo-Mysore Wars were a series of wars fought in India over the last three decades of the 18th century between the Kingdom of Mysore and the British East India Company, represented chiefly by the Madras Presidency. The fourth war resulted in the overthrow of the house of Hyder Ali and Tipu Sultan (who was killed in the final war, in 1799), and the dismantlement of Mysore to the benefit of its pro-British allies. The First Anglo-Mysore War saw Hyder Ali inflicting crushing defeats on the combined armies of the

Marathas, the Nizam of Hyderabad and the British. The Kingdom of Mysore gained large tracts of land to the north after this war.

The Second Anglo-Mysore War saw the rise of Tipu Sultan as a powerful military leader. Soldiers from Mysore decimated British armies in the east, repelled a joint Maratha-Hyderabad invasion from the north and captured territories in the south. The war was ended in 1784 with the Treaty of Mangalore, at which both sides agreed to restore the others' lands to the status quo ante bellum.

In the Third Anglo-Mysore War, Tipu Sultan, the ruler of Mysore and an ally of France, invaded the nearby state of Travancore in 1789, which was a British ally. The resultant war lasted three years and resulted in a resounding defeat for Mysore. The war ended after the 1792 siege of Seringapatam and the signing of the Treaty of Seringapatnam according to which Tipu had to surrender half of his kingdom to the East India Company.

The Fourth Anglo-Mysore War saw the defeat of the kingdom of Mysore. Mysore's alliance with the French was seen as a threat to the East India Company and Mysore was attacked from all four sides. Tipu's troops were outnumbered 4:1 in this war. Mysore had only 35,000 soldiers, whereas the British commanded 60,000 troops. The Nizam of Hyderabad and the Marathas launched an invasion from the North. The British won a decisive victory at the Battle of Seringapatam in 1799. Tipu was killed during the defence of the city. Much of Tipu Sultaun's territory was annexed by the British, the Nizam and the Marathas. The core of it, around Mysore and Seringapatam, was handed over to the Indian prince belonging to the Wodeyar dynasty, whose forefathers had been overthrown by Hyder Ali, and whose descendants ruled the Kingdom of Mysore until 1947 when it joined the Union of India.

The Battles of Plassey (1757) and Buxar (1764) which established British dominion over East India, the Anglo-Mysore wars (1766-1799) and the Anglo-Maratha Wars (1775-1818) consolidated the British claim over South Asia, resulting in the British Empire in India, though pockets of resistance among the Sikhs, Afghans and Burmese would last well into the 1880s.

The First Anglo-Mysore War (1766-1769) was a war in India between the Kingdom of Mysore and the British East India Company. Hyder Ali, ruler of Mysore, had begun to occupy the serious attention of the British government in Calcutta. In 1766 the

British entered into an agreement with the Nizam of Hyderabad to equip him with troops to be used against the common threat.

War

Shortly after this alliance been formed when a secret arrangement was made between the two Indian powers, and Colonel Smith's small force was met with a united army of 50 000 men and 100 guns. Superior British training and military discipline, however, prevailed, first in the battle of Chengam (September 3, 1767), and again still more remarkably in that of Tiruvannamalai (Trinornalai).

Following the loss of his recently built fleet and forts on the western coast, Hyder Ali now offered overtures for peace; on the rejection of these, bringing all his resources and strategy into play, he forced Colonel Smith to raise the siege of Bangalore, and brought his army within 5 miles of Madras.

Peace Treaty

The result was the treaty of April 1769, providing for the mutual restitution of all conquests, and for mutual aid and alliance in defensive war.

Aftermath

This war was followed by the Mysore-Maratha war from 1769 to 1772 which saw Mysore cede some territory to the Marathas. The British did not assist Mysore in this war, in what Hyder Ali considered a violation of the agreement between himself and the British. He blamed Mysore's losses on the British and his grievances played some role in the outbreak of The Second Anglo-Mysore War (1780–1784) was a conflict in India between the Kingdom of Great Britain and the Kingdom of Mysore. At the time, Mysore was a key French ally in India, and the Franco-British conflict raging on account of the American Revolutionary War helped spark Anglo-Mysorean hostilities in India.

Outbreak of War

Following the outbreak of hostilities between France and Britain during the American Revolutionary War in 1778, both France and Britain began waging war against each other's colonies. Britain embarked on a plan to drive the French from India, capturing Pondicherry and other French outposts in 1778. They then captured the French controlled port at Mahe on the Malabar coast in 1779. Mahe was of great strategic importance to Hyder, who received French supplied arms and munition through the port, and Hyder had explicitly told the British was under his protection. Hyder set about forming a confederacy against the British, and was joined by the Marathas and the Nizam of Hyderabad. In July Hyder invaded Karnataka with an army of 80,000, mostly cavalry. He descended through the passes of the Ghats amid burning villages, before laying siege to British forts in northern Arcot. The British responded by sending a force of 5,000 to lift the sieges. Meanwhile Hyder sent part of his army under the command of his eldest son, Tipu Sultan, to intercept a British force from Guntur sent to reinforce Colonel Hector Munro's army 145 miles (233 km) to the north at Madras.

Recovery of Chittur

On the morning of 10 September 1780, the British force from Guntur under the command of Colonel William Baille came under heavy fire from Tipu's guns near Pollilur. Baille formed his force into a long square formation at began to move slowly forward. However, Haiders cavalry broke through the formation's front, inflicting many casualties and forcing Baille to surrender. Out of the British force of 3,820 men, 336 were killed. The defeat was considered to be the East India Company's most crushing loss in India at that time. Munro reacted to the defeat by retreating to Madras, abandoning his baggage and dumping his cannons in the water tank at Conjeevaram, a small town some 50 kilometres (31 mi) south of Madras. Instead of following up the victory and pressing on for Madras, Hyder Ali instead turned to the fortress at Arcot, which he captured on 3 November. This decision gave the British time to shore up their defences in the south, and despatch reinforcements under the command of Sir Eyre Coote to Madras.

Suffren meeting with Hyder Ali in 1783, J.B. Morret engraving, 1789. Tipu also defeated on Colonel Braithwaite at Annagudi near Tanjore on 18 Feb 1782. This army consisted of 100 Europeans 300 cavalry, 1400 sepoys and 10 field pieces. Tipu seized all the guns and took the entire detachment as prisoners. In December 1781 Tipu had successfully seized Chittur from British hands. These operations gave Tipu valuable military experience, that became more Hyder died in December 1782. Warren Hastings sent from Bengal Sir Eyre Coote, who, though repulsed at Chidambaram, defeated Haidar three times in succession in the battles of Porto Novo, Pollilur and Sholingarh, while Tipu was forced to raise the siege of Wandiwash, and Vellore was provisioned. Tipu defeated Brathwaite on the banks of the Coleroon in February 1782. The arrival of Lord Macartney as governor of Madras in the summer of 1781 included news of war with the Dutch Republic. Macartney ordered the seizure of the Dutch outposts in India, and the British captured the main Dutch outpost at Negapatam after three weeks of siege in November 1781 against defences that included 2,000 of Hyder's men. This forced Hyder Ali to realize that he could never completely defeat a power that had command of the sea, since British naval support contributed to the victory. Hyder had sent his son Tipu to the west coast to seek the assistance of the French fleet when he suddenly died in December 1782 at Chittur. Tipu quickly returned and took over the war effort.

Treaty of Mangalore

The British captured Coimbatore in 1783, but neither they nor Mysore were able to obtain a clear overall victory. The war was ended on 11 March 1784 with the signing of the Treaty of Mangalore, at which both sides agreed to restore the others' lands to the *status quo ante bellum*. The treaty is an important document in the history of India, because it was the last occasion when an Indian power dictated terms to the British, who were made to play the role of humble supplicants for peace. Warren Hastings called it a humiliating pacification, and appealed to the king and Parliament to punish the Madras Government for "the faith and honour of the British nation have been equally violated." The British would not reconcile to this humiliation, and worked hard from that day to subvert Tipu's power. The great advantage was the psychological impact of his victory with the British, the mode of conclusion was highly satisfactory to him. The march of the Commissioner all the way from Madras to Mangalore seeking peace made Munro remark that such indignities were throughout poured upon the British" that limited efforts seemed necessary to repudiate the Treaty at the earliest time."

Third Anglo-Mysore War

The Third Anglo-Mysore War (1789–92) was a war in South India between the Kingdom of Mysore and the English East India Company. It was the third of four Anglo-Mysore Wars. Tipu Sultan, the ruler of Mysore and an ally of France, invaded the nearby state of Travancore in 1789, which was a British ally. The resultant war lasted three years and resulted in a resounding defeat for Mysore. France, embroiled in the French Revolution and thwarted by British Naval power, was unable to provide as much assistance as Tipu had expected. One notable military advance championed by Tipu Sultan was the use of mass attacks with rocket brigades, called *kushoons*, in the army. These weapons sufficiently impressed the British during the Third and Fourth Mysore Wars to inspire William Congreve to develop Congreve rockets. The war resulted in a sharp curtailment of Mysore's borders to the advantage of the Marathas, the Nizam of Hyderabad, and the Madras Presidency. The districts of Malabar, Salem, Bellary, and Anantapur were ceded to Madras Presidency. The war ended after the 1792 siege of Seringapatam and the signing of the Treaty of Seringapatnam according to which Tipu had to surrender half of his kingdom to the British company and send his two sons to them as the hostages of war. A fourth and final war was fought in 1799.

Fourth Anglo-Mysore War

The Fourth Anglo-Mysore War (1798–1799) was a war in South India between the Kingdom of Mysore and the British East India Company under the Earl of Mornington. Napoleon's landing in Egypt in 1798 was intended to threaten India, and Mysore was a key to that next step and as the ruler of Mysore, Tipu Sultan was a staunch ally of France. Although Horatio Nelson crushed Napoleon's ambitions at the Battle of the Nile, three armies-one from Bombay, and two British (one of which contained a division that was commanded by Colonel Arthur Wellesley the future 1st Duke of Wellington)-nevertheless marched into Mysore in 1799 and besieged the capital, Srirangapatnam after some engagements with the Tipu's armies. On 8 March, a forward force managed to hold off an advance by Tipu at the Battle of Seedaseer. On 4 May, the armies broke through the defending walls and Tipu Sultan, rushing to the breach, was shot and killed. Tipu was betrayed in this war by one of his commanders, Mir Sadiq, a traitor who was bought by the British. He sent the army to collect wages at the height of the battle thus giving the British a chance to enter through the hole made through bombardment of the wall.

5

The Three Anglo-Maratha Wars

First Anglo-Maratha War

The First Anglo-Maratha War was the first of three Anglo-Maratha wars fought between the British East India Company and Maratha Empire in India. The war began with the Treaty of Surat and ended with the Treaty of Salbai.

Background

After the death of Madhavrao Peshwa in 1772, his brother Narayanrao became Peshwa of the Maratha Empire. However, Raghunathrao, Narayanrao's uncle, had his nephew assassinated in a palace conspiracy that resulted in Raghunathrao becoming Peshwa, although he was not the legal heir.

Narayanrao's widow, Gangabai, gave birth to a posthumous son, who was legal heir to the throne. The newborn infant was named 'Sawai' Madhavrao (*Sawai* means "One and a Quarter"). Twelve Maratha chiefs, led by Nana Phadnis directed an effort to name the infant as the new Peshwa and rule under him as regents.

Raghunathrao, unwilling to give up his position of power, sought help from the British at Bombay and signed the Treaty of Surat on 6 March 1775. According to the treaty, Raghunathrao ceded the territories of Salsette and Bassein to the British, along with part of the revenues from Surat and Bharuch districts. In return, the British promised to provide Raghunathrao with 2,500 soldiers. The British Calcutta Council condemned the Treaty of Surat, sending Colonel Upton to Pune to annul it and make a new treaty with the regency. The Treaty of Purandhar (1 March 1776) annulled that of Surat, Raghunathrao was pensioned and his cause abandoned, but the revenues of Salsette and Broach districts were retained by the British. The Bombay government rejected this new treaty and gave refuge to Raghunathrao. In 1777 Nana Phadnis violated the treaty with the Calcutta Council by granting the French a port on the west coast. The British replied by sending a force towards Pune. The tangle was increased by the support of the London authorities for Bombay, which in 1778–79 again supported Raghunathrao. Peace was finally restored in 1782.

Battle of Wadgaon

The East India Company's force from Bombay consisted of about 3,900 men (about 600 Europeans, the rest Asian) accompanied by many thousands of servants and specialist workers. They were joined on the way by Raghunath's forces, adding several thousand more soldiers, and more artillery. The Maratha army included forces contributed by all the partners in the federation, tens of thousands in all, commanded by the brilliant Tukojirao Holkar and General Mahadji Shinde (also known as Mahadji Sindia). Mahadji slowed down the British march and sent forces west to cut off its supply lines.

When they found out about this, the British halted at Talegaon, a few hours' brisk march from Pune, but days away for the thousands of support staff with their ox-drawn carts. Now the Maratha cavalry harassed the enemy from all sides. The Marathas also utilized a scorched earth policy, burning farmland and poisoning wells. The British began to withdraw from Talegaon in the middle of the night, but the Marathas attacked, forcing them to halt in the village of Wadgaon (now called Vadgaon Maval), where the British force was surrounded on 12 January 1779. By the end of the next day, the British were ready to discuss surrender terms, and on 16 January signed the Treaty of Wadgaon that forced the Bombay government to relinquish all territories acquired by the Bombay office of the East India Company since 1773.

British Response

Reinforcements from northern India, commanded by Colonel Goddard, arrived too late to save the Bombay force. The British Governor-General in Bengal, Warren Hastings, rejected the treaty on the grounds that the Bombay officials had no legal power to sign it, and ordered Goddard to secure British interests in the area. Goddard's 6,000 troops captured Ahmedabad in February 1779, and Bassein in December 1780. Another Bengal detachment led by Captain Popham captured Gwalior in August 1780. Hastings sent yet another force to harass Mahadji Shinde, commanded by Major Camac; in February 1781 the British beat Shinde to the town of Sipri, but every move they made after that was shadowed by his much larger army, and their supplies were cut off, until they made a desperate night raid in late March, capturing not only supplies, but even guns and elephants. Thereafter, the military threat from Shinde's forces to the British was much reduced.

Treaty of Salbai

After the defeat, Shinde proposed a new treaty between the Peshwa and the British that would recognize the young Madhavrao as the Peshwa and grant Raghunathrao a pension. This treaty, known as the Treaty of Salbai, was signed on 17 May 1782, and was ratified by Hastings in June 1782 and by Phadnis in February 1783. The treaty also returned to Shinde all his territories west of the Yamuna. It also guaranteed peace between the two sides for twenty years and thus ending the war.

Second Anglo-Maratha War

The Second Anglo-Maratha War (1803–1805) was the second conflict between the British East India Company and the Maratha Empire in India.

Background

The overarching ambition of Raghunathrao, Peshwa Baji Rao II's father, and the latter's own incompetence since coming into his inheritance, had long caused much internecine intrigue within the Maratha confederacy; Peshwa Baji Rao II no longer commanded the deference his predecessors had.

In October 1802, Peshwa Baji Rao II was defeated by the Holkar ruler of Indore, at the Battle of Poona. He fled to British protection, and in December the same year concluded the Treaty of Bassein with the British East India Company, ceding territory for the maintenance of a subsidiary force and agreeing to treaty with no other power. The British also had to check the French influence in India.

The War

This act on the part of the Peshwa, their nominal overlord, horrified and disgusted the Maratha chieftains; in particular, the Sindia rulers of Gwalior and the Bhonsle rulers of Nagpur and Berar contested the agreement. They were defeated, respectively, at Laswari and Delhi by Lord Lake and at Assaye and Argaon (now referred to as Adgaon) by Sir Arthur Wellesley. The Holkar rulers of Indore belatedly joined the fray and compelled the British to make peace.

Conclusion

On 17 December 1803, Raghuji Bhonsale (II) of Nagpur signed the Treaty of Deogaon with the British after the Battle of Laswari and gave up the province of Cuttack including Balasore.

On 30 December 1803, the Scindia signed the Treaty of Surji-Anjangaon with the British after the Battle of Assaye and Battle of Argaon and ceded to the British Ganges-Jumna Doab, the Delhi-Agra region, parts of Bundelkhand, Broach, some districts of Gujarat, fort of Ahmmadnagar.

Yashwantrao Holkar, however began hostilities with the English by securing the alliance of the Raja of Bharatpur. By the Treaty of Rajghat, Holkar got back most of his territories. The Holkar Maharajas retained control and overlordship over much of Rajasthan.

Third Anglo-Maratha War

The Third Anglo-Maratha War (1817 – 1818) was a final and decisive conflict between the British East India Company and the Maratha Empire in India, which left the Company in control of most of India.

The war began with an invasion of Maratha territory by the British Governor General, Lord Hastings, supported by a force under Sir Thomas Hislop, in the course of operations against Pindari robber bands. The Peshwa of Pune's forces, followed by those of the Bhonsle of Nagpur and Holkar of Indore, rose against the British, but British diplomacy convinced the Scindia of Gwalior to remain neutral, although he lost control of Rajasthan. British victory was swift, resulting in the breakup of the Maratha Empire and the loss of Maratha independence to the British. The Battle of Koregaon gave decisive victory to the British; the Peshwa was pensioned off and most of his territory was annexed to the Bombay Presidency, although the Maharaja of Satara was restored as ruler of a princely state until its annexation to Bombay state in 1848. The northern portion of the Nagpur Bhonsle dominions, together with the Peshwa's territories in Bundelkhand, were annexed to British India as the Saugor and Nerbudda Territories. The Maratha kingdoms of Indore, Gwalior, Nagpur, and Jhansi became princely states, acknowledging British control.

The Third Anglo-Maratha War left the British in control of virtually all of present-day India south of the Sutlej River. In addition, the famed Nassak Diamond was acquired by the East India Company as part of the spoils of the war.

The Early Administrative Structure from Diarchy to Direct Control

Regulating Act, 1773 was a parliamentary enactment defining the powers and responsibilities of the various organs of the EAST INDIA COMPANY including its territorial control over Bengal. Before the conquest of Bengal, the East India Company was having immensely profitable trade in Bengal. The proprietors of the company's shares used to receive attractive dividends regularly. But ever since the conquest of Bengal, the company was running at a loss. Instead of pursuing lawful business for their employers, the company's servants had kept themselves engaged in plundering the resources of the country and thus making themselves rich overnight. The FAMINE of 1769/70 in the midst of the company's ravages had awakened the administration of Prime Minister Lord North to the realisation that parliamentary interference must be made into the affairs of the company in order to save the company and the new kingdom from ruin. An opportunity came when the renewal of the company's charter fell due in 1773 and when the company also applied to government for a 'rescue loan'. Parliament granted the loan and with it imposed a law regulating the affairs of the company at home and overseas. The Act made many intricate provisions, but the ones that are most relevant to the company's Bengal kingdom are as follows:

1. That, for the government of the presidency of FORT WILLIAM in Bengal, there shall be a Governor General, and a Council consisting of four councillors with the

democratic provision that the decision of the majority in the Council shall be binding on the Governor General.

2. That WARREN HASTING shall be the first Governor General and that Lt. General John Clavering, George Monson, Richard Barwell and PHILIP FRANCIS shall be four first Councillors.
3. That His Majesty shall establish a SUPREME COURT OF JUDICATURE consisting of a Chief Justice and three other judges at Fort William, and that the Court's jurisdiction shall extend to all British subjects residing in Bengal and their native servants.
4. That the company shall pay out of its revenue salaries to the designated persons in the following rate: to the Governor General 25000 sterling, to the Councillors 10,000 sterling, to the Chief Justice 8000 sterling and the Judges 6000 sterling a year.
5. That the Governor General, Councillors and Judges are prohibited from receiving any gifts, presents, pecuniary advantages from the Indian princes, zamindars and other people.
6. That no person in the civil and military establishments can receive any gift, reward, present and any pecuniary advantages from the Indians.
7. That it is unlawful for collectors and other district officials to receive any gift, present, reward or pecuniary advantages from zamindars and other people.

The provisions of the Act clearly indicate that it was directed mainly to the malpractice and corruption of the company officials. The Act, however, failed to stop corruption and it was practised rampantly by all from the Governor General at the top to the lowest district officials. Major charges brought against Hastings in his impeachment trial were those on corruption. Corruption divided the Council into two mutually hostile factions-the Hastings group and Francis group. The issues of their fighting were corruption charges against each other. Consequently, pitt's India act, 1784 had to be enacted to fight corruption and to do that an incorruptible person, lord Cornwallis, was appointed with specific references to bring order in the corruption ridden polity established by the company.

Pitts India Act

Pitt's India Act of 1784 was the enactment of the British Parliament to bring the administration of the British East India Company under the control of the British Government. It was made necessary to address the shortcoming of the East India Company Act (also known as the Regulating Act of 1773). The Regulating Act had been enacted to primarily weed-out corruption in the East India Company in the Bengal. Pitt's India Act provided for the appointment of a Board of Control and provided for a joint government of the Company and the Crown.

Background

By 1773, the East India Company was in dire financial straits and asked for assistance from the British Government. Faced with corruption and nepotism amongst the company officials in India, the British Government enacted the Regulating Act in 1773 to control the activities of the East India Company. The Act set up a system whereby it supervised (regulated) the work of the East India Company but did not take power for itself. It had, however, proven to be a failure within a few years and the British government decided to take a more active role in the affairs of the Company.

India Act (1784)

A governing Board was constituted with six members two of whom were members of the British Cabinet and rest from the Privy Council. The Board also had a President, who soon became, effectively, the minister for the affairs of the East India Company. The Board had all the powers and control over all the acts and operations relating to the civil, military and revenues of the Company. The governing council of the Company was reduced to three members and the Governor General was authorised to veto the majority decisions. The Governors of Bombay and Madras were also deprived of their independence. Calcutta was given greater powers in matters of war, revenue, and diplomacy, thus becoming in effect the administrative capital of Company possessions in India. By a supplementary the Bill passed in 1786, Lord Cornwallis was appointed as the second Governor-General, and he then became the effective ruler of British India under the authority of the Board of Control and the Court of Directors. The constitution set up by the Pitt's India Act did not undergo any major changes during the existence of the Company's rule in India.

The Pitt's Act

After the Regulating Act of 1773 to regulate the affairs of the Company in India, the second important step taken by the British Parliament was the appointment of a Board of Control under Pitt's India Bill of 1784. It provided for a joint government of the Company (represented by the Directors), and the Crown (represented by the Board of Control).

A Board of six members was constituted with two members of the British Cabinet and four of the Privy Council. One of who was the President and who soon became, in effect, the minister for the affairs of the East India Company. The Board had all the powers and control over all the acts and operations, which related to the civil, military and revenues of the Company.

The Council was reduced to three members and the Governor-General was empowered to overrule the majority. The Governors of Bombay and Madras were also deprived of their independent powers. Calcutta was given greater powers in matters of war, revenue, and diplomacy, thus becoming in effect the capital of Company possessions in India.

By a supplementary the Bill passed in 1786, Lord Cornwallis was appointed as the first Governor-General, and he then became the effective ruler of British India under the authority of the Board of Control and the Court of Directors. The constitution set up by the Pitt's India Act did not undergo any major changes during the existence of the Company's rule in India.

The Charter Act of 1813 abolished the trading activities of the Company and henceforth became purely an administrative body under the Crown. Thereafter, with few exceptions, the Governor-General and the Council could make all the laws and regulations for people (Indians and British).

The salient features relating to the governance of the kingdom of Bengal were:

1. There shall be a Board of Control consisting of maximum six parliamentarians headed by a senior cabinet member to direct, superintend and control the affairs of the company's territorial possessions in the East Indies.
2. The Court of Directors shall establish a Secret Committee to work as a link between the Board and the Court.

3. The Governor General's council shall consist of three members one of whom shall be the commander-in-chief of the King's army in India. In case the members present in a meeting of the council shall any time be equally divided in opinion, the Governor General shall have two votes (one his own and another casting vote).
4. The government must stop further experiments in the revenue administration and proceed to make a permanent settlement with zamindars at moderate rate of revenue demand. The government must establish permanent judicial and administrative systems for the governance of the new kingdom.
5. All civilians and military officers must provide the Court of Directors a full inventory of their property in India and in Britain within two months of their joining their posts.
6. Severe punishment including confiscation of property, dismissal and jail, shall be inflicted on any civilian or military officer found guilty of corruption.
7. Receiving gifts, rewards, presents in kind or cash from the rajas, zamindars and other Indians are strictly prohibited and people found guilty of these offences shall be tried charged with corruption.

Parliament directly appointed Lord Charles Cornwallis to implement the Act. Immediately after his joining as Governor General in 1786, Cornwallis embarked upon the responsibility of reform works reposed on him by parliament. In 1793 he completed his mission. He introduced permanent settlement, announced a judicial code, established administrative and police systems and then left for home in the same year.

Charter Acts enabled the English east India company to come to the 'East Indies' for trade and commerce as a company endowed with exclusive rights and subsequently to rule India up to 1858. A charter for overseas trade had to be obtained by a commercial company for several reasons, the most important of which was the marine support of the Kingdom against all pirates and invaders in foreign lands and seas. Besides, it was a source of income for the Crown.

The sovereign required all British companies sailing out overseas to register themselves as bona fide companies on payment of tributes which constituted a substantial source of income for the kingdom. To make the overseas business attractive to investors, the Crown granted monopoly rights to the British overseas maritime companies. The monopoly charter to a company meant that trading rights in its chartered territories were denied to other British private traders.

On the last day of the year 1600 the East India Company was chartered as a company by the name of 'the Governor and Company of Merchants of London Trading into the East Indies'. The number of founding stock subscribers was 217. The first governor, Thomas Smythe, and twenty-four committeemen were specifically mentioned in the charter. The charter provided that the committee must be elected annually. The exclusive trade with India was granted tentatively for fifteen years. The great journey towards establishing an empire in the east by a private chartered company was thus begun.

In 1609, the company sought from the king a perpetual trading right in India. In view of the progressive growth of the company and profitable business transacted in the eastern waters, the king granted a charter endowing the company with a monopoly right tenable in perpetuity, unless it should prove unprofitable to the kingdom. The right, however, could be revoked on serving three years' notice.

During Cromwell's regime the company had faced considerable difficulties. Cromwell was thinking to revoke the comapany's charter and declare 'East Indies trade' open to all. But finally it could manage a new charter from the Long Parliament. Under this charter the company was turned into a permanent joint stock company. It, however, enjoyed a prosperous time after the Restoration. The Stewart kings often borrowed money from the company without paying it back. The charters granted between the years 1661 and 1683 strengthened the position of the company in many ways, giving it the right to coin money, erect fortifications, exercise jurisdiction over English subjects residing in the east, make war or peace, and form alliances with non-Christian peoples. It is on the basis of this charter that the company had waged war against Mughal Bengal in the 1680s, made settlements and fortifications in Calcutta in the 1690s and became a territorial power in the 1760s and '70s. The first Charter Act after the establishment of dominion in Bengal was the Townshend's Act of

1767. This Act recognised the acquisition of the *Diwani* of Bengal, Bihar and Orissa in lieu of an annual tribute to His Majesty's exchequer. The company was now both a commercial as well as territorial power. Henceforth all the Charter Acts, also known as India Acts, were aimed at curbing progressively its political powers and commercial privileges. By enacting the regulating act of 1773, parliament had started the process of bringing the company's state under its own control. Under this Act, the governor of fort william was given primacy over other presidencies. He was designated as 'Governor General and Council of the Presidency of Fort William in Bengal'. A four member Council was appointed by parliament to assist the Governor General.

The parliamentary control that was established under the Regulating Act increased progressively under the Charter Acts of 1781, 1784 and 1793. Under the Charter Act of 1784 (pitt's India act) the Governor General was armed with extraordinary powers. Under this Act the Governor General's designation was changed into 'Governor General in Council' and the commander-in-chief of the King's army in India became an ex-officio member of the Council.

The Calcutta government was further directed to establish a permanent system of government without indulging in exterminations any more. Lord Cornwallis was appointed Governor General under this Act. The system of appointing the Governor General directly by parliament had indeed very materially curbed the privileges of the court of directors. The company lost the monopoly right under the Charter Act of 1813, which made India open to free trade. However, the company still retained the monopoly of China trade. But this residue privilege was also abolished under the Charter Act of 1833. Henceforth, the East India Company as a business concern had to compete with others on equal footing. The Charter Act of 1853 had abolished the company's trading right and privilege of patronage.

From now on, the civilians of the company's civil service were to be recruited by competitive examinations. From 1853, the company was to rule India on behalf of the Crown and parliament according to rules set by parliament. Finally, the company had a painless death when parliament abolished the company altogether under the India act, 1858 and undertook the responsibility of ruling British India directly. The Governor General of India was redesignated under this Act as the 'Governor General and Viceroy of India'. A cabinet minister with the designation of Secretary of State for India in Council was henceforth to rule India through the office of the Governor General and Viceroy. [Sirajul Islam]

The voice of free trade and the changing character of British colonial rule

After gaining the right to collect revenue in Bengal in 1765, the Company largely ceased importing gold and silver, which it had hitherto used to pay for goods shipped back to Britain. In addition, as under Mughal rule, land revenue collected in the Bengal Presidency helped finance the Company's wars in other part of India. Consequently, in the period 1760-1800, Bengal's money supply was greatly diminished; furthermore, the closing of some local mints and close supervision of the rest, the fixing of exchange rates, and the standardization of coinage, paradoxically, added to the economic downturn.

During the period, 1780-1860, India changed from being an exporter of processed goods for which it received payment in bullion, to being an exporter of raw materials and a buyer of manufactured goods. More specifically, in the 1750s, mostly fine cotton and silk was exported from India to markets in Europe, Asia, and Africa; by the second quarter of the 19th century, raw materials, which chiefly consisted of raw cotton, opium, and indigo, accounted for most of India's exports. Also, from the late 18th century British cotton mill industry began to lobby the government to both tax Indian imports and allow them access to markets in India. Starting in the 1830s, British textiles began to appear in—and soon to inundate—the Indian markets, with the value of the textile imports growing from £5.2 million 1850 to £18.4 million in 1896. The American Civil War too would have a major impact on India's cotton economy: with the outbreak of the war, American cotton was no longer available to British manufacturers; consequently, demand for Indian cotton soared, and the prices soon quadrupled. This led many farmers in India to switch to cultivating cotton as a quick cash crop; however, with the end of the war in 1865, the demand plummeted again, creating another downturn in the agricultural economy.

At this time, the East India Company's trade with China began to grow as well. In the early 1800s demand for Chinese tea had greatly increased in Britain; since the money supply in India was restricted and the Company was indisposed to shipping bullion from Britain, it decided upon opium, which had a large underground market in China and which was grown in many parts of India, as the most profitable form of payment. However, since the Chinese authorities had banned the importation and consumption of opium, the Company engaged them in the First Opium War, and at its conclusion, under the Treaty of Nanjing, gained access to five Chinese ports, Guangzhou, Xiamen, Fuzhou, Shanghai, and Ningbo; in addition, Hong Kong was ceded to the British Crown. Towards the end of the second quarter of the 19th century, opium export constituted 40% of India's exports.

Another major, though erratic, export item was indigo dye, which was extracted from natural indigo, and which came to be grown in Bengal and northern Bihar. In late 17th and early 18th century Europe, blue apparel was favoured as a fashion, and blue uniforms were common in the military; consequently, the demand for the dye was high. In 1788, the East India Company offered advances to ten British planters to grow indigo; however, since the new (landed) property rights defined in the Permanent Settlement, didn't allow them, as Europeans, to buy agricultural land, they had to in turn offer cash advances to local peasants, and sometimes coerce them, to grow the crop. The European demand for the dye, however, proved to be unstable, and both creditors and cultivators bore the risk of the market crashes in 1827 and 1847. The peasant discontent in Bengal eventually led to the *Indigo rebellion* in 1859-60 and to the end of indigo production there. In Bihar, however, indigo production continued well into the 20th century; the centre of indigo production there, Champaran district, became the staging ground, in 1917, for Mohandas Karamchand Gandhi's first experiment in nonviolent resistance against the British Raj. East India Company

British involvement in India during the 18th century can be divided into two phases, one ending and the other beginning at mid-century. In the first half of the century, the British were a trading presence at certain points along the coast; from the 1750s they began to wage war on land in eastern and southeastern India and to reap the reward of successful warfare, which was the exercise of political power, notably over the rich province of Bengal. By the end of the century British rule had been consolidated over the first conquests and it was being extended up the Ganges valley to Delhi and over most of the peninsula of southern India. By then the British had established a military dominance that would enable them in the next fifty years to subdue all the remaining Indian states of any consequence, either conquering them or forcing their rulers to become subordinate allies....India became the focal point of the Company's trade.

At the beginning of the 18th century English commerce with India was nearly a hundred years old. It was transacted by the East India Company, which had been given a monopoly of all English trade to Asia by royal grant at its foundation in 1600. Through many vicissitudes, the Company had evolved into a commercial concern only matched in size by its Dutch rival. Some 3000 shareholders subscribed to a stock of £3 200 000; a further £6 million was borrowed on short-term bonds; twenty or thirty ships a year were sent to Asia and annual sales in London were worth up to £2 million. Twenty-four directors, elected annually by the shareholders ran the Company's operations from its headquarters in the City of London.

Towards the end of the 17th century India became the focal point of the Company's trade. Cotton cloth woven by Indian weavers was being imported into Britain in huge quantities to supply a worldwide demand for cheap, washable, lightweight fabrics for dresses and furnishings. The Company's main settlements, Bombay, Madras and Calcutta were established in the Indian provinces where cotton textiles for export were most readily available. These settlements had evolved from 'factories' or trading posts into major commercial towns under British jurisdiction, as Indian merchants and artisans moved in to do business with the Company and with the British inhabitants who lived there.

Regional Politics

The East India Company's trade was built on a sophisticated Indian economy. India offered foreign traders the skills of its artisans in weaving cloth and winding raw silk, agricultural products for export, such as sugar, the indigo dye or opium, and the services of substantial merchants and rich bankers. During the 17th century at least, the effective rule maintained by the Mughal emperors throughout much of the subcontinent provided a secure framework for trade.

A New Empire in India

The Anglo-French conflicts that began in the 1750s ended in 1763 with a British ascendancy in the southeast and most significantly in Bengal. There the local ruler actually took the Company's Calcutta settlement in 1756, only to be driven out of it by British troops under Robert Clive, whose victory at Plassey in the following year enabled a new British satellite ruler to be installed. British influence quickly gave way to outright rule over Bengal, formally conceded to Clive in 1765 by the still symbolically important, if militarily impotent, Mughal emperor.

...the governors of the Company's commercial settlements became governors of provinces...

What opinion in Britain came to recognise as a new British empire in India remained under the authority of the East India Company, even if the importance of the national concerns now involved meant that the Company had to submit to increasingly close supervision by the British state and to periodical inquiries by parliament. In India, the governors of the Company's commercial settlements became governors of provinces and, although the East India Company continued to trade, many of its servants became administrators in the new British regimes. Huge armies were created, largely composed of Indian sepoys but with some regular British regiments. These armies were used to defend the Company's territories, to coerce neighbouring Indian states and to crush any potential internal resistance.

Company Government

The new Company governments were based on those of the Indian states that they had displaced and much of the effective work of administration was initially still done by Indians. Collection of taxes was the main function of government. About one third of the produce of the land was extracted from the cultivators and passed up to the state through a range of intermediaries, who were entitled to keep a proportion for themselves.

In addition to enforcing a system whose yield provided the Company with the resources to maintain its armies and finance its trade, British officials tried to fix what seemed to them to be an appropriate balance between the rights of the cultivating peasants and those of the intermediaries, who resembled landlords. British judges also supervised the courts, which applied Hindu or Islamic rather than British law. There was as yet little belief in the need for outright innovation. On the contrary, men like Warren Hastings, who ruled British Bengal from 1772 to 1785, believed that Indian institutions were well adapted to Indian needs and that the new British governments should try to restore an 'ancient constitution', which had been subverted during the upheavals of the 18th century. If this were done, provinces like Bengal would naturally recover their legendary past prosperity.

The ignorance and superstition...should be challenged...

By the end of the century, however, opinions were changing. India seemed to be suffering not merely from an unfortunate recent history but from deeply ingrained backwardness. It needed to be 'improved' by firm, benevolent foreign rule. Various strategies for improvement were being discussed. Property relations should be reformed to give greater security to the ownership of land. Laws should be codified on scientific principles. All obstacles to free trade between Britain and India should be removed, thus opening India's economy to the stimulus of an expanding trade with Europe. Education should be remodelled. The ignorance and superstition thought to be inculcated by Asian religions should be challenged by missionaries propagating the rationality embodied in Christianity. The implementation of improvement in any systematic way lay in the future, but commitment to governing in Indian ways through Indians was waning fast.

6

Liberal Political Theory

Introduction

Throughout the years of his involvement in the colonial administration of India from 1819-1835 in the East India Company, James Mill persistently held a conviction that India needed enlightenment and progress. The paper attempts to unravel how Mill applied his utilitarianismand theory of progress to justify the British rule in India. This issue has been neglected or taken for granted in the literature on Mill's viewon the Indians and British India; In section I, I unravel Mill's grand vision in bringing about the global happiness of humankind with particular reference to Asian nations. It shows why Mill believed that if non-European peoples in Asia, including India, were enlightened through interacting with the Europeans, they would progress and the global happiness would be increased. Then I discuss why Mill thought that the Indians would progress more readily if the whole continent of India was brought under British rule.

Before taking up the post in the East India Company in 1819, Mill delineated in sundry journal writings and his massive *History of British India* (hereafter as *History*) a dilemma which the British Indian government had to resolve if they intended to keep British India and extended their rulership to the remaining parts of India. On the one hand, Britain suffered substantial economic loss and political disadvantages in governing India. On the other hand, India would progress and the Indians would be able to have more happiness under British rule than when they were governed by their native kings. Thus, if only the benefits which the Indians would gain from British rule were taken into account, it was desirable for the British to rule the Indians. However, whether the British should take a total control of India depended on whether there would be an overall utility or disutility. Section II examines why Mill believed that from the utilitarian perspective, there would be an overall utility if the British kept British India, which included the provinces of Bengal, Bombay, and Madras, and if the British extended their rule to the remaining parts of India. I attempt to unravel the consistency of Mill's and Bentham's accounts in arguing for an emancipation of the British colonies in America while supporting an extension of British rule to the whole continent of India. In section III, I delineate what Mill thought to be the best means for the British to subjugate the whole continent of India. Basically, there were two ways to extend British rule: either by making conquest over the native states or through inducing the voluntary consent of the Indians. I shall show why Mill thought that it was not justified for the British to wage offensive wars against the independent native states for the purpose of subjugating the Indians, and why the only legitimate way was in Mill's view to induce the consent of the native princes.

Global Happiness and the Desirability of a Foreign Rule

The Enlightenment of Non-European Peoples

Throughout his life Mill's ultimate concern was the happiness of humankind as a whole, or as I shall call it, global happiness. Global happiness will be obtained if all races of peoples of the globe are 'civilized' in the utilitarian sense. Mill had a conviction that all non-European peoples would become 'civilized' if the European knowledge, arts, manners, and institutions were diffused to them. Mill was particularly concerned with how to bring enlightenment to what he believed to be 'half-civilized' peoples, such as peoples in India and other Asian nations. Mill believed that India and other Asian nations, such as China and Japan, needed enlightenment and progress. Mill acknowledged that 'even to Voltaire, a keen-eyed and sceptical judge, the Chinese, of almost all nations, are the objects of the loudest and most unqualified praise'. However, in Mill's view, Voltaire's high praise of the Chinese culture originated from an orientalist bias which was similar to that of Sir William Jones who suggested wrongly that India had been quite advanced in many respects of civilization. Mill acknowledged that in ancient time, as India developed, the social structure and other institutions progressed accordingly. For instance, the division of castes in India was multiplied at some stage in ancient India from four basic castes to a number of thirty-six by admitting 'impure' people borne from mixed marriage of the basic castes. Mill thought that the progress of the Indians up to that stage was impressive and it was 'an important era in the history of Hindu society' in that ancient period. But Mill contended that 'having reached this stage, it does not appear that it [India] has made, or that it is capable of making, much further progress'. According to Mill's scale of civilization, the Chinese was at a similar level of progress as that of the Indians, the Persians, and Arabians:

'There can be no doubt that they [The Indians] are in a state of civilization very nearly the same with that of the Chinese, the Persians, and the Arabians; who, together, compose the great branches of the Asian population; and of which the subordinate nations, the Japanese, the Cochin-Chinese, Siamese, Burmans, and even Malays and Tibetans are a number of corresponding and resembling offsets.'.

And being 'resembling offsets' of the Chinese, the Japanese and other South East Asian peoples were of an even lower level of progress in their civilizations. From Mill's perspective, China, Japan, and other Asian nations needed as much enlightenment as India. Mill was quite certain that just as the Europeans could attain a civilized mode of existence, other peoples of the human race could also attain that level of advancement so that they would have a similar amount of happiness as what the Europeans had been enjoying. Mill believed that once China had been enlightened, the civilized manners and institutions which the Europeans brought them would in the long run have had spread to other Asian nations. Mill requested his readers to imagine what would happen if the European manners, arts, and institutions were diffused to China, and subsequently to other Asian peoples:

'what glorious results might be expected for the whole of Asia, that vast proportion of the earth, which, even in its most favoured parts, has been in all ages condemned to semi-barbarism, and the miseries of despotic power?'

From Mill's perspective, the more the Asian peoples would be enlightened, the happier they would be. Of course, the European manners, arts, and institutions were in Mill's view far from perfect when they were assessed from the utilitarian perspective. From Mill's perspective, only when the moral and the political ideals and practices of the utilitarian liberal doctrine were implemented in Europe and all over the world could the maximization of global happiness be foreseeable.

Given his concern with India even before taking up the administrative job in the East India Company in 1819, Mill's immediate objective was surely to bring European enlightenment to India. As early as in 1813, Mill denounced in a reviewarticle the claim that the Indians could not be enlightened; as he queried: 'Why every thing is unchangeable so long as nothing occurs which is calculated to produce a change'. Holding firmly a conviction in the malleability of human nature, Mill thought that if the Indians of the independent native states developed an extensive interaction with the Europeans, they would inevitably receive from the Europeans substantial positive impact on their social progress. Mill believed that the extent of progress which the Indians might attain through interacting with the Europeans would be no less than what the Mahomedans had brought them:

'an intercourse with Europeans is not likely to produce effects less considerable, than intercourse with a people so nearly on the same level of civilization with themselves, as the Mahomedans'.

In Mill's view, a widespread settlement of Englishmen in India would speed up the enlightenment process of the Indians. Mill claimed that the 'formation of an European – of a British – population in India' increased the 'advantages which would accrue to the vast population of India, and the still more vast population of Asia and Africa'. Mill fervently believed that the enlightenment of India would bring the European civilization close to the 'doors' of other Asian peoples who needed as much enlightenment from the Europeans as India:

'The pace of civilization [in other Asian nations] would be quickened beyond all example. The arts, the knowledge, and the manners of Europe would be brought to their doors, and forced by an irresistible moral pressure on their acceptance. The happiness of the human race would be this prodigiously augmented; and the progress, perhaps, of even the most cultivated nations, greatly accelerated.'

For Mill, the enlightenment of the Indians would thus conduce to a progressive development of other Asian peoples.

It should be noticed that Mill envisaged a more direct way which facilitated the interaction between the Europeans and the Asian peoples, such as the Chinese and the Japanese. Mill believed that if there existed 'a navigable passage across the isthmus of Panama', the Asian peoples would be enlightened more readily. This is because Asian nations, such as China and Japan, would be subject more effectively to the influence of the European civilization. Mill asked, 'Is it too much to hope, that China and Japan themselves, thus brought so much nearer the influence of European civilization – much more constantly and powerfully subject to its operation – would not be able to resist the salutary impression, but would soon receive important changes in ideas, arts, manners and institutions?'

In Mill's view, if this navigable passage existed, the fulfilment of the hope in enlightening China and Japan seemed 'to rise even to certainty'; and Britain would be able to influence these Asian nations effectively: 'the connexion thus formed between the two countries [Britain and China], would still further tend to accelerate the acquisition of enlightened views and civilized manners in China herself'. It seemed that Mill envisaged an enlightenment of China, Japan, and other Asian nations through building up commercial and other interactions with them. This required merely constant and frequent peaceful commercial interaction between the Europeans and the Chinese and the Japanese. But I shall show that from Mill's perspective, it would benefit these Asian nations more if they were brought directly under British rule. To see why Mill would have thought so, we should now turn to see why Mill believed that it was desirable for the Indians to be directly governed by a more advanced civilization.

The Desirability of a Foreign Rule in India

The desirability for the Indians to be ruled by a more advanced civilization was revealed in Mill's opinion on Mogul rule in India. With regard to Mogul rule in India, Mill found it significant to examine:

'Whether by a government, moulded and conducted agreeably to the properties of Persian civilization, instead of a government moulded and conducted agreeably to the properties of Hindu civilization, the Hindu population of India lost or gained'. For Mill, before the Moguls ruled India, the individual progress and the societal progress of the Hindu Indians had been retarded by their superstitions in Hinduism. But as I now show, Mill believed that the Indians gained progress both at the individual level and at the social level under the Mogul sovereigns. Consider individual progress first. Gain or loss in individual progress of the Indians was measured in terms of the extent of the improvement of human nature which the Hindu Indians received from the Moguls. In speaking of the advantages to the Indians as they were governed by the Moguls, Mill asserted that it would 'not admit of any long dispute, that human nature in India gained, and gained very considerably, by passing from a Hindu to a Mogul government'. And the improvement of human nature was assessed with reference to the cultivation of the four qualities of mind, namely, intelligence, temperance, justice, and generosity (EE, PP 32,34). Aprogressive development of these four qualities would be conducive to the individual happiness and the total happiness of the Indian society. Thus, what Mill meant was that the Indians got the four qualities cultivated more progressively when they were under Mogul rule than when they were governed by the Hindu despots. According to Mill, since these four qualities of the Indians were better cultivated under the Mogul sovereigns, it could be inferred that the Indians who were under the Mogul sovereigns had more happiness than those who were under the Hindu rulers.

Nowlet us turn to the societal progress of the Indians who were under Mogul rule, Mill thought that the Moguls were in nearly all respects of civilization, including the worldview, political arrangement, legal system, and other attainments, superior to the Hindus. It was to the benefits of the Hindu Indians when they were under the Mogul rule because they were brought with the more advanced Persian civilization:

'The Persian language was the language they [the Moguls] used; the Persian laws, and the Persian religion, were the laws and religion they had expoused; it was the Persian literature to which they were devoted; and they carried along with them the full benefit of the Persian arts and knowledge, when they established themselves in Hindustan.'

Mill believed that in bringing with them all important respects of the Persian civilization to the Hindus, the Moguls brought substantial social progress in India. Mill rejected the claim that the Hindus were very advanced before their being conquered by the Moguls but had declined since then. Mill argued that 'those, who affirm the high state of civilization among the Hindus previous to their subjugation to foreigners, held fast their opinion, that wherever the Hindu have been found in a situation always except from the dominion of foreigners, they appear, and with an uniformity which admits of no exception, in a state of civilization inferior to those who have long been the subjects of a Mohammedan throne'.

For Mill, it was evident that the Hindu Indians who were not subject to the Mogul rule were at a lower stage of societal progress than that of those who had been subjected to the Mogul rule. The message which Mill in effect attempted to convey was that it was justifiable for a people of an advanced civilization to govern a people of a retarded progress in civilization. Nevertheless, Mill seemed to have anticipated a nationalist argument from the perspective of the Indians. According to this argument, the Hindu Indians were justified to reject Mogul rule or other foreign rule because the ruling people were foreigners. Against this argument, Mill stressed the unreasonableness of the intention to reject a government simply because it was formed by foreigners: 'For the aversion to a government, because in the hands of foreigners; that is, of men who are called by one rather than some other name, without regard to the qualities of the government, whether better or worse; is a prejudice which reason disclaims.'

What mattered was in Mill's view whether the government governed benevolently so as to bring progress and happiness to the Indians. Mill believed that the European civilization was surely a better candidate for the Indians than that of the Moguls. Given the collapse and the gradual disintegration of the Mogul Empire, there were two alternatives available to the Indians: either to revert to the Hindu despotism, or to accept European rule, French or British in particular. According to Mill's logic, it was justifiable for the Europeans to take over the government of India from the degenerating Mogul Empire. The fact that the British had attained a much higher progress suggested that it was unreasonable for the Indians to object to the British governance simply because the British were foreigners. Now, it is not implausible to draw out an implication for other Asian nations. As Mill believed that it was desirable for not only the Indians but also other non-Europeans to have their institutions transformed in accordance with the utilitarian liberal doctrine, it seemed natural to imagine that for Mill, the case of India presented a model for China and other Asian nations. If China and Japan were at a similar level of progress as India, it was justified from Mill's perspective for China, Japan, and other even more backward Asian nations to be governed by the European nations so that they might be enlightened more readily.

With regard to India, it seems plausible to suggest further that from Mill's perspective, it was desirable for the British to subjugate the whole continent of India because it was to the benefit of the Indians if they were governed by the British. But what should also be taken into account was the utility to Britain. Around the period when Mill finished the *History*, a substantial portion of India had already been subjected to the dominion of the East India Company. The immediate concern of Mill and Bentham was whether British India should be kept under British rule or whether they should be emancipated.

British India and the Extension of British Rule

Utility and the Emancipation of Colonies

To assess Mill's view on whether it was desirable for Britain to keep British India, we should bear in mind that there was a distinction between two kinds of colonies with which Mill was mostly concerned. On the one hand, there were colonies, such as those in America, which originated from the widespread settlement of English, French, Spanish and other Europeans. Given the substantial extermination of the indigenous Amerindians, the majority of the population in these settler colonies was of European origin. On the other hand, there were colonies such as British India and Egypt where the native people constituted the majority of the population. Mill's attitude towards these two kinds of colonies was, as I shall demonstrate, very much in agreement with that of Bentham. With regard to these two kinds of colonies, the issue which concerned Mill and Bentham was whether the European nations 'ought to have them'. From the utilitarian perspective, it was necessary to weigh the utility or disutility in keeping colonies against the utility or disutility in emancipating them in order to determine whether it was desirable for the mother nations to retain their colonies. If there was an overall disutility in keeping the colonies, it would not be desirable for the mother nations to retain them. But if there was an overall utility in keeping the colonies, it would be desirable for the mother nations to retain them despite the fact that the mother nations suffered in keeping them. For Bentham and Mill, keeping colonies brought neither economic nor political advantages to the mother nations. In Bentham's words, colonies 'in general yield no advantage to the mother country'. From the financial point of view, as Mill argued in his *Essay on Colony* which appeared in 1820, it was a matter of fact that colonies yielded no tribute to the mother country, 'a government always spend as much as it finds it possible or safe to extract from the people.... If the government of the mother country is sure to spend up to the resources of the country; and if a still stronger necessity operates upon the government of the colony to produce this effect, how can it possibly afford any tribute?'

More important, Mill contended that 'there is, if not an absolute, at least, a moral impossibility, that a colony should ever benefit the mother country, by yielding it a permanent tribute', because even if it might happen that colonies yielded tributes, the tributes should be retained for the governance of the colonies. Mill and Bentham thought that Britain suffered economic disadvantages in keeping British India as its colony. Mill had been repetitively complaining about the financial deficits of the East India Company for many years even before the publication of his *History* and his subsequent appointment in the East India Company in 1819. The deficits were due to the costs involved in the administration its Indian dominion and in wars designed to extend its sovereignty.

With regard to the political advantage and disadvantage in keeping British India, Bentham listed out several reasons in his *Principles of International Law* as early as in 1786-9 to explain why it was in the political interest of the British to give up British India:

1. Saving the danger of war;
2. Getting rid of the means of corruption resulting from the patronage, civil and military;
3. Simplifying the government;
4. Getting rid of prosecutions that consume the time of parliament, and beget suspicion of injustice.

In discussing the emancipation of Spanish colonies in America Bentham elaborated these advantages which he thought Spain would enjoy if they grant independence to their colonies in America. The most important one which the mother nations suffered was the wars which were waged to contest for colonies; as Mill believed, colonies were a 'grand source of wars', or as Bentham claimed, colonies increased 'the chances of war'. Having shown that keeping colonies brought no advantages but only disadvantages, political or economic, to the mother country, we may proceed to discuss the utility that the colonies and the whole humankind would have obtained if they were retained or reliquished.

From the utilitarian perspective, far from being economically disadvantageous to the well-established colonies in America, their emancipation brought economic benefits to the mother nations and the colonies. Mill claimed that the independence of the British colonies of the United States had been commercially 'far more profitable to' the British than its subjection. Furthermore, Mill contended that instead of hindering global trade, granting independence to well-established Europeanized colonies, such as the case of the United States, had enhanced it. Mill was convinced that the independence of the United States presented an evidence to affirm that newly independent nations offered valuable chances for enhancement of commercial connections and free trade among nations which in turn increased the economic prosperity of all involved nations. In supporting the emancipation of Spanish America, Mill argued that the independence of Spanish America would not only enhance trade between Spain and its colonies but also present a commercial opportunity for other nations and hence increase the global trade. Of course, it would happen only if the newly formed government in the Spanish America was 'a just and beneficent government' which acknowledged the utility of the freedom of trade.

With regard to British India, given the economic backwardness of the Indians, granting self-governance would in Mill's view not bring much enhancement of trade to other nations. And more important, given their strict adherence to the traditional economic practices and laws which were prescribed in the Hindu sacred texts, it was not very likely that a just and beneficent government, which would enhance trade, might be established. What should be done was rather to terminate the monopoly of the East India

Company in the Indian trade so that not only other English merchants but also merchants from all other nations could join the Indian trade. If the monopoly of the East India Company was terminated, competition and freedom of trade would increase the prosperity of all involved nations. With regard to the political advantages and disadvantages, Bentham contended in his *Principles of International Law* that in the case of all those distant well-established colonies in America, it would be impossible for the mother nations in Europe 'to govern them so well as they would govern themselves, on account of the distance'. Bentham believed that it was not in the interest of the well-established Europeanized colonies to be governed by the people of the mother nations who never knew, nor could ever know, either their inclinations or their wants. Thus, there was a great disutility to the distant well-established colonies if they were kept governed by their mother nations.

Nevertheless, there was in Mill's and Bentham's view an important difference between the well-established Europeanized colonies and the British India, namely, that the European well-established colonies in America were all ready for self-government, whereas British India was not. In his *Emancipate Your Colonies!* written early around 1792-3, Bentham advised the French to grant their colonies in the West Indies independence because they were 'ripe for self-government' but not to give their colonies in India back to the Indians themselves:

'whatever applies to the West Indies, applies to the East with double force. The islands present no difficulty: the population there is French: they are ripe for self-government. There remains the continent: you know-how things are changed there: – the power of Tipu is no more. Would the tree of liberty grow there, if planted? Would the declaration of rights translate into Shanskrit? Would *Bramin, Chetree, Bice, Sooder,* and *Hallachore* meet on equal ground? If not, you may find some difficulty in giving themto themselves.'

In Bentham's view, if the Indians were left to their own native princes, they would inevitably be ruled by despots. In contrast to the situation in the well-established Europeanized colonies, it was not in the interest of the Indians if they governed themselves. As Mill asserted: 'whatever may be our sense of the difficulties into which we have brought ourselves, by the improvident assumption of such a dominion, we earnestly hope, for the sake of the natives, that it will not be found necessary to leave them to their own direction'.

Mill thought that even though Britain suffered in keeping British India, it was in the interest of the Indians. Furthermore, Mill believed that instead of leaving the Indians to govern themselves, if the British governed them directly would enlighten India, and this would in turn facilitate a rapid diffusion of European knowledge, arts, manners, and institutions to other Asian nations, and would thereby enhance the happiness of the humankind. So far I believe I have shown that it was desirable in Mill's view for the British to keep their dominion in India. Let us proceed to discuss: to what extent Mill committed himself to an extension of British rule to the whole continent of India, and by what means Mill thought it to be legitimate for the British Indian government to extend its sovereignty to the independent and semi-independent native states.

Conquest, Consent, and the Extension of British Rule

There were basically two ways for the British Indian government to bring enlightenment to the Indians in various independent native states through extending British rule to these states: either by conquest or by inducing voluntary subjection. I shall discuss first whether Mill thought that it was legitimate for the British to extend their sovereignty to and thereby impose their institutions upon the Indians of the independent native states by conquest. To examine this issue, we should begin by examining Mill's account of just war and then study how he applied it to the situation in India. Throughout his life, Mill never attempted to conceal his passionate contempt against war. In Mill's eyes, wars inevitably produce evils:

'Nobody is now so profligate as to vindicate war on the ground of its being a positive good. It is spoken of as at best a necessary evil. It is a painful means, only to be endured for the sake of the end; namely, protection against the injuries of other nations.'

War can never be justified unless it is used to prevent more evils, 'that of repelling actual and unprovoked invasion'. Generally speaking, war may be justly waged against other nations only if 'some right of the nation is violated'. Awar is just if the objective of this war is to seek for a 'compensation for an injury received' and for the 'security that a fresh injury shall not be committed'. However, even if some injury is done, a recourse to war is in Mill's view not always justified. For example, if a compensation has been made to the injured nation by the offending nation, no war is justified. More important, even in the cases when compensation could not be gained except through revenge, it does not necessarily justify war. Mill claimed: 'When it has suffered real injury, and when there is no doubt about the matter, the principle of utility says, Consider whether the evil which you have suffered is likely to be compensated by war. If the evils of the war are likely to outweigh the gains, it is better to abstain from war, and to pass by the injury. When the happiness of the people is the object in pursuit, this is the rule which will be followed.'

Thus, even if it is just for the injured nation to wage war against offensive nations, it is not desirable to do so if more evils than gains would be done to itself. Waging offensive wars against other nations cannot in Mill's view be justified by appealing to the principle of utility. Even if it may be conducive to the overall happiness of humankind for a nation to conquer another nation, such a conquest cannot be justified because of the injustice involved. Mill summerized: 'To pursue what is useful to itself, and to avoid injustice towards other nations, is the grand concern of every community'. To see how Mill applied these considerations in the context of India, let us begin with the system of neutrality firstly prescribed in the Pitt's Indian Act in 1784.

Since the enactment of the Pitt's Act, a system of neutrality had been the official British international policy in India and was declared repeatedly in the Act of 1793. The two acts prohibited the Governor-Generals of British India from making any attempt to pursue schemes of conquest and extension of dominion in India. In order to comply with the Acts, the British Indian government should adopt a policy of neutrality in the sense that the British Indian government 'should stand aloof from all connection with native princes, should form no alliances with them, should take no part in their quarrels, and should never draw the sword for any purpose but that of self defence, when its territory is actually invaded'. Mill agreed with the basic principle that the British government should abstain from making any conquest in India and from waging any wars except those which were launched for defensive purposes. Mill praised the fundamental rationale behind the policy of neutrality, namely, the prevention of war. But Mill did not quite agree with an unconditional submission to the policy of neutrality because he believed that the system of neutrality was in many occasions impracticable in India.

Since Mill's ultimate concern was peace, any policy which tended to produce peace instead of war should in Mill's view be chosen. Accordingly, how the number and the extent of wars could be minimized in India involved a pragmatic consideration of the actual situation in India. Mill believed that to adopt a policy which departed from the policy of neutrality did not inevitably render wars more frequently. Mill claimed that, in some cases, a 'system of vigilant interference', instead of a system of neutrality, should be adopted. Mill contended that the 'system of vigilant interference' was not offensive in nature but as defensive as the system of neutrality 'in spirit':

'By keeping a watchful eye upon the princes of the country marking the individual from whom danger is most imminent, and hedging him round, by contracting alliances with his neighbours, so that he must force his way to you through a rampart of foes, you are obviously both repressing the desire to attack, and lessening the danger, should war be inevitable.'

Mill believed that this system was in principle no more than 'the policy of foresight and prevention'. Nevertheless, Mill admitted that 'by opening a door to defensive policy on this ground, we open a door to offensive policy also'. Let us discuss further the abuses which Mill had in mind. For almost a decade before his appointment in the East India Company in 1819, Mill had been condemning the aggressive British policy and the subsequent violent conquest over the native princes in a series of review articles. Mill thought that the 'system of vigilant interference' was open to abuse in the hands of the governors-general: 'the power of interfering in the affairs of the princes of India, might be made use of by Governors General, not for the purpose of maintaining the security and tranquillity of the Anglo-Indian dominions, but for the gratification of private ambition, or private revenge, or private avarice, or private partiality and favour'.

Mill persistently discredited the contemptible personal ambitions of the governors-general, especially Lord Wellesley who was the governor-general from 1786 to 1805. It is worth pursuing further to see to what extent Mill thought that it was not reasonable for Lord Wellesley to depart from the system of neutrality. Mill contended that if Lord Wellesley's intention to extend the British influence could be used as a justification for his aggressive policy, the political ambition of his enemy, Dowlut Rao Scindia, could also be used to claim justice for himself.

With regard to Lord Wellesley's unnecessary departure from the policy of neutrality, Mill held: 'in proportion as we recede from a system of neutrality, we shall find daily more causes for interference, fresh claims for protection, and new wrongs to revenge. Who is there so blind as not to perceive that it leads, by a natural but inevitable progression, to the entire subjugation of all India?'

The formation of the alliance with the Peshwa under the Governor-General-ship of Lord Wellesley finally gave rise to the second Mahratta war. What was wrong was not the alliance which Lord Wellesley formed with the Peshwa but his private ambitions which were hidden behind the apparent intention of bring benevolent rule in India. Mill compared Lord Wellesley's apparent intention to govern India benevolently with that of the French Bonarparte to govern the world beneveolently:

'The truth is, that independent states are generally extremely ungrateful to the great men in their neighbourhood, who take the trouble of forming plans for their future welfare. They have an unlucky propensity to being happy in their own way, and to managing their own affairs themselves. The benevolent plans of the French emperor for the improvement and happiness of the human race, are perversely counteracted by every nation who can, and who dare counteract them. The administration of Lord Wellesley was a period of uninterrupted warfare. We are perfectly aware of the millennium which was intended to succeed to all this disturbance; but we never could tell exactly when this millennium was to begin.'

For Mill, even though it might be granted that the intentions of the French emperor and Lord Wellesley in bringing about benevolent governance by establishing European institutions over the whole world and in India respectively were sincere, it should not be done through offensive conquest. In Mill's view, the only legitimate means to subjugate the independent native princes and thereby extend appropriate British institutions to their states was to induce their consent: 'One thing, indeed, is to be considered, that in a great part of all that is said by the Governor-General, it is pretty distinctly implied, that to render these Indian princes dependent upon the British government was not an injury to them, but a benefit. If this were allowed to be true; and if it were possible, in other indulgences, to make up to a prince for the loss of his independence; yet, in such cases, the consent of the prince in question would seema requisite, even were his subject people, may proceed to impose force of this kind of benefit upon any other ruler at his pleasure, this allegation would prove to be neither more nor less than another of the pretexts, under which the weak are always exposed to become the prey of the strong. For Mill, the sovereignty of the independent native princes should be respected. And only when the Indians attacked British India or had become aggressive and were ready to attack British India might the British justifiably wage war against them and thereby subjugate them. Otherwise, to induce their consent to the British governance was the only legitimate means to extend British rule to the independent native states.

7

Sikh Empire

The Sikh Empire was a state in the northwestern part of the Indian Subcontinent (present-day India and Pakistan) from 1799 to 1849. It consisted of a collection of autonomous Punjabi Misls, which were governed by Misldars, mainly in the Punjab region.

History

Ranjit Singh was crowned on April 12, 1801 (to coincide with Baisakhi). Sahib Singh Bedi, a descendant of Guru Nanak Dev, conducted the coronation. Gujranwala served as his capital from 1799. In 1802 he shifted his capital to Lahore & Amritsar. Ranjit Singh rose to power in a very short period, from a leader of a single Sikh misl to finally becoming the Maharaja (Emperor) of Punjab.

There was strong collaboration in defence against foreign incursions such as those initiated by Ahmed Shah Abdali and Nadir Shah. The city of Amritsar was attacked numerous times. Yet the time is remembered by Sikh historians as the "Heroic Century". This is mainly to describe the rise of Sikhs to political power against large odds. The circumstances were hostile religious environment against Sikhs, a tiny Sikh population compared to other religious and political powers, which were much larger in the region than the Sikhs.

Misl

Misl refers to a fighting clan. The period from 1716 to 1799 in Punjab was a highly turbulent time politically and militarily. This was caused by the overall decline of the Mughal Empire, particularly in Punjab, caused by Sikh military action against it.

This left a power vacuum that was eventually filled by the Sikh Confederacy. This Confederacy was made up of individual Sikh kingdoms that were ruled by Sikh barons. Each of these barons had his own army, which was commanded by and loyal to him. Each individual army had its own specific name, but the armies were referred to in general as misls.

General Military Structure

Each Misl was made up of members of soldiers, whose loyalty was given to the Misl's Baron (Misldar). A Misl could be composed of a few hundred to tens of thousands soldiers. Every soldier was free to join any Misl he chose and free to cancel his membership of the Misl to whom he belonged. He could, if he wanted, cancel his membership of his old Misl and join another (provided certain procedures were followed). The Barons would allow their armies to combine or coördinate their defences together against a hostile force if ordered by the Misldar Supreme Commander. These orders were only issued in military matters affecting the whole Sikh community. These orders would normally be related to defence against external threats, such as Afghan military attacks (typically initiated by Afghan Kings).

The head Barons of each kingdom, in a council, elected the Misldar Supreme Commander. Previous Supreme Commanders include Nawab Kapur Singh and Sultan Ul Quam Baba Jassa Singh Ahluwalia. The Sikh Confederacy is a description of the political structure, of how all the Barons' Kingdoms interacted with each other, (politically), together in Punjab.

Prominent Misls

1. Bhangi or Bhuma Misl first led by Chajja Singh and then Sardar Hari Singh Bhangi of Panjwad near Amritsar-(Strength-20,000 regular horsemen)
2. Karorh Singhia Misl (also known as Panjgarhia), first led by Sardar Karora Singh-(Strength-10,000 regular horsemen)
3. Nakai Misl, first led by Sardar Hira Singh Nakai-(Strength-7,000 regular horsemen)
4. Ahluwalia Misl, first led Sadhu Singh and then by Sardar Sultan ul Quam Baba Jassa Singh Ahluwalia-(Strength-6,000 regular horsemen)

5. Ramgarhia Misl, first led by Sardar Nand Singh and then by Jassa Singh Ramgarhia-(Strength-5,000 regular horsemen)
6. Kanahiya Misl, first led by Sardar Jai Singh Kanhaiya-(Strength-5,000 regular horsemen)
7. Dallewalia Misl, first led by Sardar Gulab Singh Dallewalia-(Strength-5,000 regular horsemen)
8. Shaheedan Misl, first led by Sardar Baba Deep Singh of Pahuwind near Patti-(Strength-5,000 regular horsemen)
9. Faizalpuria or Singhpuria Misl, first led by Sardar Nawab Kapur Singh-(Strength-5,000 regular horsemen)
10. Shukarchakia Misl, first led by Sardar Naud Singh-(Strength-5,000 regular horsemen)
11. Nishanwalia Misl, first led by Sardar Dasaundha Singh-(Strength-2,000 regular horsemen)
12. Phulkian Misl, first led by Ala Singh-(Strength-4,000 regular horsemen). *(Expelled in August 1765).*

Ahluwalia

Ahluwalia is one of twelve Sikh Misls, or fighting clans, founded by the misldar (leader of the misl) Jassa Singh Ahluwalia in mid-eighteenth century Punjab, who also found the Kapurthala State. Some Hindu Punjabis also use Ahluwalia as their last name.

History and Traditions

The term Ahluwalia came into use after the rise of a resident of the Ahlu village (located 11 miles SE of Lahore), Jassa Singh Ahluwalia as a misldar of the Sikh Kingdom of Punjab. Hence his descendants and followers came to be known by Ahluwalia or Walias.

Walia is short form of Ahluwalia. Later, descendants of other non-Sikh residents of the village also started using Ahluwalia, now a sizable community among Punjabis.

Ahluwalia Chiefs

Kapurthala 1777 Kapurthala state founded Rulers (title Sardar) Ahluwalia dynasty:

- 1777 – 20 Oct 1783 Jassa Singh (1718–1783)
- 20 Oct 1783 – 1801 Bagh Singh (1747–1801).

Rajas Ahluwalia dynasty:

- 1801 – 20 Oct 1837 Fateh Singh (1784–1837)
- 20 Oct 1837 – 13 Sep 1852 Nihal Singh (1817–1852)
- 13 Sep 1852 – 12 Mar 1861 Randhir Singh (1831–1870).

Rulers (title Raja-i Rajgan) Ahluwalia dynasty:

- 12 Mar 1861 – 2 Apr 1870 Randhir Singh (s.a.)
- 2 Apr 1870 – 3 Sep 1877 Kharrak Singh (1850–1877)
- 3 Sep 1877 – 12 Dec 1911 Jagatjit Singh Bahadur (1872–1949).

Maharaja Ahluwalia dynasty:

- 12 Dec 1911 – 15 Aug 1947 Jagatjit Singh Bahadur.

Jassa Singh Ahluwalia

Sultan ul Quam Nawab Jassa Singh Ahluwalia (1718–1783) was a prominent Sikh leader during the period of the Sikh Confederacy. He was also Misldar of the Ahluwalia Army (misl). This period was an interlude, lasting roughly from the time of the death of Banda Bahadur in 1716 to the founding of the Sikh Empire in 1801. The period is also sometimes described as *the Age of the Misls.* He founded the Kapurthala State in 1772.

Early Life

Sultan ul Quam Nawab Jassa Singh Ahluwalia was born at a village called Ahl/Ahlu/Ahluwal near Lahore, established by his ancestor, Sadda Singh, a disciple of the sixth Sikh Guru, Guru Har Gobind. Hence, the name *Ahluwalia* stuck to him. His father, Sardar Badar Singh died in 1723 A.D., when Ahluwalia was hardly five years old. His mother entreated Mata Sundari, widow of Guru Gobind Singh, to take him into her care. Mata Sundari agreed to do so. She brought him up affectionately, instructing him in the arts of war and peace. He studied Sikh scriptures under Bhai Mani Singh. Later, Mata Sundari asked Nawab Kapur Singh to take charge of the promising youth. Nawab Kapur Singh was pleased with Jassa Singh's supreme devotion to the faith and a sense of duty and humility. He appointed him as a storekeeper with his forces. Ahluwalia participated in many battles as well where he proved himself to be a natural leader. Nawab Kapur Singh appointed him as his successor on the eve of his death in 1753. Elated at his successful helmsmanship, the Khalsa honoured Jassa

Singh with the title of *Sultan-ul-Qaum* (King of the community), when they captured Lahore in 1761.

The Raids of Ahmed Shah Abdali

Ahmed Shah Abdali, Nadir Shah's seniormost general, succeeded to the throne of Afghanistan, when Shah was murdered in June, 1747. He established his own dynasty, the Sadozai, which was the name of the Pashtun khel to which he belonged to.

Starting from December, 1747 till 1769, Abdali made a total of nine incursions into India. His repeated invasions destroyed the Mughal administration of the Punjab and the rest of Northern India. At the Third Battle of Panipat, he dealt a drippling blow to Maratha pretensions in the North. Thus he created a power vacuum in the Punjab, which was filled by the Sikhs.

The Sixth Afghan Invasion, 1762

On February 5, 1762, the Sikhs were especially the target of Ahmad Shah Abdali's sixth invasion into India. News had reached him in Afghanistan of the defeat of his general, Nur-ud-Din Bamezai, at the hands of the Sikhs who were fast spreading themselves out over the Punjab and had declared their leader, Baron Jassa Singh Ahluwalia, king of Lahore. To rid his Indian dominion of them once and for all, he set out from Kandahar. Marching with alacrity, he overtook the Sikhs as they were withdrawing into Malwa after crossing the Satluj.

The moving caravan comprised a substantial portion of the total Sikh population and contained, besides active fighters, a large body of old men, women and children who were being escorted to the safety of the interior. Surprised by Ahmad Shah, the Sikhs threw a cordon round those who needed protection, and prepared for the battle. In this formation and continuing their march, they fought the invaders and their Indian allies (The Nawabs of Malerkotla, Sirhind, etc.) desperately. Sardar Charhat Singh Sukerchakia (the grandfather of Maharaja Ranjit Singh), Sardar Hari Singh Dhillon and Sardar Jassa Singh Ahluwalia led their forces with skill and courage. Jassa Singh sustained sixty-four wounds on his body, but he survived. Sardar Charhat Singh rode to exhaustion, five of his horses one after another.

Ahmad Shah succeeded, in the end, in breaking through the cordon and carried out a full scale massacre. His orders were for everyone in native dress to be killed at sight. The soldiers of Malerkotala and Sirhind were to wear green leaves of trees on their heads to distinguish themselves from the Sikhs. Near the village of Kup, in the vicinity of Malerkotla, about 20,000 Sikhs died at the end of a single day's action (February 5, 1762). This battle is known in Sikh history as the *Wadda Ghalughara*(The Great Holocaust).

The Battle of Amritsar

Despite the Ghalughara disaster, by the month of May, the Sikhs were up in arms again. Under Jassa Singh, they defeated the Afghan *faujdar* of Sihind at Harnaulgarh. By autumn, the Sikhs had regained enough confidence to foregather in large numbers at Amritsar to celebrate Diwali. Abdali made a mild effort to win over them and sent an envoy with proposals for a treaty of peace. The Sikhs were in no mood for peace and insulted the emissary. Abdali did not waste any time and turned up at the outskirts of Amritsar.

The Battle of Amritsar (October 17, 1762) was fought in the grey light of a sun in total eclipse. It ended when the sunless day was blacked out by a moonless night with the adversaries retiring from the field: The Sikhs to the fastness of the jungles of the *Lakhi*(the forests of a hundred thousand trees located in Central Punjab) and Abdali behind the walled safety of Lahore.

The Formation of the Dal Khalsa and the Misls

Until now, the Sikh forces were divided into 65 *jathas* (bands). Baron Nawab Kapur Singh reorganised them into twelve bands, each of with its own name, flag and leader. These Armies or jathas, which came to known later on as Misls (literally "equal", also "an example") together were, however, given the name of the Dal Khalsa (or the Army of the Khalsa). Baron Jassa Singh Ahluwalia was nominated as the Supreme Commander of the Sikh Confederacy in addition to being Baron of the Ahluwalia Army (misl).

The Eighth Afghan Invasion, 1766

In November 1766 Abdali came to the Punjab for the eight time with the avowed object of "crushing the Sikhs". The Sikhs had recourse to their old game of *Dhai-phut* ('hit, run and turn back to hit again') tactics (later made famous at the Battle of

Chillianwala against the British). They vacated Lahore, but faced squarely the Afghan general Jahan Khan at Amritsar. The Sikhs inflicted a humiliating defeat, and forced him to retreat, with five thousand Afghan soldiers killed. Jassa Singh Ahluwalia with an army of about twenty thousand Sikhs roamed in the neighbourhood of the Afghan camp, plundering it.

Death

Jassa Singh continued with his campaigns. After Abdali's ninth and last invasion in 1769, Jassa Singh wrested Kapurthala in 1774 from Rao Ibrahim Bhatti and made it his headquarters. Jassa Singh died in Amritsar in 1783 AD. Being issueless, he was succeeded by Bhag Singh, whose son, Fateh Singh became a close collaborator of Ranjit Singh.

Ramgarhia

The Ramgarhia community is an ethnic tribe of the Punjab region in South Asia which started from the Ramgarhia Misl. The founder of the Ramgarhia Misl was Baron Nand Singh Sanghania and its members were Sikhs from different tribes (Khatris, Jatts, Rajputs, Tarkhan) Ramgarhia is mainly associated with the Tarkhan tribe because only of its later famous Baron Jassa Singh Ramgarhia Tarkhans commonly known as Ramgarhias

History of the Ramgarhia Misl

The founder of the Ramgarhia Misl was Jassa Singh Ramgarhia of Guga village near Amritsar. Jassa Singh Ramgarhia was succeeded by, Sardar Bhagwan Singh Bhambhra who belonged to village the grandfather of Jassa Singh, was the resident of Suringh which is situated about nineteen miles east of Khem Karan, in the present district of Amritsar. Jassa Singh Ramgarhia was initiated into the Khalsa faith by Guru Gobind Singh Ji himself from whose hands he took *Amrit/pahul* (the Sikh baptismal oath) and fought some battles at Guru Ji's side. After the death of the Guru, he joined the forces of Banda Bahadur and took part in almost every religious battle under his flag against the Mughal Empire. In 1716 AD, he died in a skirmish. After him his son, Sardar Bhagwan Singh became the head of the family, and with 200 followers entered the Imperial Mughal forces under the Governor of Lahore. Owing to his ability he rose to be a distinguished officer. He died fighting for his master in 1739 at Lahore, when Nadir Shah invaded

India and the Governor resisted him ineffectually. He had five sons. Baron Jassa Singh, the eldest, now became the head of the family. He was appointed a Risaldar by the Governor of Lahore, and the following villages were given to him : Jagir Valla, Verka, Sultanwind, Tung and Chabba (all of these are now in the Amritsar district). On the death of Khan Bahadur, the Governor of Lahore, in 1746, Baron Jassa Singh, together with his followers, joined his Sikh brethren at Amritsar.

Sardar Jassa Singh

At this time the celebrated Adina Beg Khan, the Imperial Governor of the Jullundur Doab, exercised great influence in the Punjab. As there was constant quarrelling between him and the Sikhs, Baron Jassa Singh was sent to him as their ambassador by the Sikhs, who considered the Sardar one of the ablest men among themselves. From all accounts Sardar Jassa Singh was a tall, handsome young man, possessing rare intellectual qualities. Khan was so pleased with him that he granted all the demands of the Sikhs, to plead for which Baron Jassa Singh had been sent. Moreover, Adina Beg took him and his brothers into his service and made him the Tahsildar over a large district. He remained for a long time in the service of the Governor.

Katra Ramgarhian

The Ramgarhian Katra (Bazar) was the natural adjunct of the Ramgarhia fort, which has been stated, was the chief seat of the family, and the head quarters of the Ramgarhia army, numbering thousands. The Bazaar arose on the space between the Ramgarh fort and the Bunga in the environs of the temple, and named Ramgarhian Katra. In the same way the Ahluwalia built a Bazaar between their fort and the temple and named it Katra Ahluwalian.

The Ramgarhian Katra is the greatest of all the Katras and covers over an area extending over 3 gates of the city. This is one more proof of the fact that the Ramgarhia forces appointed to guard the temple were more numerous than those of any other Misl. This Katra constitutes one fourth of the city. It is till known by that old name and the signboards with the inscription (Katra Ramgarhian) are put up by the Municipality on its boundaries. In this way the memory of this great house is kept to this day.

The Ghallughara

When Prince Timur, son of Ahmad Shah Abdali, marched against Adina Beg, the latter retreated towards the hills to the north and Baron Jassa Singh and his brothers left him and went to Amritsar, where they joined the forces of Nand Singh Sanghania. The younger brother of Sardar Jassa Singh was at this time killed in action with the Afghans near Majitha.

After the terrible blow dealt to the Sikhs by Abdali, in the Battle of Ghallughara ('Holocaust'), in which 17,000 Sikhs fell, the three brothers, Jassa Singh, Mali Singh and Tara Singh, with Jai Singh Kanhaiya (Leader of the Kanhaiya Misl), were reduced to the necessity of hiding in jungles and subsisting on whatever chance threw in their way.

They had, however, the temerity to visit Amritsar to bathe in the sacred tank, and pillaged the suburbs of the city. When attacked by the Shah's troops they fired off their matchlocks and fled to the jungles.

After the departure of Ahmad Shah, Jassa Singh with his brothers Mali Singh and Tara Singh, and Jai Singh Kanhaiya emerged from their jungle retreat, and collecting their followers ravaged the country far and wide, building forts and establishing military outposts. When Khawaja Obed, the Governor of Lahore, attacked the Sikh fort at Gujranwala, he was opposed by the united forces of the Ramgarhias and Kanhaiyas and the guns, ammunition and treasure left by the Governor were equally divided by the Barons of the two Misls.

Victory and Continued Occupation of Lahore

The Afghan prince and his guardian, seeing that all their attempts to disperse the Sikhs had failed, and that the number of the insurgents was daily increasing by thousands, and realising that the forces at their own disposal, however well armed and disciplined, were not strong enough to stand before them, considered it prudent to evacuate Lahore and retire towards the Chenab. They retreated in the night, unknown even to their own Hindustani troops, whom they distrusted, and in such haste that the royal family fell into the hands of the enemy, though they were subsequently released. This took place about the middle of 1758. The triumphant Sikhs occupied Lahore under their celebrated leader, Baron Jassa Singh Ramgarhia

Jassa Singh Ramgarhia

Jassa Singh Ramgarhia (1723-1803) was a prominent Sikh leader during the period of the Sikh Confederacy. He became the Commander of the Ramgarhia Sikh Cavalry misl (unit or group of Sikhs). This period was an interlude, lasting roughly from the time of the death of Banda Bahadur in 1716 to the founding of the Sikh Empire in 1801. The period is also sometimes described as the *Age of the Misls.*

Early Life

Jassa Singh Ramgarhia was born at Thoka *Ichogil* village in 1723, near the city of Amritsar into a Tarkhan family. His grandfather, Hardas was a resident of *Sur Singh,* a large village in the Lahore district. Hardas Singh took *Pahul* (the Sikh baptismal oath) from the hands of Guru Gobind Singh and leaving the plough, became one of the Guru's personal attendants. After the death of the Guru, he joined the forces of Banda Bahadur and took part in almost every battle under the Sikh Jathedar's (commander) flag against the Mughal Empire's forces. Jassa Singh Ramgarhia was five years old when Banda Bahadur was executed in Delhi.

In 1716 his grandfather, Hardas Singh died in a skirmish. His son, Bhagwan Singh then became the head of the family, and with two hundred followers entered the Imperial Mughal forces under the Governor of Lahore—Khan Bahadur. Where owing to his abilities he became a distinguished officer. During Nadir Shah's invasion of India in 1739 he died in a battle near Lahore. Khan Bahadur surrendered to the Persian invader's forces and was left in place as Governor.

Bhagwan Singh had five sons, Jai Singh, Jassa Singh, Khushal Singh, Mali Singh and Tara Singh. Jassa Singh, the eldest, now became the head of the family. He was appointed a Risaldar by Khan Bahadur. He and his brothers were given the following five villages (one village to each brother): Valla went to Jassa Singh, his four brothers were given Verka, Sultanwind, Tung and Chabba. All of these are now in the Amritsar district. On the death of Khan Bahadur in 1746, Jassa Singh, together with his followers, joined his Sikh brethren at Amritsar.

The Dal Khalsa: the Buddha Dal and the Taruna Dal

In 1733, the Mughal government decided, at the insistence of

Zakarya Khan, to stop the persecution of the Sikhs and made an offer of a grant to them. The title of Nawab was conferred upon their leader, with a jagir consisting of the three parganas of Dipalpur, Kanganval and Jhabal.

After some mutual discussion, the Panj Piare (five revered Sikhs)-Baba Deep Singh, Jassa Singh Ramgarhia, Hari Singh Dhillon, Bhai Karam Singh and Bhai Buddh Singh decided to make Kapur Singh the Supreme Leader of the Sikhs. Kapur Singh was thus chosen for the title and became *Nawab Kapur Singh.*

Word was sent round to Sikhs passing their days in distant jungles and deserts that peace had been made with the government and that they could return to their homes. Nawab Kapur Singh undertook the task of consolidating the disintegrated fabric of the Sikh *Jathas*. They were merged into a single central fighting force (The Dal) divided into two sections-The *Budha Dal,* the army of the veterans, and the *Taruna Dal,* the army of the young. Hari Singh Dhillon was elected leader of the Taruna Dal. The former was entrusted with the task of looking after the holy places, preaching the word of the Gurus and inducting converts into the Khalsa Panth by holding baptismal ceremonies. The Taruna Dal was the more active division and its function was to fight in times of emergencies and fighting Afghan armies of Ahmed Shah Abdali.

Jassa Singh Ramgarhia and Sultan ul Quam Baba Jassa Singh Ahluwalia were then youngsters who led regiments under Hari Singh Dhillon in the Taruna Dal, reporting to Nawab Kapur Singh at Diwali and Vaisakhi.

The Rise of the Misls

The Taruna Dal rapidly grew in strength and soon numbered more than 12,000. To ensure efficient control, Nawab Kapur Singh split it into five parts, each with a separate command. The first group was led by Baba Deep Singh, the second by Karam and Dharam Singh, the third by Kahan Singh and Binod Singh of Goindwal, the fourth by Dasaundha Singh of Kot Budha and the fifth by Vir Singh Ranghreta and Jivan Singh Ranghreta. Each group had its own banner and drum, and formed the nucleus of a separate political state. The territories conquered by these groups were entered in their respective papers at the Akal Takht by Sultan ul Quam Baba Jassa Singh Ahluwalia. From these documents or misls, the principalities carved out by them came to known as

Misls. Seven more groups were formed subsequently and, towards the close of century, there were altogether twelve Sikh Misls ruling the Punjab.

The Ramgarhia Misl

In 1716 Ahmed Shah Durrane left Lahore, Adina Beg the Afghan Governor of Punjab was hunting for the heads of the sikhs, they dispersed and scattered in all directions. Jassa Singh and others in the band took refuge in the mud fort of Ram Rauni near Amritsar where they were surrounded and attacked during the ensuing period. In 1758 Adina Beg died and there was a power vacuum in Punjab and those who escaped from fort of Ram Rauni assumed the name of Ramgarhias and Jassa Singh became its head. The Misal (Confederacy) was called Ramgarhia.

The main concentration of the Misl was in and around the Riarki area of Amritsar, Gurdaspur and Batala (in Majha). Ramgarhia constructed and fortified the mud fortress of *Ram Rauni* just outside Amritsar.

It was named in honour of the founder of the city, the fourth Sikh Guru, Guru Ram Das. His Misl contained more than 10000 cavalry who were always on the move, helping the Dal Khalsa whenever the Mughals or Afghans attacked. Whilst the Mughal administration controlled the cities, it were the Sikhs who were in control of the villages. Twenty years earlier, Banda Bahadur had wreaked havoc on the Mughal administration by abolishing all taxes and the *Zamindari* system. Now only a "dasvand" (10% of income) was levied on the Sikhs-as protection tax to pay for the armies. Maharaja Sr. Jassa Singh Ramgarhia was 1st Sikh maharaja and Hargobindpur was his capital.

Mir Mannu becomes the New Subedar of the Punjab

Mir Mannu became the new governor of the Punjab on April 9, 1748. He appointed Kaura Mal as his new Diwan (minister). After taking control of the administration of the provinces, he employed his army to fight the Sikh misls or *fighting orders. The Sikhs left the territory and moved to other states. The Sikh Chiefs asked Jassa Singh Ramgarhia to liaise with the* subedar*(governor) of the Jullundur Doab, Adina Beg Khan. While drawing his salary from Mughals, Adina Beg Khan joined forces with the Jassa Singh Ramgarhia against the Mughals.*

The Siege of Ram Rauni

The Sikhs gathered in Amritsar on Diwali, 1748. Adina Beg proceeded towards Amritsar and besieged Ram Rauni. Mir Mannu came down from Lahore with an army to assist Beg in the siege.

Jassa Singh used the good offices of Diwan Kaura Mal and had the siege lifted. The fort was strengthened and re-named *Ramgarh*. Jassa Singh, having been designated the *Jathedar* of the fort, became popular as *Ramgarhia*.

Fighting Tyranny

Mannu intensified his violence and oppression against the Sikhs. There were only 900 Sikhs when he surrounded the Ramgarh fort again. The Sikhs fought their way out bravely. The army demolished the fort. The hunt for and torture of the Sikhs continued until Mannu died in 1753.

Manu's death left Punjab without any effective Governor. It was again an opportune period for the Sikhs to organize themselves and gain strength. Jassa Singh rebuilt the fort and took possession of some areas around Amritsar. The Sikhs took upon themselves the task of protecting the people in the villages from the invaders. The money they obtained from the people was called *Rakhi* (protection charges).

The new Governor, Prince Timur, the son of Ahmed Shah Abdali, despised the Sikhs. In 1757, he again forced the Sikhs to vacate the fort and move to their hiding places. The fort was demolished, the Harimandir was blown up, and the sacred pool was filled with debris.

The Governor decided to replace Adina Beg. Beg asked the Sikhs for help and they both got a chance to weaken their common enemy. Adina Beg won the battle. The Sikhs rebuilt Ramgarh and repaired the Harimandir. Beg was well acquainted with the strength of the Sikhs and he feared they would oust him if he allowed them to grow stronger, so he lead a strong army to demolish the fort. After fighting valiantly, the Sikhs decided to leave the fort. Beg died in 1758.

The Ramgarhia Misl Estate

Jassa Singh Ramgarhia occupied the area to the north of Amritsar between the Ravi and the Beas rivers. He also added the Jalandhar region and Kangra hill areas to his estate. He had his capital in Sri Hargobindpur. The large size of Jassa Singh's territory aroused the jealousy of the other Sikh Misls.

Intra Misl Wars

Although Jai Singh Kanhaiya and Jassa Singh Ramgarhia were once close friends, their rivalries led to a pitched battle between them and their allies. The chiefs of the Bhangi Misls joined the Ramgarhias and their associates. Jai Singh Kanhaiya was joined by Charhat Singh Sukerchakia and Sultan ul Quam Baba Jassa Singh Ahluwalia. The Ramgarhia side lost the battle.

Later, Ahluwalia while hunting one day, happened to enter Ramgarhia territory where Jassa Singh's brother arrested him. Jassa Singh apologized for the misbehavior of his brother, and honorably returned Ahluwalia with gifts. However, their old differences increased further. The other chiefs also took a grim view of this act.

Due to mutual jealousies, fights continued among the Sikh Sardars. In 1776, the Bhangis changed sides and joined Jai Singh to defeat Jassa Singh. His capital at Sri Hargobindpur was taken over and he and his forces were pursued from village to village. Finally he lost all his territory. He choose to cross the river Satluj, going over to Amar Singh, the ruler of Patiala.

Amar Singh welcomed the Ramgarhia sardar in order to make use of his bravery, fighting skill, and ruling experience. He gave him the areas of Hansi and Hissar which Jassa Singh handed over to his son. He himself joined Amar Singh to take control of the villages on the west and north of Delhi, now forming parts of Haryana and western Uttar Pradesh. Jassa Singh Ramgarhia entered Delhi in 1783. Shah Alam II, the Mughal emperor, extended him a warm welcome. Ramgarhia left Delhi after receiving gifts from him.

Meanwhile to the north, differences over how to divide the Jammu state revenues, resulted in long time friends and neighbours Maha Singh, Jathedar of the Sukerchakia Misl and Jai Singh, Jathedar of the Kanahya Misl, becoming enemies. This rancor resulted in a war which would change the course of Sikh history.

Maha Singh requested Jassa Singh Ramgarhia's aid. In the ensuing battle, Jai Singh Kanahya lost his son, Gurbaksh Singh in the fighting with the Sukerchakias and the Ramgarhias.

The Unification of the Misls

Sada Kaur, the newly widowed wife of Gurbaksh Singh, proved to be a great statesperson. Seeing the end of Khalsa power if such internescine battles continued, she now worked to unite the waring misls in order to form a united, *formidable* force. She was able to convince Maha Singh to adopt the path of friendship by offering the hand of her daughter, then only a child, to his son, himself just a young boy, Ranjit Singh the future Maharaja of the Punjab. The balance of power now shifted in favour of this united Misl as other sardars also joined the union. Ranjit Singh was now the leader of the most powerful Sikh Misl ever.

Establishment of the Sikh Kingdom of the Punjab

When the Afghan invader, Shah Zaman, came in 1788, the Sikhs, however, were still divided. The Ramgarhia and Bhangi Misls were not willing to help Ranjit Singh to fight the invader, so the Afghans took over Lahore and looted it. As soon as the Afghans went back, Ranjit Singh occupied Lahore in 1799 but the Ramgarhias and Bhangis did not accept him as the leader of all the Sikhs. They got the support of their friends and marched to Lahore to challenge Ranjit Singh. The forces, who were 12 miles outside the city, were finalizing their plans to attack, when the Bhangi leader died. This discouraged Jassa Singh and he returned to his territory.he was a best Sikh ever

Death

Maharaja Jassa Singh Ramgarhia was eighty years old when he died in 1803. His son, Sr. Jodh Singh Ramgarhia, developed good relations with Ranjit Singh and they never fought again.

Trivia

Because of Jassa Singh Ramgarhia's Tarkhan roots, Tarkhans who became Sikhs, came to be known as Ramgarhias.

Baba Deep Singh

Babe Deep Singh is revered among Sikhs as one of the most hallowed martyrs in Sikhism and as a highly religious person. He is remembered for his sacrifice and devotion to the teachings of the Sikh Gurus. He was the first jathedar(Head) of Damdami Taksal a 300 years old religious school of the Sikhs which was allegedly founded by last Sikh Guru, Guru Gobind Singh (although no research or historical document supports this was founded by Guru Gobind Singh).

His name is also found as *Deep Singh* (without the "*Baba*" honorific) and *Baba Deep Singh Ji.*

Early Life

Baba Deep Singh was born in 1682 to a Sikh couple, *Bhagata* (father) and *Jioni* (mother). He lived in the village of Pohuwind in the district of Amritsar.

He went to Anandpur on the day of Vaisakhi in 1699, where he was baptized as Khalsa by Guru Gobind Singh. Deep Singh took *Khande di Pahul* or Amrit Sanchar (ceremonial initiation into Khalsa). As a youth, he spent considerable time in close companionship of Guru Gobind Singh. He started learning weaponry, riding and other martial skills. From Bhai Mani Singh, he began learning, reading and writing Gurmukhi and the interpretation of the Gurus' words. After spending two years at Anandpur, he returned to his village in 1702 and married and settled down. He was summoned by Guru Gobind Singh at Talwandi Sabo in 1705, where he helped Bhai Mani Singh in making copies of the Guru Granth Sahib. Before departing for Deccan, Guru Gobind Singh installed him as the caretaker of Gurdwara Damdama Sahib.

Warrior

Misldar: In 1709, Baba Deep Singh joined Banda Bahadur during the assaults on the towns of Sadhaura and Sirhind. In 1733, Nawab Kapur Singh appointed him a leader of an armed squad(*jatha*). On the Vaisakhi of 1748, at the meeting of the *Sarbat Khalsa* in Amritsar, the 65 *jathas* of the Dal Khalsa were reorganized into twelve Misls. Baba Deep Singh was entrusted with the Leadership of the *Shaheedan* Misl.

The Demolition of the Harimandir Sahib

In April 1757, Ahmad Shah Durrani raided Northern India for the fourth time. While he was on his way back to Kabul from Delhi with precious booty and young men and women as captives, the Sikhs made a plan to relieve him of the valuables and free the captives. The squad of *baba* Deep Singh was deployed near Kurukshetra. His squad freed a large number of prisoners and raided Durrani's considerable treasury. On his arrival in Lahore, Durrani, embittered by his loss, ordered the demolition of the Harimandir Sahib. The shrine was blown up and the sacred pool filled with the entrails of slaughtered cows. Durrani assigned the Punjab region to his son, Prince Timur Shah, and left him a force of ten thousand men under General Jahan Khan.

Baba Deep Singh, aged 75-years old, felt that it was up to him to atone for the sin of having let the Afghans desecrate the shrine. He emerged from scholastic retirement (he had been making copies of the *Guru Granth Sahib*), and declared to a congregation at Damdama Sahib that he intended to rebuild the temple. Five hundred men came forward to go with him. Deep Singh offered prayers before starting for Amritsar: "May my head fall at the Darbar Sahib." As he went from hamlet to hamlet, many villagers joined him. By the time *baba* Deep Singh reached Tarn Taran Sahib, ten miles from Amritsar, over five thousand peasants armed with hatchets, swords, and spears accompanied him.

Martyrdom-Two Versions

According to the Sikh legend, Baba Deep Singh had vowed to avenge the desecration of the Golden Temple by the Afghan army. In 1757, he led an army to defend the Golden Temple. The Sikhs and the Afghans clashed, in the battle of Amritsar, at the village of Gohalwar on November 11, 1757, and in the ensuing conflict Baba Deep Singh was decapitated.

Version One

The first version has it that Deep Singh continued to fight after having been decapitated, slaying his enemies with his head in one hand and his sword in the other. In this version, only upon reaching the sacred city of Amritsar did he stop and finally die. This tale recalls the words of the first Guru, Guru Nanak:

Shouldst thou wish to play the game of love, come unto my Path with thy head on thy palm. And, once you step unto this path, You may well give up thy head, rather than the cause.

Version Two

In the other version it is said:

> *"Fighting bravely Singhs pushed the army back and reached village Chabba where General Attal Khan came forward and*

inflicted a blow on Baba Deep Singh ji which made his neck lean to one side. A Sikh reminded him, "You had resolved to reach the periphery of the pool." On hearing the talk of the Sikh, he supported his head with his left hand and removing the enemies from his way with the strokes of his double-edged sword with his right hand, reached the periphery of Harmindar Sahib where he breathed his last. The Singhs celebrated the Diwali of 1757 A.D. in Harminder Sahib".

The Sikhs recovered their prestige by defeating the Afghan army and the latter were forced to flee.

The spot where the legend Baba Deep Singh's head fell is marked in the Golden Temple complex, and Sikhs from around the world pay their respects there. Baba Deep Singh's 30 kg Khanda (double-edged sword), which he used in his final battle, is still preserved at Takht Sri Hazur Sahib, one of the five centres of temporal Sikh authority.

Nawab Kapur Singh

Nawab Kapur Singh (1697–1753) is considered one of the pivotal figures in Sikh history, under whose courageous leadership the Sikh community traversed one of the darkest periods of its history. He was the organizer of the Sikh Confederacy and the Dal Khalsa.

Nawab Kapur Singh is regarded by Sikhs as a leader and general par excellence. The period, starting from the massacre in Delhi of Banda Singh and seven hundred other Sikhs, was followed by severe action against the Sikhs, including massacres of young men, women and children. However, every fresh adversity only stimulated their will to survive.

Early Life

Nawab Kapur Singh was born into a Virk family of Jats in 1697. His native village was *Kaloke*, now in Sheikhupura district, in Punjab (Pakistan). Kapur Singh was eleven years old at the time of Guru Gobind Singh's death and nineteen at the time of the massacre of Banda Bahadur and his followers in Delhi. Later, when he seized the village of *Faizullapur*, near Amritsar, he renamed it *Singhpura* and made it his headquarters. He is thus, also known as Kapur Singh Faizullapuria, and the small principality he founded, as Faizullapuria or Singhpuria.

Initiation into the Khalsa Fold

Kapur Singh underwent amrit-initiation at a large gathering held at Amritsar on Baisakhi Day, 1721 from Panj Piarey led by Bhai Mani Singh. His father, Dalip Singh, and brother, Dan Singh, were also among those who were initiated into the Khalsa fold on that day.

Campaign against Zakarya Khan

Kapur Singh soon gained a position of eminence among the Sikhs, who were then engaged in a desperate struggle against the Imperial Mughal government. Zakarya Khan, who had become the Mughal governor of Lahore in 1726, launched a policy of persecution against the Sikhs.

In those days, pursued by the bounty-hunters, as the governor of Lahore had put a price on a Sikh's head, the Sikhs roamed the jungles of Central Punjab in small groups. Kapur Singh headed one such band. To assert their high spirits despite being hounded by government forces and bounty-hunters, and with a view to paralysing the administration and obtaining food for their companions these groups would launch attacks on government treasuries and caravans moving from one place to another. Such was their success in this endeavour that the governor was soon obliged to make terms with them.

The Title of Nawab

In 1733, the Mughal government decided, at the instance of Zakarya Khan, to revoke all repressive measures issued against the Sikhs and made an offer of a grant to them. The title of Nawab was conferred upon their leader, with a jagir consisting of the three parganas of Dipalpur, Kanganval and Jhabal.

After some mutual discussion, the Sikhs accepted the offer. Kapur Singh was unanimously elected as the leader and chosen for the title. He was reluctant, but could not deny the unanimous will of the community. As a mark of respect, he placed the robe of honour('Siropa') sent by the Mughals at the feet of five revered Sikhs-amongst whom were Baba Deep Singh, Bhai Karam Singh and Bhai Buddh Singh (great-great-grandfather of Maharaja Ranjit Singh-before putting it on. The dress included a shawl, a turban, a jewelled plume, a pair of gold bangles, a necklace, a row of pearls, a brocade garment and a sword.

The Formation of the Dal Khalsa

Word was sent round to Sikhs passing their days in distant jungles and deserts that peace had been made with the government and that they could return to their homes. Nawab Kapur Singh undertook the task of consolidating the disintegrated fabric of the Sikh *Jathas*. They were merged into a single central fighting force (The Dal) divided into two sections-The *Budha Dal*, the army of the veterans, and the *Taruna Dal*, the army of the young, Sardar Hari Singh Dhillon was elected its leader. The former was entrusted with the task of looking after the holy places, preaching the word of the Gurus and inducting converts into the Khalsa Panth by holding baptismal ceremonies. The Taruna Dal was the more active division and its function was to fight in times of emergencies.

Nawab Kapur Singh's personality was the common link between these two wings. He was universally respected for his high character. His word was obeyed willingly and to receive baptism at his hands was counted an act of rare merit.

The Rise of the Misls

Under its leader, Hari Singh, the Taruna Dal rapidly grew in strength and soon numbered more than 12,000. To ensure efficient control, Nawab Kapur Singh split it into five parts, each with a separate centre. The first batch was led by Baba Deep Singh Shaheed, the second by Karam Singh and Dharam Singh, the third by Kahan Singh and Binod Singh of Goindwal, the fourth by Dasaundha Singh of Kot Budha and the fifth by Vir Singh Ranghreta and Jivan Singh Ranghreta. Each batch had its own banner and drum, and formed the nucleus of a separate political state. The territories conquered by these groups were entered in their respective papers at the Akal Takht by Sultan ul Quam Baba Jassa Singh Ahluwalia. From these documents or misls, the principalities carved out by them came to known as Misls. Seven more groups were formed subsequently and, towards the close of century, there were altogether twelve Sikh Misls ruling the Punjab.

The Singhpuria Misl

The founder of the rule-by-Misl system was Nawab Kapur Singh. Nawab Kapur Singh was a great warrior. He fought many battles. The last battle that he fought was the battle of Sirhind. After the fall of Sirhind in 1763, a considerable portion of present-day Rupnagar District came under the Singhpuria Misl. These areas included *Manauli, Ghanuli, Bharatgarh, Kandhola, Chooni, Machli, Bhareli, Bunga* and *Bela.*

By 1769, the Singpuria Misl had the following territories in its possession:-Some parts of the districts of Jalandhar and Hoshiarpur in Doaba, Kharparkheri and Singhpura in Bari-Doab and Abhar, Adampur, Chhat, Banoor, Manauli Ghanauli, Bharatgarh, Kandhola, Chooni, Machhli Bhareli, Banga, Bela, Attal Garh and some other places in the province of Sirhind.

Lakhpat Rai

The entente with the Mughals did not last long and, before the harvest of 1735, Zakarya Khan, sent a strong force and occupied the Jagir. The Sikhs were driven out of Amritsar into the Bari Doab and then across the Satluj into Malwa by Diwan Lakhpat Rai, Zakarya Khan's minister. They were welcomed by Sardar Ala Singh of the Phulkian Misl of Malwa. During his sojourn in Malwa, Nawab Kapur Singh conquered the territory of Sunam and made it over to Ala Singh. He also attacked Sirhind and defeated the Mughal governor. Nawab Kapur Singh led the Sikhs back to Majha to celebrate Diwali at Amritsar. He was pursued by Lakhpat Rai's army near Amritsar and forced to turn away. The Taruna Dal promptly came to his help. The combined force fell upon Lakhpat Rai before he could reach Lahore and inflicted a severe defeat. His nephew, Duni Chand, and two important Faujdars, Jamal Khan and Tatar Khan, were killed in the battle.

Nadir Shah

In the summer of 1739, Nadir Shah, the Persian invader, was returning home after plundering Delhi and Punjab. The Dal lay in wait, not far from the route he had taken. When he reached Akhnur, on the Chenab (in the present-day Jammu region), they swooped down upon the rear guard, relieving the invaders of much of their booty. On the third night they made an even fiercer attack and rescued from their hands, thousands of girls who were escorted back to their families. For a long part of his return journey, the Sikhs pursued Nadir Shah in this manner.

Zakarya Khan's Campaign Continues

Zakarya Khan continued to carry out his policy of repression with redoubled zeal. A pitiless campaign for a manhunt was started.

Sikhs heads sold for money and the Mughals offered a prize for each head brought to them. According to the historian, Ratan Singh Bhangu, "He who informed where a Sikh was received ten rupees, he who killed one received fifty."

To cut off the Sikhs from the main source of their inspiration, the Harimandir at Amritsar was taken possession of and guarded by Mughal troops to prevent them visiting it. Sikhs were then living in exile in the Shiwalik hills, the Lakhi Jungle and in the sandy desert of Rajputana. To assert their right to ablution in the holy tank in Amritsar, they would occasionally send riders, who, in disguise or openly cutting their way through armed guards, would reach the temple, take a dip in the tank and ride back with lightning speed. Zakarya Khan, sent a strong force under Samad Khab to seek out the Sikhs. The force was defeated and their leader, Samad Khan who had been the target of the Sikhs' wrath since he had on June 24, 1734 executed Bhai Mani Singh was killed.

Nawab Kapur Singh now made a plan to capture Zakarya Khan. With a force of 2000 men all of whom were in disguise, he entered Lahore and went on to the Shahi Mosque where, according to intelligence received, the Mughal governor was expected to attend the afternoon prayer. But Zakarya Khan did not visit the mosque. Kapur Singh was disappointed at the failure of the mission. Throwing off the disguise and shouting their war cry of Sat Sri Akal, the Sikhs marched out of Lahore and vanished into thejungle.

The Chota Ghalughara

Meanwhile, Khan and his minister, Lakhpat Rai, again launched an all-out campaign and set forth with a large army. The Sikhs were brought to bay in a dense bush near Kahnuwan, in theGurdaspur District. They put up determined fight, but were overwhelmed by the superior numbers of the enemy and scattered with heavy losses. They were chased into hills. More than 7000 died. "To complete revenge" says Syed Mohammad Latif, another historian of the Punjab, "Lakhpat Rai brought 1000 Sikhs in irons to Lahore, having compelled them to ride on donkeys, bare-backed, paraded them in the bazars. They were, then taken to the horse-market outside Delhi Gate, and there beheaded one after another without mercy." So indiscriminate and extensive was the killing that the campaign is known in Sikh history is known as the *Chhota*

Ghalughara or the lesser holocaust. The *Wadda Ghalughara* or the greater holocaust was to come later.

Ahmed Shah Abdali

In 1748, a section of the Dal Khalsa under Charhat Singh Sukerchakia, grandfather of Ranjit Singh gave chase to the fleeing troops of Ahmad Shah Abdali.

Death

Nawab Kapur Singh requested the community to relieve him of his office, due to his old age, and at his suggestion, Jassa Singh Ahluwalia was chosen as the supreme commander of the Dal Khalsa. Kapur Singh died in 1753 at Amritsar and was succeeded by his nephew (Dhan Singh's son), Khushal Singh.

Khushal Singh who succeeded him as the leader of the misl. Sardar Khushal Singh played a significant role in expanding the territories of the Singhpuria Misl on both the banks of the Satluj river. The most important of the possessions of Khushal Singh were Patti, Bhartgarh, Nurpur, Bahrampur and Jalandhar. Khushal Singh also occupied Ludhiana. He had to divide the district of Banur with Patiala. He died in 1795 leaving his misl stronger than ever it was and with territorial possessions far larger than those he had inherited.

Khushal Singh was succeeded by his son Budh Singh. When Abdali returned home after his ninth invasion of India, the Sikhs had occupied more territories in the Punjab. Sheikh Nizam-ud-din was the ruler of Jalandhar at that time. Sardar Budh Singh defeated Nizam-id-din on the battle-field and occupied Jalandhar. He also took possooession of Bulandgarh, Behrampur, Nurpur and Haibatpur-Patti. This victory brought him yearly revenue of three lakhs of rupees.

However, Budh Singh could not equal Khushal Singh's talents. The Singhpuria Misl began to decline and ultimately all its possessions on the west of Satluj were annexed by Maharaja Ranjit Singh. On his possessions on the east of the Satluj, however, the British extended their protection to him.

Budh Singh died in 1816, leaving seven sons behind him. His eldest son, Amar Singh, retained possession of Bhartgarh and divided the rest of the territories among his six brother as under:-

- Bhopal Singh was given the estate of Ghanauli.

- Gopal Singh: Manauli.
- Lal Singh: Bunga.
- Gurdyal Singh: Attalgarh.
- Hardyal Singh: Bela
- Dyal Singh: Kandhola.

The descendants of these Sardars still live on their respective estates.

Trivia

The village of Kapurgarh in Nabha is named after Nawab Kapur Singh.

Phulkian Sardars

The Phoolka family had descended from the celebrated Phool, their eponym, from whom descended the rulers of Patiala, Jind, Nabha as well as the Chiefs of Bhadaur, Malaudh and Badrukhan and the Sardars of Juindan, Laudhgarh, Dyalpura, Rampura and Kot Duna. The early progenitors of the Phoolka House were scions of the Princely Rajput family of Jaisulmer who left their desert homes around the time of Rai Pithora and established themselves around the country of Hisar, Sirsa and Bhatner. Maharaja Ala Singh of Patiala descended from Phool and to his genius must be ascribed the remarkable and rapid rise of the family in the first stages of its history. The Phoolka Sardars trace their genealogy from the Raja of Jaisalmer Rawal Jaisal, Yadu Bhatti Rajput of Chandra Vanshi clan and descendants of Lord Krishna, *Avatar* of Lord Vishnu.

Common Founder

Phool, a Sidhu Brar was the founder of this family. Phool's eldest son Tiloka was the ancestor of the Nabha, Jind and Badrukhan royal families and his second son Rama sired six sons and out of Dunna, Ala Singh and Bakhta sprang the princely states of Bhadaur, Patiala and Malaudh which were the most important of the Cis-Satluj States belonging to Phoolkian Misl. Collaterally, the descendants of Phool were connected with the rulers of Faridkot, the extinct Kaithal family, and the feudatories of Arnauli, Jhumba, Saddhuwal, and, north of the Sutlej, Attari. These numerous branches of a vigorous stock belonged to the great Sidhu-Brar tribe, the most powerful Jat clan south of the Sutlej.

Maharawal Jaisal to Phool

Maharawal Jaisal, having founded the State of Jaisalmer in 1156 A.D. was driven from his kingdom by a rebellion and took refuge with Prithvi Raj Chauhan, the last Hindu King of Delhi and later settled near Hissar. Hemhel, his son, sacked that town and overran the country up to Delhi but was repulsed by Shams-ud-din Altamash. Subsequently, in 1212, that ruler made him governor of the Sirsa and Bhatinda country. But his great-grandson Mangal Rao, having rebelled against the Muhammadan sovereign of Delhi, was beheaded at Jaisalmer. His grandson, Khiwa, sank to the status of a Jat by contracting a marriage with a woman of that class; and though the great Siddhu-Barar tribe in the following centuries spread itself far and wide over the Malwa country up to and even beyond the Sutlej, the descendants of Khiwa fell into poverty and obscurity, until one of them, Sanghar, entered the service of the emperor Babur with a few followers. Sanghar himself fell at First Battle of Panipat in 1526 A.D. when Babur defeated Ibrahim Lodhi ; but the Mughal emperor rewarded his devotion by granting his son Baryam the chaudhriyat or intendancy of the waste country southwest of Delhi and thus restored the fortunes of the family. The grant was confirmed by Humayun ; but in 1560 Baryam fell fighting against the Muhammadan Bhattis, at once the kinsmen and hereditary foes of the Siddhu tribe. Baryam was succeeded as Chaudhry by his son Mahraj and his grandson Mohan who were both engaged in constant warfare with the Bhattis, until Mohan was compelled to flee to Hansi and Hissar, whence he returned with a considerable force of his tribesmen, defeated the Bhattis at Bhedowal, and on the advice of the Sikh Guru Har Gobind founded Mahraj in Ferozepore District. But the contest with the Bhattis was soon renewed, and Mohan and his son Rup Chand were killed by them in a skirmish about 1618. His second son Kala succeeded to the Chaudhriyat and became the guardian of Phool and Sandali, the sons of Rup Chand.

Blessed by the Gurus

Phool along with his brother Sandali became orphans in 1618 A.D. and both were taken under the wings of their Uncle Chaudhary Kala who founded Mehraj on the advice of the sixth Guru Hargobind. They both visited Guru Hargobind as youngsters, it is said that their uncle told them to rap their bellies to indicate to the Guru the poverty and hunger they were enduring. On being told his name was Phool which means flower, the Guru Hargobind said, " *The name shall be a True Omen, and he shall bear many blossoms.*" The Guru blessed Phool and is said to have told him that he would make a King. When Shah Jehan's army attacked the Guru in 1635 at Lehra near Mehraj, Kala along with his clan sided firmly with him. The Guru ended victorious. A happy Guru Har Gobind asked Kala to fence as much land he wanted to. By evening, Kala had marked twenty-two villages and put his fence (Morhi) into the ground. The Bhullar Jats, who considered themselves to be the original dwellers and owners of this area removed his fence and threw it into a well. When Kala complained against this to the Guru, he remarked: *"Bhai Kala, your roots have reached to the other world."* Hence, Kala founded a village and named it as Mehraj.

The Guru Har Rai had blessed him thus: *You feel'eth hunger now, worry no more...your house shall be a very big Charity House....donating and feeding many.......the horses of you Armies shall graze in grasslands spanning the area between the Yamuna and Sutlej* and the prophecy of the Guru was fulfilled.

The sons of Phool, Tilok Singh and Ram Singh were blessed with *Khande da Pahul* by Guru Gobind Singh himself at Damdama Sahib. Guru Gobind Singh in a Hukamnama (royal edict) addressed to the two sons of Phool, Rama & Tiloka on 2 August, 1696, called upon them for aid in his fight with the Hill Rajas proclaiming " *tera ghar mera asey* " meaning Your House is My Own bestowing special status on the HOUSE of PHOOL. It is said that it is because of this blessing from Guru Sahib that the other 11 Misls never attacked the Phulkian States despite some provocations. They were blessed with the *Apaar kirpa* of Guru Gobind Singh evidence of which can be seen in the Patiala Hukumnama sent by Guru Sahib in 1696 A.D. Its translation into English reads:

There is one God. The Guru is great. It is the order of the Guru. Bhai Rama and Bhai Tiloka, the Guru will protect all. You are required to come with your contingent. I am much pleased with you. Your house is my own. On seeing this letter you should come in my presence. Your house is my refuge. You should come to me immediately. On seeing this letter you should arrive with horsemen. You must come. A Sirpau (robe of honour or Jorra) for you is being sent. This was the initiation of the prestigious Sikh Sirpau or Siropa, as it is popularly known. Bhai Tiloka and Bhai Rama had been the most ardent devotees of Guru Gobind Singh and had won Guruji's favour by showing extraordinary valour in battles and were baptised by Guruji himself at Damdama Sahib.

Phoolkian Dynasty Genealogy

- I. Buddha. Patriarch of the Yadu Race of Chandra Vanshi Clan. Espoused Ella, a princess of Surya race.
- II. Prururwa. Rajput King of the Yadu race and founder of Mathura which remained their seat of power. Had issue:
- III. Ayu. Had issue.... and several generations later....
- IV. Hari Krishna. Founded Dwarka (computed by Historians to be about 1100 years before Christ). Yadu's Exterminated in the conflict of Dwarka. Had eight wives.
- V. Pridema. Son of Hari & Rookhmani (his first wife). Married a princess of Vidarbha who bore him two sons:

  (i) Anurad

  (ii) Bujra.

  Had issue two sons:

  (i) Naba

  (ii) Khira.

  Yadu Rajput King of Mathura & Dwarka. Son of Burja Chandra Vanshi (Lunar Clan). Compelled to flee to Marusthali (conjectured to be Merv, now a part of Iran) from Dwarka by other Rajput tribes long subjugated by the Yadus. Had issue:
- VIII. Prithibaho.

Had issue:

- IX. Bahubal. Espoused Kamlavati, his chief queen daughter of Vijaya Sinh, Prince of Malwa who bore him one son Bahu (meaning strong).
- X. Bahu. Died by a fall from his horse. Had issue:
- XI. Subahu. Married daughter of Raja Mund Chauhan of Ajmer who bore him a son Rijh but poisoned and killed her husband.
- XII. Raja Rijh. Ruled Marusthali (Land of The Dead in Sanskrit) for twelve years. Married Soobhag Sundri, daughter of Ber Sinh Prince of Malwa. Invaded &

vanquished Farid Shah of Khorasan (Persia, Iran) who lost 30,000 men and Raja Rijh lost 4,000 in two battles. Had issue:

- XIII. Raja Guj (Gaja). Occupied Ghazni, Afghanistan making it his stronghold. Married Hansavati, daughter of Judbhan. Erected a huge fortress amidst the mountains and called it Gujni after himself as foretold by the Guardian Goddess of the Yadu race. Lost Ghazni to Khorasan who held it for sometime. Fought a fierce battle with Shah of Khorasan Shah Mamraiz & Sekander Roomi resulting in the destruction of thirty two thousand men.Conquered all the countries to the west. Invaded Kandrupkel in Kashmir and later married the daughter of its Prince by whom he had a son, Salbahan
- XIV. Salivaahan. Driven out from Ghazni by Mamnenez, King of Khorasan. Married daughter of Jaipal Tuar of Delhi. Had fifteen sons; all went on to be Rajas & set up their own Kingdoms. Conquered Punjab & established his capital at Sialkot. Expelled from Kabul but returned to defeat the Indo-Scythians in a decisive battle at Kohror near Multan and regained Ghazni. Established the Saka era from the date of battle & assumed title of Sakari (foe-of-the-Sakas) Founded city of Salabhana near Lahore in S.V.72. His eldest son was Baland.
- XV. Bal Band (Baland). Left Ghazni to the charge of his grandson, Chakito who later became King of Baloch Bukhara from whom descended the Chakito Mughals. Shifted his capital to Salbahanpur and had issue seven sons. Invaded by the Kings of Syria & Khorasan but repulsed their attacks. Kullar, his third son had eight sons most of whom embraced Islam. Jinj, his fourth son had seven sons.
- XVI. Bhatti Rao. Succeeded his father Baland. Changed the patronymic of Yadu to Bhatti and thenceforth known as Bhatti or Bhati Rajputs. Conquered fourteen Princes around his Kingdom and added to his fortunes. Held court at Lahore. Had issue two sons:

  (i) Mangal Rao

  (ii) Musur Rao.

- XVII. Mangal Rao. Pushed back by King of Ghazni, Dhundi. Moved to Mer with his tribe (in the Great Indian Thar Desert). Had issue six sons: (i) Majam Rao (ii) Kulursi (iii) Moolraj (iv) Seoraj (v) Bhul (vi) Kewala
- XVIII. Majam Rao. Solemnized marriage with daughter of Soda prince of Amerkote. Laid the foundation of a castle across the Sutlej and named it Tannote after Tunna Mata but died before its completion. Had issue three sons: (i) Kehar (ii) Moolraj (iii) Gogli
- XIX. Kehar Rao. Married daughter of Allansi Deora of Jhallore. Renowned for his exploits. Invaded the Barahas in 730 A.D. In 731 A.D.,completed the construction of fort at Tanote making it his capital. Had issue five sons: (i) Tunno (ii) Otirao (iii) Chunnur (iv) Kafrio (v) Thaem
- XX. Tunno Rao. Found hidden treasure & erected a fortress naming it Bijnot in A.D.757 in Cholistan Desert S.787 Died after a reign of eighty years.
- XXI. Rao Biji Bhati. Succeeded Tunno in 814 A.D. Engaged in continual feud with the Langahas & Barahas whom he plundered. Later, Bijirao & eight hundred of his kin and Clan treacherously massacred by his enemies. 336 vikram samvat (~ AD 392)
- XXII. Rawal Deoraj. Escaped to Boota, his maternal abode after the carnage. Founded Hanumangarh (then Bhatner in Rajasthan) Ruled 853-908 A.D.. Was the first to take the title of Rawal (King) Founded the city of Dera Rawal and Derawar Fort in 853 A.D. Conquered Lodorva from Lodra Rajputs in 9th century (Rajasthan). Excavated several lakes in Khadal including Tunnosirr and Deosirr. Slain by Choona Rajputs while on a hunt having reigned for fifty five years. Had two sons:

  (i) Mundh

  (ii) Chedu.
- XXIII. Rawal Mundh (Munda). Ruled 908-979 A.D. Had issue:
- XXIV. Rawal Bacheraj (Bachera). Married daughter of Raja Vallabh Sen Solanki of Patan in 1011 A.D. Ruled 979-1044. Founded Bhatinda in 965 A.D. (then known as Tabarhindh).

In 1008 A.D., tributary of King Anandapal of Delhi. Invaded by Mahmud. Had issue five sons:

(i) Doosaj
(ii) Singh
(iii) Bapirao
(iv) Ankho
(v) Malpasao.

- XXV. Rawal Doosaji. King of Laudorva (Rajasthan) Ruled 1044-1123 A.D. Had issue:
- XXVI. Rawal Bijairaj Ii.Ruled 1123-1148 A.D. Had issue two sons:

(i) Jaisal
(ii) Vijayraj (Lanjha).

- XXVII. Maharawal Jaisal Ji. Ruled 1153-1168 A.D. Founded the Golden City of Jaisalmer in 1156 A.D., fulfilling the prophecy of Lord Krishna, the head of Yadav Clan, who foretold Arjuna that his descendent would build his kingdom atop the Trikuta Hill. He was later driven from his kingdom by a rebellion and wandered northwards to settle near Hissar. Had issue four sons:

(i) Rawal Salvahan II Crowned in 1168 A.D. Jaisalmer State (Bhatti) Throne usurped by his son Bijil
(ii) Rawal KALHAN Crowned in 1190
(iii) Rai Hemhal (Hemraj)
(iv) Pem

- XXVIII. Rai Hemhal (Hemraj). Born 1150 A.D. Sacked Hisar in 1180. Supported Mohammed of Ghor when he invaded India. Sacked and overran the country up to Delhi, but was repulsed by Altamash. Subsequently, in 1212, made Governor of Sirsa & Bhatinda country by Shams-Ud-Din Altamash, the third Tartar King of Delhi. Ousted the Panwar Rajputs from the area of Muktsar. Died 1219 A.D
- XXIX. Jaidrath (Jandra)

Had issue twenty one sons; Batera being the eldest.

- XXX. Pate Rao (Batera)

Had issue:

- XXXI. Mangal Rao (Manjalrab) Having rebelled against the Mohammedan Sovereign of Delhi, was beheaded at Jaisalmer.
- XXXII. Anand Rao (Undra)
- XXXIII. Khiwa Rai (Kot). Built Khiva Khota. Sank to the status of a Jat by contracting marriage with Rajo, a Saräo-Basehrä lady from Neli Dulkot of ordinary class. Had issue:
- XXXIV. Sidhu

Born 1250. Also ancestor of Sidhu Jats. Fell into poverty and obscurity. Had issue four sons: (i) DHAR (Debi) Kaithal Jhumba Arnauli Sadhowal (ii) BHUR (iii) SUR (iv) RUPACH

- XXXV. Bhur

Had issue:

- XXXVI. Bir

Had issue two sons :

(i) Sidtilkara became an ascetic.

(ii) Satrach (Satra)

- XXXVII. Satrach (Satra). Had issue two sons:

(i) Jertha

(ii) Lakumba. Lakumba had one son HARI who is the ancestor of Attari & Harike families.

- XXXVIII. JERTHA (Charta)

Had issue:

- XXXIX. Mahi (Maho).

Had issue:

- XL. Kala (Gala)

Had issue:

- XLI. Mehra.

Had issue:

- XLII. Hambir (Hamira).

Had issue:

- XLIII. Rao Barar.

A known marauder and warrior. Also ancestor of Brar Jats. Regained Bathinda after defeating the Bhattis. He also rebelled against the Delhi government.Made Bidowali in Bathinda his stronghold. He and his men attacked Timur near Tohana during Timur's terrible raid on Northern India in 1398 A.D. resulting in heavy losses. Died 1415 in Bidowali. Had two sons: (i) Paur (ii) Dhul ancestor of Faridkot Royal family

- XLIV. Paur.

Had issue:

- XLV. Bairath (Bairi).

Had issue:

- XLVI. Kayen (Kao).

Had issue three sons:

(i) Baho

(ii) Mehna

(iii) Kilja.

- XLVII. Baho.

Had issue:

- XLVIII. Sanghar.

Entered the service of Emperor Babar with his followers. Killed on 21 April 1526 in Battle of Panipat when Babur defeated Ibrahim Lodhi. Had issue:

- XLIX. Ch.Bariyam (Beeram).

Granted the title of Chaudhary by Emperor Babar in 1526 and Chaudhriyat of the waste country southwest of Delhi which was reconfirmed by Emperor Humayun in 1554.Helped Humayun in his final victory against Sikandar Shah Sur in 1555. Fell fighting the Mohammedan Bhattis, their traditional foes along with Suttoh, his grandson and only son of Mehraj. Died 1560 A.D. Had issue two sons:

(i) Ch. Mehraj (Maharaj)

(ii) Geraj.

- L. Ch. Mehraj (Maharaj).

Succeeded his father Bariyam as Chaudhary & engaged in warfare with the Bhattis. Had issue:

- LI. Ch. SUTTOH (Satu).

Died 1560. Had issue three sons:

(i) Ch.Pukkoh (Pakhu)

(ii) Lukha

(iii) Chaha.

- LII. Ch.Pukkoh (Pakhu)

Killed fighting at Bhidowal. Had issue two sons:

(i) Ch. Mohan

(ii) Habbal.

- LIII. Ch. Mohan.

Fell into arrears with the Government & compelled to flee to Hansi and Hisar. Returned with a considerable force and defeated the Bhattis at Bhidowal. Founded Mehraj on the advice of Sixth Guru Hargobind naming it after his great-grandfather. Killed along with his son Rup Chand in a skirmish with Bhattis in 1618 A.D.

Had issue two sons:

(i) Ch. Ch. Rup Chand.

(ii) Ch. Kala

- LIV. Ch. Rup Chand.

Died 1618. Killed by the Bhattis. Had issue two sons: (i) Phool (ii) Sandali Kala succeeded to the Chaudriyat after the death of his brother and became the guardian of his two sons Phool & Sandali.

- LV. Ch. Phool

1603-1652 Fought for Sixth Guru Hargobind against Mohammedan Delhi Sovereign in War of Gurusar 1635 A.D. & emerged victorious. The Guru blessed Phool and is said to have told him that he would make a King. The Guru Har Rai also blessed him and proclaimed that his descendants shall rule the entire area between the Yamuna and Sutlej.

Founded Rampura Phul in 1627 (now in Distt.Bhatinda). He was often in conflict with local chiefs which enraged the Governor of Sirhind who summoned him and put him behind bars. Received royal firman from Emperor Shah Jahan and Prophecy of Guru was to be fulfilled. Killed by accident after feigning death in funeral pyre to escape imprisonment in 1652 A.D. Had issue six sons:

(i) Ch.Tiloka Died 1705. Ancestor of Nabha, Jind & Badrukhan.

(ii) Ch.Rama Died 1714. Ancestor of Bhadaur, Patiala,Malaudh & Kot Duna.

(iii) Rughu Ancestor of Laudgarhias
(iv) Channu
(v) Jhandu
(vi) Takht Mal Gumti Jagirdars.

Appellation of dynasty 'Phoolkian' is derived from their common founder Phool whose descendants were the great ruling & feudal families known as Phoolkian Chiefs who used Phoolkian from Phool, as their eponym.

- LVI. Ch.Rama.

Successfully raided the Bhattis and others including Hassan Khan & Muslim chief of Kot. Captured Kot and Bhatian. Obtained the intendancy of the Jangal tract from Mohameddan Governor of Sirhind. Choudhary Ram Singh founded Bhai Rupa in 1680 and built Rampur. Rama & Tiloka were baptized with *Khande da amrit* at the hands of the Tenth Sikh Guru, Guru Gobind Singh at Damdama Sahib. Guru Gobind Singh in a self written Hukamnama addressed to the two sons of Phool, Rama & Tiloka on 2 August, 1696 called upon them for help in his fight with the Hill Rajas proclaiming " *tera ghar mera asey*."

Rama & Tiloka later helped Banda Singh Bahadur with men and money in his early exploits (1710-16) Rama was killed at Maler Kotla in 1714. Married Sabi daughter of Bhuttar zamindar of Nanun who bore him six sons:

- Chaudhuri Dunna 1676-1726. Educ. privately. Granted Shahnaki in jagir. Founded Kot Duna. Appointed as Imperial Chaudhary of Sangrur, Dhanaula, Bhadaur, Hadaya, and other districts. Ancestor of the Bhadaur and Kot Duna families. He died at Bhadaur, 1726, having had issue, five sons.
- Subbah of Dhabali. Born 1679. Married Begi Kaur. He died 1729, having had issue, one son.
- H.H. Sri Raja-i-Rajgan, Maharaja ALA, Mahendra Bahadur, Yadu Vansha Vatans Bhatti Kul Bushan, Maharaja of Patiala. 1691-1765. Ancestor of Patiala family. In a fight against the powerful Mahomeddan Chief of Kot and Jagraon, aided by the Afghans of Maler Kotla and the Imperial Faujdar of the Jullundur Doab, Ala Singh gained a brilliant victory, which spread his fame far and wide. He entered into

friendly relations with Ahmad Shah Abdali who overran Punjab defeating the Marathas. Abdali presented Ala a robe of honour and conferred upon him the title of Raja.

- Bakhta 1683-1757. Founded Kotla Koura. m. a lady from the Man Jat clan. Ancestor of Malaudh family. Had issue, one son: Sardar Man Singh, of Malaudh. Born 1725. Conquered Malaudh from Maler Kotla Afghans in 1754 A.D. He died 1778, having had issue, two sons:

  1. Sardar Dalel Singh, of Malaudh. Born 1761, educ. privately. Forced to share a third of his estate with his brother, following the intervention of the Sardar of Bhadaur and the Maharaja of Patiala. Assisted the British during the Anglo-Nepalese War in 1815. A religious minded ascetic, he only employed fakirs and mahants in his service, and outlawed hunting on his estates. In 1806, Maharaja Ranjit Singh, passing through the country, summoned the Sardar Dalel Singh. On his refusal to come as he was engaged in prayers & devotion, Ranjit Singh was incensed and seized his eldest son Fateh Singh making him carry a heavy load for a long distance releasing him only when the Sardar had paid him Rs. 22,000 as fine or harrzana. He died 1824, having had issue, three sons.
  2. Sardar Bagh Singh of Ber. Born 1770. He died 1820, having had issue, two sons.

     (v) Mian Buddha. He d.s.p. 1714.

     (vi) Mian Ram Singh Laddha. Blessed as Ram Singh by Guru Gobind Singh in 1707. He died 1742, having had issue, one son.

Sons of Phool

Phool left six sons, of whom Tiloka was the eldest, and from him are descended the families of Jind and Nabha. From Rama, the second son, sprang the greatest of the Phoolkian houses, that of Patiala besides Bhadaur,Kot duna and Malaudh. In 1627 Phool founded and gave his name to a village which was an important town in the State of Nabha. His two eldest sons founded Bhai Rupa while Rama also built Rampur. The last named successfully raided the Bhattis and other enemies of his line. He then obtained from the Muhammadan governor of Sirhind the intendancy of the Jar gal tract. The other four sons succeeded to only a small share of their father's possessions.Rughu laid foundation stone of Village Bangi Rughu near Talwandi Sabo in district bathinda Rawal Jaisal's third Prince was Mokal who's son was Hansraj or Hans the Phulkian Sardars Sidhu-Brar bans are their heirs. 'As Per the Book "Bhati Rajputo Ka Gauravmaye Itihaas" by hukam singh *bhati*

Phoolkian States

The Phoolkia Sardars had always been on the right side of the Mughal government in Delhi. Patiala, Jind, and Nabha received royal titles from the declining Mughal power. They came under the loose domination of the new military machine of Mahadji Scindia and later under the British who took Delhi in 1803. Phulkian Sardars approached the British Government for seeking protection against the rising power of Maharaja Ranjit Singh. Although Ranjit Singh was very moderate towards the Phulkian Rajas, in due course, with the rising power of Ranjit Singh, they became suspicious of his designs and hence sought British protection. Accordingly, the leaders of the Cis-Satluj Sikh states including the rulers of Patiala, Nabha and Jind decided in a conclave to send a deputation to the British Resident in Delhi, Mr. Seton. They presented their memorandum to the British Resident on 1 April 1809 and pledged their loyalty to every succeeding power in Delhi and formally sought protection of the British.

The British were very glad to entertain their offer and accordingly they signed the Treaty of Amritsar on 25 April 1809 with Maharaja Ranjit Singh. The Maharaja agreed not to carry out his military exploits in the Cis-Satluj territories. Under the British Empire, Honours or Rewards bestowed on the Native Princes of India, grants were made to the Maharaja of Patiala and the Rajas of Jind and Nabha consisting of, first, a Sunnud from the Governor General confirming to him and his heirs forever his possessions and all the privileges attached to them and secondly, the recognition of his right, in failure of direct heirs, to adopt a successor from the Phoolka family. This right of adoption was granted to the Chiefs of Patiala, Jind, and Nabha in 1860, together with the further concession that, in the event of the Chief of any one State dying without male issue and without adopting a successor, the chiefs of the other two, in concert with the Political Agent, could choose a successor from among the Phoolkian family. Succession in those cases was subject to the payment to the British Government of a nazarana or fine equal to one-third of the gross revenue of the State. The Political Agent for the Phoolkian States and Bahawalpur was at Patiala.

Eleven of the descendants of Phool of the Phoolkian family in the Cis-Sutlej States who had Rank, Position and were entitled seats to attend the Durbars of the Viceroy 1864-1885 were:

1. Maharaja Mahindar Singh, Patiala;
2. Raja Raghbir Singh, Jind;
3. Raja Bhagwan Singh, Nabha;
4. Sirdar Sir Attar Singh, Bhadour;
5. Sirdar Kehr Singh, Bhadour;
6. Sirdar Achhal Singh, Bhadour;
7. Sirdar Uttam Singh Rampuria, Malaud;
8. Sirdar Mit Singh, Malaudh;
9. Sirdar Hakikat Singh, Ber, Malaud;
10. Sirdar Diwan Singh and
11. Sirdar Hira Singh, Badrukhan.

The Bhadour Chiefs sat in Durbar as feudatories of Pattiala; the Badrukhan Chiefs of Jhind, and the Malaudh Sirdars as British Jagirdar Chiefs.

Misl Dallewalia

Dallevalla Misl derived its name from the village of Dalleval, near Dera Baba Nanak on the left bank of River Ravi, 50 km northeast of Amritsar to which its founder, Gulab Singh (Gulaba Khatri before he converted a Khalsa), belonged. At the time of the formation of the Dal Khalsa in 1748, Gulab Singh who had already fought bravely against Nadir Shah in 1739 and in the Chhota Ghallughara in 1746, was declared head of the Dallevalia dera, later called misl.

The Dallevalla and Nishananvali jathas were stationed at Amritsar to protect the holy city. In 1757 when Ahmad Shah Durrani was returning homeward laden with the booty from Delhi, Mathura and Agra, Gulab Singh made frequent night attacks on his baggage train. Commanding a band of 400 men, he plundered Panipat, Rohtak, Hansi and Hissar.

On the death in 1759 of Gulab Singh, his trusted associate, Tara Singh Ghaiba, succeeded him as head of the misl. Tara Singh proved to be an able leader of men and a fearless fighter. One of his first exploits was to attack a detachment of Ahmad Shah Durrani's army and rob it of its horses and arms while crossing the Beus river near his native village, Kangt in Kapurthala district. In 1760, he crossed the Sutlej and seized the towns of Dharamkot and Fatehgarh. On his return to the Doab, he took Sarai Dakkhani from the Afghan chief Saif ud-din of Jalandhar and marched eastwards seizing the country around Rahon. He made Rahon his headquarters now. He next captured Nakodar from Manj Rajputs and several other villages on the right side of the Sutlej, including Mahatpur and Kot Badal Khan. In 1763, Tara Singh joined the Bhangi, Ramgarhia and Kanhaiya misls against the Pathan Nawab of Kasur and, in the sack of the town, collected four lakhs of rupees as his share of the booty. He joined other Sikh sardars in laying siege to Sirhind (January 1764) and razing it to the ground after defeating its faujdar, Zain Khan.

The Dallevalla misl under Tara Singh and his co-generals and associates held a major portion of the upper Jalandhar Doab, and the northern portions of Ambala and Ludhiana, with some portions of Firozpur. Tara Singh's cousin Dharam Singh captured Kohlan and a cluster of villages in the centre of which he founded the village of Dharamsinghvala where he set up his permanent headquarters. Other members of the misl seized Tihala, on the left bank of the Sutlej. Saundha Singh from among them captured Khanna in Ludhiana district; Hari Singh took Ropar, Sialba, Avankot, Sisvan and Kurah. He also occupied the forts of Khizrabad and Nurpur. Buddh Singh of Garh Shankar captured Takhtgarh. Desu Singh of the misl occupied Mustafabad, Arnaull, Siddhuval, Bangar, Amlu and Kullar Kharial. In 1760, he established his headquarters at Kaithal. van Singh of the same clan captured Sikandra, Akalgarh and Barara. Sahib Singh and Gurdit Singh, two Sansi brothers, seized Ladva and Indri. Bhanga Singh became master of Thanesar and Bhag Singh and Buddh Singh took Pehova. Tara Singh Ghaiba however remained the central figure of the misl. He became a close friend and associate of Maharaja Ranjit Singh and took part in his early Malva campaigns. After his death in 1807 at the age of 90, Dallevala territories were annexed by Ranjit Singh.

Misl Bhangian

Bhangi Misl was one of the twelve misls or eighteenth-century Sikh principalities acquired its name from the addiction of its members to a drug called bhang or hemp. The founder of the jatha, i.e. band of warriors, that later acquired the dimensions of a misl was Chhajja Singh of Panjvar village, near Amritsar who had converted to Sikhism. He was succeeded by Bhuma Singh, a Dhillon Jatt of the village of Hung, near Badhni in present day Moga district, who won a name for himself in skirmishes with Nadir Shah's troops in 1739. On Bhuma Singh's death in 1746, his nephew and adopted son, Han Singh, assumed the leadership of the misl. At the formation of the Dal Khalsa in 1748, Hari Singh was acknowledged head of the Bhangi masl as well as leader of the Taruna Dal. He vastly increased the power and influence of the Bhangi misl which began to be ranked as the strongest among its peers. He created an army of 20,000 dashing youths, captured Panjvar in the Tarn Taran parganah and established his headquarters first at Sohal and then at Gilvah, both in Amritsar district. Hari Singh kept up guerrilla warfare against the invading hosts of Ahmad Shah Durrani. In 1763, he along with the Kanhaiyas and Ramgarhias, sacked the Afghan strong hold of Kasur. In 1764, he ravaged Bahawalpur and Multan. Crossing the River Indus, he realized tribute from the Baluchi chiefs in the districts of Muzaffargarh, Dera Ghazi Khan and Dera Ismail Khan. On his way back home, he reduced Jhang, Chiniot and Sialkot. Hari Singh died in 1765, fighting against Baba Ala Singh of Patiala.

Hari Singh was succeeded by Jhanda Singh, his eldest son, under whom the Bhangi misl reached the zenith of its power. In 1764, Jhanda Singh had invaded Multan and Bahawalpur, but failed to drive out the Durrani satrap Shuja Khan Saddozai. Jhanda Singh marched on Multan again in 1772 forcing the Nawab to flee. Multan was declared Khalsa territory and the city was parcelled out between Jhanda Singh and his commander Lahina Singh. Jhanda Singh next subdued Jhang, Kala Bagh and Mankera. He built a brick fort at Amritsar which he named Qila Bhangian and laid out fine bazars in the city. He then proceeded to Rasulnagar, where he recovered from the Muhammadan Chattha rulers the famous gun Zamzama which came to be known as Bhangian di Top. But Jhanda Singh was soon involved in the internal feuds of the warring misl. He was killed in 1774 in a battle with the

Kanhaiyas and the Sukkarchakkias at Jammu where he had marched to settle a standing succession issue. He was succeeded by his brother Ganda Singh who, dying of illness at the time of a battle with the Kanhaiyas at Dinanagar, was in turn succeeded by his minor son, Desa Singh, under whose weak leadership began the decline of the dynasty.

Several Bhangi sardars set themselves up as independent chiefs within their territories. Desa Singh was killed in action against Mahan Singh Sukkarchakkia in 1782. A leading Bhangi sardar now was Gurbakhsh Singh Rowranvala who had fought hand in hand with Hari Singh Bhangi in several of his battles. After his death, his adopted son Lahina Singh, and Gujjar Singh son of his daughter, divided his estates. In 1765, they had joined hands with Sobha Singh Kanhaiya and occupied Lahore. The city was partitioned among the three sardars who though temporarily driven out in 1767 by Ahmad Shah Durrani, had continued in authority.

In January 1797 Ahmad Shah's grandson, Shah Zaman, led out an expedition and seized the city. But soon after the departure of the Durrani Shah for Kabul, Lahina Singh and Sobha Singh (Gujjar Singh had died in 1791), returned and reestablished their rule. The same year, 1797, Lahina Singh died and was succeeded by his son Chet Singh and about the same time Sobha Singh died and was succeeded by his son Mohar Singh. But the new rulers failed to establish their authority.

People groaned under oppressive taxes and extortions and local Muhammadan Chaudharis and mercantile Khatris made a common cause and invited Ranjit Singh and Sada Kaur to come and occupy the city. On 7 July 1799, Ranjit Singh arrived with 5,000 troops at the Shalamar Gardens. The Bhangi sardars left the town hastily and Ranjit Singh became master of the capital of the Punjab, laying the foundation of Sikh monarchy.

Reverting to the main branch of the Bhangi misl Desa Singh, son of Ganda Singh, was succeeded by his minor son Gulab Singh, who administered the misl through his cousin Karam Singh. Gulab Singh enlarged the city of Amritsar where he resided, and, on attaining years of discretion, overran the whole Pathan colony of Kasur, which he subdued, the Pathan chiefs of Kasur, Nizamuddin and Qutb-ud-Din Khan, brothers, entering the service of the conqueror. In 1794, however, the brothers, with the aid of their

Afghan countrymen, recovered Kasur. Gulab Singh died in 1800 and was succeeded by his son, Gurdit Singh, a 10-year old boy who conducted the affairs of the misl through his mother and guardian, Mai Sukkhan. Maharaja Ranjit Singh who after having taken possession of Lahore in 1799 was launched on a career of rapid conquest had his eyes on Amritsar where Bhangis still held their sway. On the excuse of taking from them the famous Zamzama gun, he marched with a strong force in 1802, Gurdit Singh, along with his mother, Mai Sukkhan, fleeing without resistance. The last Bhangi chief to fall was Sahib Singh of Gujrat who was dismissed with a grant of a few villages. By 1810 all Bhangi territories Lahore, Amritsar, Sialkot, Chiniot, Jhang, Bhera, Rawalpindi, Hasan Abdal, Gujrat—had merged with the kingdom of Ranjit Singh. The descendants of Bhangi sardars are today concentrated mainly in the Amritsar district of the Punjab.

Misl Singhpuria (Faizullpuria)

Singhpuria (or Faizullapuria) Misl was founded by Kapur Singh, a Virk Jatt of the village of Kaleke, now in Sheikhupura district of Pakistan Punjab. The misl got its name from Faizullapur, a village in Amritsar district which Kapur Singh had wrested from its Muslim chief, Faizulla Khan, and, conquering the country around, given it the name of Singhpura. Kapur Singh was eleven years old at the time of Guru Gobind Singh's passing away. His physical courage and warlike spirit were valuable qualities in those days of high adventure. He soon gained a position of eminence among Sikhs then engaged in a desperate struggle against the Mughal rulers. When in 1734 Zakriya Khan, the Mughal governor of Lahore, decided to make peace with the Sikhs, he offered them a jagar and title of Nawab for their leader. The Khalsa chose with one voice Kapur Singh to receive the title.

Nawab Kapur Singh now proceeded to restructuring the Sikh fighting force. The whole body of the Khalsa was formed into two sections, the Buddha Dal, army of the veterans, and the Taruna Dal, army of the young. The cstentewith the Mughals did not last long and, before the harvest of 1735, Zakariya Khan sent a force and occupied the jagzr. Nawab Kapur Singh and his band were driven away towards the Malva by Lakhpat Rai, the Hindu minister at the Mughal court at Lahore. During his sojourn in the Malva, Nawab Kapur Singh conquered the territory of Sunam and made it over to Ala Singh of Patiala. He also attacked Sirhind and defeated the Mughal governor. Returning to Amritsar, he successfully routed, in 1736, the force led by Lakhpat Rai, killing two important faujdars, Jamal Khan and Tatar Khan, in the battle. With 2,000 followers Nawab Kapur Singh entered, in disguise, the city of Lahore with a view to capturing the governor, Zakariya Khan. Driven back, Nawab Kapur Singh proceeded towards Delhi, the imperial capital. He overran Faridabad, Balabhgarh and Gurgaon and laid contributions on Jhauar, Dojana and Pataudi. In 1748 at the time of the organization of the Dal Khalsa, a confederation of various misls, Nawab Kapur Singh handed over leadership of the Sikhs to Jassa Singh Ahluvalia and himself continued to guide the destinies of the newly formed Singhpuria house or misl. On his death in 1755, charge of the misl came into the hands of his nephew Khushhal Singh who made further territorial acquisitions. Capturing Jalandhar in 1759, he made it his capital, and seized the parganahs of Haibatpur and Patti from the Pathan chief of Kasur. At the time of the conquest of Sirhind by Sikhs in January 1764, he got Bharatgarh, Machhall, Ghanauli, Manauli and several other villages as his share of the booty. Khushhal Singh and Rija Amar Singh of Patiala took from the Nawab of Rishikot 23 villages around Chhat and Banur which remained under their joint control for several years. The Singhpuria territory yielded annually two lakhs in the Bari Doab, one lakh in the Jalandhar Doab and one and a half lakh in the Sirhind province. Khushhal Singh died in 1795 and was succeeded by his son Buddh Singh. But like other sardars, Buddh Singh also succumbed to the rising power of Ranjit Singh who occupied his Bari Doab and Jalandhar Doab territories. He was forced to shift to his estates below the River Sutlej, with Manauli as his new headquarters. Buddh Singh died in 1816 leaving behind seven sons. The cis Sutlej remnants of the Singhpuria misl were eventually annexed by the British.

Misl Kanhaiya

Kanhaiya Misl was founded by Jai Singh, a Sandhu Jatt of the village of Kahna, 21 km southwest of Lahore on the road to Firozpur. He had an humble origin, his father Khushhal (Singh) eking out his livelihood by selling hay at Lahore. Jai Singh received the vows of the Khalsa at the hands of Nawab Kapur Singh and joined the derah or jatha of Amar Singh Kingra. It is commonly believed that the name of the misl, Kanhaiya, was derived from the name of Jai Singh's village, Kahna, although another explanation connects it with the Sardar's own handsome appearance which earned him the epithet (Kahn) Kanhaiya, an endearing title used for Lord Krisna. The Kanhaiya misl under Jai Singh became the dominant power in the Punjab, seized a part of Riloki comprising the district of Gurdaspur and upper portions of Amritsar. He first made his wife's village, Sohian, in Amritsar district, his headquarters from where he shifted to Batala and thence to Mukerian. His territories lay on both sides of the Rivers Beas and Ravi. Jai Singh extended his territory up to Parol, about 70 km southeast of Jammu, and the hill chiefs of Kangra, Nurpur and Datarpur became his tributaries.

In 1778, he with the help of Mahan Singh Sukkarchakkia and Jassa Singh Ahluvalia, drove away Jassa Singh Ramgarhia to the desert region of Hansi and Hissar. In 1781 Jai Singh and his associate Haqiqat Singh led an expedition to Jammu and received a sum of 3,00,000 rupees as tribute from its new ruler, Brij Raj Dev. On Jai Singh's death in 1793 at the age of 81, control of the Kanhaiya clan passed into the hands of his daughter-in-law Sada Kaur, his son Gurbakhsh Singh having predeceased him. Sada Kaur whose daughter Mahitab Kaur was married to Ranjit Singh was mainly instrumental in the Sukkarchakkia chief's rise to political power in the Punjab.

In July 1799, she helped Ranjit Singh occupy Lahore defeating the Bhangi chiefs, Mohar Singh, Sahib Singh and Chet Singh. Supported by Sada Kaur, Ranjit Singh made further acquisitions and assumed the title of Maharaja in April 1801. In the campaigns of Amritsar, Chiniot, Kasur and Kangra as well as against the turbulent Pathans of Hazara and Attock, Sada Kaur led the armies side by side with Ranjit Singh. The entente however did not last long and the two began to drift apart. The marriage of Sada Kaur's daughter to Ranjit Singh did not prove a happy one. The differences came into the open when Sada Kaur started secret negotiations with the British through Sir Charles Metcalfe and Sir David Ochterlony to secure herself the status of an independent chief. Ranjit Singh started making inroads into the Kanhaiya territory and confiscated their wealth Iying at Atalgarh (Mukerian). Batala was made over as a jagir to his son Sher Singh, while the rest of

Sada Kaur's estates were placed under the governorship of Desa Singh Majlthia. Sada Kaur died in confinement in 1832.

The leader of another section of the Kanhaiya misl was Haqiqat Singh, son of Baghel Singh, a Siddhu Jatt, hailing from the village of Julka, near Kahna, the birthplace of Jai Singh. A friend and associate of Jai Singh in many of his campaigns of conquest, Haqiqat Singh was also his rival. Emerging an independent chief, he occupied Kalanaur, as Kahngarh, Adalatgarh, Pathankot and several other villages. In 1760, Haqiqat Singh destroyed Churlanvala and founded another village instead naming it Sangatpura and constructed a fort at Fatehgarh. Haqiqat Singh died in 1782 and his only son Jaimal Singh, then a minor, succeeded to his estates. Haqiqat Singh's grand daughter, Chand Kaur, was married to Prince Kharak Singh, eldest son of Maharaja Ranjit Singh. Jaimal Singh died in 1812, leaving no son. Ranjit Singh seized his wealth stored up in the fort of Fatehgarh, allowing the revenue of the district as subsistence allowance to his widow. All the remaining Kanhaiya territories were conferred on Prince Kharak Singh

Karora Singhia Misl

Karora Singhia Misl was named after Karora Singh, a Virk Jatt of Barki in Lahore district. The founder of the jatha or band of warriors that subsequently acquired the size and power of a misl, was Shiam Singh of Narli who had battled with the invading forces of Nadir Shah in 1739. He was succeeded by Karam Singh, an Uppal Khatri of the village of Paijgarh in Gurdaspur district. Karam Singh fell fighting against Ahmad Shah Durrani in January 1748 and was succeeded by Karora Singh. Karora Singh confined his activities to the tract lying south of the Kangra hills in Hoshiarpur district, and had seized several important towns such as Hoshiarpur, Hariana and Sham Chaurasi before he died in 1761.

Baghel Singh who succeeded Karora Singh as leader of the Karorsinghias is celebrated in Sikh history as the conqueror of Mughal Delhi. A Dhalival Jatt, Baghel Singh arose from the village of Jhabal, in Amritsar district, to become a formidable force in the cis-Sutlej region. According to Syad Muhammad Latlf, he had under him 12,000 fighting men. Soon after the Sikh conquest of Sirhind in January 1764, he extended his arms towards Karnal, occupying a number of villages including Chhalaudl which he later made his headquarters. In February 1764, Sikhs in a body of 40,000 under the command of Baghel Singh and other leading warriors crossed the Yamuna and captured Saharanpur. They overran the territory of Najib ud-Daulah, the Ruhilla chief realizing from him a tribute of eleven lakh of rupees. In April 1775, Baghel Singh with two other sardars, Rai Singh Bhangi and Tara Singh Ghaiba, crossed the Yamuna to overrun the country then ruled by Zabita Khan, son and successor of Najib ud-Daulah. Zabita Khan in desperation offered Baghel Singh large sums of money and proposed an alliance jointly to plunder the crown-lands.

The combined forces of Sikhs and Ruhilas captured villages around the present site of New Delhi. In March 1776, they defeated the imperial forces near Muzaffarnagar. The whole of the Yamuna-gangetic Doab was now at their mercy. When in April 1781, Mirza Shafi, a close relative of the Mughal prime minister, captured the Sikh military post at Indri, 10 km south of Ladva, Baghel Singh retaliated by attacking Kahl Beg Khan of Shahabad who surrendered with 300 horse, 800 foot and two pieces of cannon. When on 11 March 1785, Sikhs entered the Red Fort in Delhi and occupied the Diwan-i-Am, the Mughal emperor, Shah Alam II, made a settlement with them agreeing to allow Baghel Singh to raise gurdwaras on Sikh historical sites and realize six annas in a rupee (37.5%) of all the octroi duties in the capital. Baghel Singh stayed in area called Sabzi Mandi, with 4,000 troops, and took charge of Chandni Chowk. He located seven sites sacred to the Sikhs and had shrines raised thereon within the space of eight months from April to November 1783.

Another Karorsinghia scion, Rai Singh, son of Mahtab Singh who had killed the notorious Masse Khan Ranghar, seized a number of villages in Samrala in the Ludhiana district after the Sikh conquest of Sirhind in 1764. Gurbaksh Singh, a Sandhu Jatt of the village of Kalsia in Kasur tahsil of Lahore district, who was a prominent companion of Baghel Singh, shared the exploits and conquests of the Karorsinghia sardar and occupied parganahs of Chhachhraun, Sialba, etc. Karam Singh and Dial Singh, also from Kalsia, took possession of the Bilaspur parganah, now in Jagadhari tahstl of Ambala district, and the parganah of Dharamkot in Firozpur district, respectively. Dulcha Singh, another member of the misl, took possession of Radaur and Damla in Karnal district. In October 1774 Dulja Singh Bahadur, "along with five other Sikh chiefs, was requested by the Mughal emperor to enter imperial service at the head of 1,000 horse and 500 foot, but he declined the offer.

The last of the prominent Karorsinghia leaders was Jodh Singh (1751-1818), son of Gurbakhsh Singh of Kalsia. Jodh Singh made considerable additions to his otherwise small inheritance. In 1807, he joined Maharaja Ranjit Singh in the attack on Naraingarh in Ambala district and later fought for him in many a battle in the Punjab. The Maharaja granted him the tracts of Garhdivala in Hoshiarpur district, and Charik in Firozpur district as rewards for his services. Jodh Singh died in the battle of Multan in 1818, and his son, Sobha, Singh, who succeeded him ruled over Kalsia state for 40 years until his death in 1758. Sobha Singh's son, Lahina Singh, who died in 1869, was followed in the chiefship by his son, Bishan Singh (d. 1883) and grandsons Jatit Singh (d. 1886) and Ranjit Singh (d. 1908). The chief figure in Kalsla during the twentieth century was Raja Ravi Sher Singh (1902-1947) who succeeded his father, Ranjit Singh, on the gaddi in 1908. The Kalsia state acceded to the Indian Union on the lapse of British paramountcy in August 1947 and joined the Patiala and East Punjab States Union (PEPSU) in 1948.

Misal Nakai

Nakai Misl was founded by Hari Singh, a Sandhu Jatt of the village of Bahirval in Chunlan tahsil of Lahore district. His village fell in the country called Nakka which lay southwest of Lahore between the rivers Rivi and Sutlej. It was through this region that the highway from Lahore to Multan, Baluchistan and Sindh passed imparting to it the name Nakka (nakka, in Punjabi, signifying a kind of gateway). Hira Singh had taken to arms while still very young. As the Sikhs sacked Kasur in 1763 and conquered Sirhind in 1764, Hari Singh occupied Bahirval, Chunlan, Dipalpur, Jambar, Jethupur, Kanganval and Khudian establishing his headquarters at Chunian. In 1767, he led out an expedition to Pakpattan, but was killed in the action that took place.

His son Dal Singh being a minor, he was succeeded by his nephew Nahar Singh who had but a tenure of nine months falling in a battle at Kot Kamalia in 1768. His younger brother Ran Singh, who succeeded him, considerably increased the power and influence of the Nakals. The territory under his control was worth nine lakhs of rupees per annum and comprised Chunlan, part of

Kasur, Sharakpur, Cugera and, at one time, Kot Kamalia. Ran Singh had a force of 2,000 horsemen, with camel swivels and a few guns. His headquarters were at Bahirval in Lahore district. Ran Singh died in 1781 and was succeeded by his eldest son Bhagvan Singh, whose sister, Raj Kaur, was married to Maharaja Ranjit Singh. Bhagvan Singh was succeeded by his younger brother, Gian Singh, who died in 1807 leaving a son, Kahn Singh. Ranjit Singh granted Kahn Singh a jagir of 15,000 rupees per annum and seized all the possessions of the family. Nakai became a prominent last name among several families. Many Nakai Sardars were converted to Islam lured by the women, power and money. A former Chief minister of Pakistan, Arif Nakai's grandfather was born as a Sikh but got converted to Islam. A Shame indeed.

Misl Nishanawali

Nishananvali Misl, owed its origin to Dasaundha Singh whose jatha were the standard-bearers of the Dal Khalsa. Hence the name of the jatha or misl Nishananvali, nishan in Punjabi meaning a flag or standard. The misl was originally based in Amritsar where it guarded the Holy Harimandar and also served as a reserve force of the Dal. Dasaundha Singh, son of Chaudhari Sahib Rai was a Gill Jatt belonging to the village of Mansur in Firozpur district, who, after the conquest of Sirhind by Sikhs in January 1764, took possession of Singhanvala, again in Firozpur district, Sahneval, Sarai Lashkari Khan, Amloh, Doraha, Zirfi, and Ambala, establishing his headquarters at the lastnamed station.

On his death in 1767, Dasaundha Singh was succeeded to the headship of the misl by his younger brother Sangat Singh who made over charge of Ambala to his cousins, Lal Singh and Gurbakhsh Singh, and himself retired to Singhavala. On Sangat Singh's death in 1774, Lal Singh's three sons Mohar Singh, Kapur Singh, and Anup Singh drove out Gurbakhsh Singh from Ambala dividing the Nishananvali territories among themselves. Mohar Singh soon became an influential figure among the cis-Sutlej chiefs. On 9 May 1785, he and Dulcha Singh made treaties of friendship with Mahadji Scindia, the all-powerful Maratha deputy of the Mughal empire, and both of them received robes of honour and cash awards from him. Among other leaders of the misal, Naudh Singh, who was severely wounded in the battle of Sirhind (January 1764), took possession of Khen close to Sirhind, Sudha Singh Bajva seized Machhivara east of Ludhiana, while Rai Singh secured 16 villages southwest of Khanna. Jai Singh, another member of the misl, captured 27 villages in Kharar. Karam Singh acquired the parganahs of Shahabad and Ismailabad in the present Kurukshetra district. Savan Singh, a cousin of Dasaundha Singh and Sangat Singh, appropriated to himself several villages around Saunti, near Amloh.

The military strength of the Nishananvali misl had risen to 12,000 horse under Sangat Singh. Its territories included Ambala, Shahabad, Saunti, Kheri, Morinda, Amloh, Khanna, Doraha, Sahneval, Machhivara and Zira. Ambala was last ruled by Daya Kaur, widow of Gurbaksh Singh who had died in 1786. Upon Daya Kaur's death in 1823, her estates and property lapsed to the British government.

Misl Shaheedan

Shahidan Misl owed its origin to Baba Dip Singh Shahid (1652-1757) belonging to the village of Pahuvind in Amritsar district. Baba Dip Singh had received the vows of the Khalsa at the hands of Guru Gobind Singh. He rejoined in 1706 Guru Gobind Singh, then at Talvandi Sabo, 28 km southeast of Bathinda and, after the latter's departure for the South, stayed on there to look after the sacred shrine, Damdama Sahib. He had four copies of the Guru Granth Sahib made from the recension prepared earlier by Bhai Mani Singh under the supervision of Guru Gobind Singh during their stay at Damdama Sahib.

In 1733, when the Mughal governor of Lahore made peace with the Sikhs offering them nawabship and a jagir, Dip Singh, now reverently called Baba, i.e. the elder, joined Nawab Kapur Singh, who had been invested with the title of Nawab, and received command of one of the five jathas that constituted the newly formed Taruna Dal. These jathas were redesignated misls in 1748 and the jatha headed by Dip Singh came to be known as Shahid misl after he met with the death of a martyr (shahid, in Punjabi). The misls, the number increasing to twelve, soon established their hegemony over different regions in the Punjab.

The Shahid misl was mostly made up of Nihangs, a class of warriors which owed its origin to Baba Fateh Singh, son of Guru Gobind Singh. They wore blue, with heavy bangles of steel upon their wrists and quoia around their heads. The Shahids had their sphere of influence south of the River Sutlej. The Shahids under Dip Singh had their headquarters at Talvandi Sabo. They also held control of the Harimandar at Amritsar. In 1757 Jahan Khan, Ahmad Shah Durrani's commander-in-chief and deputy to his son, Taimur Shah, the governor of the Punjab, invested the town, razed the Sikh fortress of Ram Rauni and desecrated the shrine filling up the sacred pool. The Shahids led by Gurbakhsh Singh had defended the holy premises valiantly, but failed to stem the onslaught. As the news reached Dip Singh at Talvandi Sabo, he set out with his jatha towards the Holy City. Many Sikhs joined him on the way so that when he arrived at Tarn Taran he had at his command a force of 5,000 men. Jahan Khan's troops lay in wait for them near Cohjvar village 8 km ahead. They barred their way and a fierce action took place. Dip Singh was mortally wounded near Ramsar, yet such was the firmness of his resolve to reach the holy precincts that he carried on the battle until he fell dead in the close vicinity of the Harimandar. This was on 11 November 1757.

After Dip Singh's death, the leadership of the misl passed on to Karam Singh, a Sandhu Jatt belonging to the village of Marahka in Sheikhupura district, now in Pakistan. In January 1764, at the conquest of the Sirhind province by the Sikhs, he seized a number of villages in the parganah of Kesari and Shahzadpur in Ambala district yielding about a lakh of rupees annually. Kararn Singh made Shahzadpur his headquarters though he lived for most of the time at Talvandi Sabo (Damdama Sahib). In 1773, he overran a large tract of land belonging to Zabita Khan Ruhlla in the upper Gangetic Doab. He captured a number of villages in Saharanpur district. After Karam Singh's death in 1784, his elder son, Gulab Singh, succeeded to the headship of the misl. On Gulab Singh's death in 1844, his son Shiv Kirpal Singh succeeded to the family estate, the misl having become extinct in 1809 after the cis Sutlej Sikh states had accepted British protection.

Before the Empire

The period from 1716 to 1799 was a highly turbulent time politically and militarily in the Punjab. This was caused by the overall decline of the Mughal Empire. This left a power vacuum that was eventually filled by the Sikhs in the late 18th century, after fighting off local Mughal remnants and allied Rajput leaders, Afghans, and occasionally hostile Punjabi Muslims who sided with other Muslim forces. Sikh warlords eventually formed their own independent Sikh administrative regions (misls), which were united in large part by Ranjit Singh.

Sarbat Khalsa

The Sarbat Khalsa is a gathering of a representative portion of the Khalsa Panth held at Amritsar in India. During the 18th century the Sarbat Khalsa was converted into the supreme central forum for decision-making relating to all issues affecting the Sikh religion and the Sikh Empire. These included Sikh philosophy, Sikh community development and central administration of the Sikh religion. The Sarbat Khalsa was also responsible for decision making and planning for strengthening the Sikh religion and Sikh politics. During the 18th century, the Sikh Confederacy existed and the Sarbat Khalsa was responsible for adjudicating disputes about property and succession in the Sikh Barons' kingdoms if they were unable to resolve them internally. Due to the powers and rights invested in the Sarbat Khalsa, during the period of the Gurus, it is seen as the most powerful body in the Sikh religion.

Formation

The Sikh Empire (from 1801-1849) was formed on the foundations of the Punjabi Army by Maharaja Ranjit Singh. The Empire extended from Khyber Pass in the west, to Kashmir in the north, to Sindh in the south, and Tibet in the east. The main geographical footprint of the empire was the Punjab. The religious demography of the Sikh Empire was Muslim (80%), Sikh (10%), Hindu (10%).

Ranjit Singh

Maharaja Ranjit Singh (November 13, 1780 in Gujranwala, Mughal Empire-June 20, 1839 in Lahore, Sikh Empire) was the first Maharaja of the Sikh Empire and was also known as Sher-e-Punjab (The Lion of the Punjab).

Early Life

Ranjit Singh was born in Gujranwala (now in Pakistan), into the family of Sandhawalia Sikh (According to some historians of Jatt origin and others Sansi caste) Clan who were Sukerchakia misldars. He belonged to Sikh clan of Northern India. As a child he suffered from smallpox which resulted in the loss of one eye.

At the time, much of Punjab was ruled by the Sikhs under a Confederate Sarbat Khalsa system, who had divided the territory among factions known as misls. Ranjit Singh's father Maha Singh was the Commander of the Sukerchakia misl and controlled a territory in west Punjab based around his headquarters at Gujranwala. Ranjit Singh succeeded his father at the young age of 12. After several campaigns, his rivals accepted him as their leader, and he united the Sikh factions into one entity.

The Maharaja

Ranjit Singh was crowned on April 12, 1801 (to coincide with Baisakhi). Sahib Singh Bedi, a descendant of Guru Nanak Dev, conducted the coronation. Gujranwala served as his capital from 1799. In 1802 he shifted his capital to Lahore. Ranjit Singh rose to power in a very short period, from a leader of a single Sikh misl to finally becoming the Maharaja (Emperor) of Punjab.

He then spent the following years fighting the Afghans, driving them out of the Punjab. He also captured Pashtun territory including Peshawar (now referred to as North West Frontier Province and the Tribal Areas). This was the first time that Peshawari Pashtuns were ruled by Punjabis. He captured the province of Multan which encompassed the southern parts of Punjab, Peshawar (1818), Jammu and Kashmir (1819). Thus Ranjit Singh put an end to more than a thousand years of Muslim rule. He also conquered the hill states north of Anandpur Sahib, the largest of which was Kangra.

When the Foreign Minister of the Ranjit Singh's court, *Fakir Azizuddin*, met the British Governor-General of India, Lord Auckland, in Simla, Lord Auckland asked Fakir Azizuddin which of the Maharaja's eyes was missing, Azizuddin replied: *"The Maharaja is like the sun and sun has only one eye. The splendour and luminosity of his single eye is so much that I have never dared to look at his other eye."* The Governor General was so pleased with this reply that he gave his gold watch to Azizuddin.

Ranjit Singh's Empire was secular, none of the subjects were discriminated against on account of their religions. The Maharaja never forced Sikhism on his subjects.

Gurudwaras Built by Maharaja Ranjit Singh

At the Harmandir Sahib, much of the present decorative gilding and marblework date back from the early 1800s. The gold and intricate marble work were conducted under the patronage of Maharaja Ranjit Singh, Maharaja of the Punjab. The *Sher-e-Punjab* (Lion of the Punjab) was a generous patron of the shrine and is remembered with much affection by the Sikhs. Maharaja Ranjit Singh deeply loved and admired the teachings of the Tenth Guru of Sikhism Guru Gobind Singh, thus he promoted the teachings of the Dasam Granth (the Tenth Granth) and built two of the most sacred temples in Sikhism. These are Takht Sri Patna Sahib, the birth place of Guru Gobind Singh, and Takht Sri Hazur Sahib, the place where Guru Gobind Singh took his final rest or mahasamadhi, in Nanded, Maharashtra in 1708.

Generals of Maharaja

Ranjit Singh encircled himself with an array of strong generals and soldiers. They were men from different clans, castes and regions and religions.

Hari Singh Nalwa

Hari Singh Nalwa (1791-1837), grandson of Kashibai, is honoured as one of the most celebrated Sikh warriors. He was born in Gujranwala, Punjab. He served as the Commander-in-Chief of Maharaja Ranjit Singh's kingdom along the Indus frontier, which bordered the Kingdom of Kabul. He took the North West Frontier of the Sikh Kingdom across the river Indus, annexing a large portion of the Afghan Kingdom. At the time of his death, the western boundary of the Sikh Kingdom touched the foothills of the Hindu Kush mountains. After him, no further conquests were made in that direction.

Early Life

Hari Singh was born into an Uppal Khatri family at Gujranwala (now in Pakistan). His parents were Gurdas Singh and Dharam Kaur (daughter of Kashibai). He became fatherless at a very young age, when his father died in 1798.

Military Career

Sir Henry Griffin called Nalwa the "Murat of the Khalsa". A British newspaper had asserted in the early twentieth century that had Nalwa the resources and the artillery of the British, he would have conquered the East and extended the boundaries of the Sikh

Kingdom to include Europe. This most famous of the great Sikh generals participated in the following conquests: Sialkot, Kasur (1807), Multan (1818), Kashmir (1819), Pakhli and Damtaur (1821-2), Peshawar (1834) and finally Jamrud (1837) in the Khyber Hills. He served as the governor of both Kashmir and Peshawar. A coin minted in Kashmir came to be known as the 'Hari Singhee'. The coin is on display in museums.

Legacy

Haripur city, tehsil and district, in Hazara, North-West Frontier Province, Pakistan, are named after him..He defeated the Afghans, something the British failed to do, and annexed a segment of what was the Kingdom of Kabul to the Sikh Kingdom.

Nalwa was the consummate example of the Sikh saint-soldier, and India owes much to his strategic genius. His descendants live in India and abroad. This runs counter to the story of Maharajah Ranjit Singh's line, which was forever destroyed by the British, who abducted his children and took them to England, where they were held hostage against the threat of India rising against British rule. Nalwa was the senior most member of Ranjit's court. His son, Jawahir Singh, led the famous charge at the Battle of Chillianwala, a battle in which the British suffered a retreat. Another son, Arjan Singh, also posed a tough challenge to the British as they struggled to annex the Punjab.

Plaudits

A very popular 19th century British newspaper, Tit-Bits, made a comparative analysis of great generals of the world and arrived at the following conclusion:

"Some people might think that Napoleon was a great General. Some might name Marshall Hendenburgh, Lord Kitchener, General Karobzey or Duke of Wellington etc. And some going further might say Halaku Khan, Genghis Khan, Changez Khan, Richard or Allaudin etc. But let me tell you that in the North of India a General of the name of Hari Singh Nalwa of the Sikhs prevailed. Had he lived longer and had the sources and artillery of the British, he would have conquered most of Asia and Europe...."

Hari Singh Nalwa's meeting with various British and a German travellers are recorded. Baron Charles von Hügel remembers him fondly in his memoirs. He met the Sardar at his residence in

Gujranwala. On that occasion the German was gifted a portrait of Nalwa in the act of killing a tiger. Hari Singh Nalwa was fluent in the Persian language. He was also conversant with Punjabi, Gurmukhi script and Pushtu, the latter being the language of the Pashtuns. He was familiar with world politics, including details about the European states.

He rebuilt the Bala Hisar Fort in Maharaja Ranjit Singh's name.

Accolades continued coming long after Sardar Hari Singh Nalwa's death. Pannikar perhaps sums him up best — "The noblest and the most gallant of the Sikh generals of his time, the very embodiment of honour, chivalry, and courage..."

Dewan Mokham Chand

"Mokham Chand, the most distinguished of the durbars generals, was the son of Waisakhi Mal, a Khatri tradesman of the village Kunjah near Gujarat.. "

"The most distinguished of the generals, by whose skill and courage Ranjit Singh rose from a subordinate chiefship to the Empire of the Punjab, was Diwan Mokham Chand. The sagacity with which the Maharaja selected his officers was reason of his uniform success... "

Ranjit Singh had seen him in action at Akalgarh three years earlier and again in the Fight against the Bhangi Sardar of Gujarat. Mokham Chand had fallen out with his Bhangi master and had come to Ranjit for employment. Ranjit welcomed him with handsome gifts of an elephant and horses and granted him the Dallewalia possessions as a Jagir. He was made commander of a cavalry unit with power to recruit 1500 foot soldiers as well.

"In the beginning of 1808 various places in the Upper Punjab were taken from their independent Sikh proprieters, and brought under the direct management of the new kingdom of Lahore, and Mokham Chand was at the same time employed in effecting a settlement of the territories which had been seized on the left bank of the Sutlej. But Ranjit Singh's systematic aggression had begun to excite fear in the minds of the Sikhs of Sirhind "

Diwan Mohkam Chand was the Commander-in-Chief of the Sikh Forces from 1806 to 1814 A.D.

He died at Phillaur on October 16, 1814. His son Moti Ram and grandson Ram Dayal also served the state with distinction.

Ghaus Mohammad

Ghaus Mohammad Khan (1915 – 1982) from Lucknow was the first Indian to reach the Quarter Finals in the Wimbledon in 1939 where he lost to American tennis player Bobby Riggs.

Veer Singh

Veer Singh Dillon (1792–1842) was a legendary Sikh warrior who was born in Gurdaspore, Punjab. He was the a general in the army of Maharaja Ranjit Singh and was the founder of one of the most highly honoured Sikh warrior famalies.

Veer Singh was awarded the Title Jallaha of Gurdaspore after his army single handedly won the eastern areas of Punjab for the Maharaja. Later when the Sikh Empire fell to the British forces, the armies of the Jallaha of Gurdaspore (now under the son of Veer Singh) were not defeated due to their strong defences. But later the British signed a treaty with the ruler in which his areas would come under the British Empire but the Jallaha would still remain the supreme commander of the military forces and also the chief administrator of the area.

Early Life

Veer Singh was born in a Dhillon Jatt Sikh family, and was raised a Nihang. He was a master in the art of Gatka a Sikh martial art. At an early age his family was forced out of Gurdaspore (now Gurdaspur a district in India) after the Raja of Kapurthala attacked the rather peaceful town. Later Veer Singh led his armies against the Raja, and won back Gurdaspore.

Military Career

Singh participated in the following conquests: Sialkot, Kasur (1807), Multan (1818), Kashmir (1819), Pakhli & Damtaur (1821-2), and finally Gurdapore (1831). He served as the governor of Peshawar for a short period and was later Jallaha (duke) of Gurdaspore.

Legacy

Almost every generation of Veer Singh's family made an impact on history of India. The army of Jallaha in Gurdaspore was the only army which sided with the Indian rebels in 1857. Subsequently, when the empire fell into the hands of the British throne, the royals of Britons did not want to lose the support of the Sikhs who by now had only the Jallaha as their leader. So in 1858 when the British Crown was ruling over India let the Jallha retain his title and position he enjoyed earlier thus avoided trouble in Punjab. But under the treaty the army of the Jallha would now consist of Royal British officers who later plagued the Sikh army. The army of Jallaha was officially included into the Royal British Forces in 1862 as the "The Royal Sikh Infantry" and "The Sikh Cavalry," (now called the Sikh regiment, part of the army of the Republic of India.) The Jallah was also officially given The Title of The "Duke of Gurdaspore" but the Jallaha preferred retaining Jallaha as his title so that he would be closer to his people. The Jallaha also refused British Army Rank of a General for himself.

He also retained the uniform for his forces, and the disc sword was retained as a part of the uniform. He urged the British officers of his forces also to wear the saffron colours on their uniform (which is still the uniform of the Sikh Regiment and the Disc sword is also still a ceremonial uniform of the Sikh Regiment in India. Veer Singh was a senior member of Ranjit's court. His sons posed a tough challenge to the British as they struggled to annex the Punjab. The armies of the Jallaha of Gurdaspore (now under the son of Veer Singh) were not defeated due to their strong defence. But later the British signed a treaty with the ruler in which his areas would also come under the British empire but Jallaha would still remain the supreme commander of the forces and also the chief administrator of the area.

The sons of Jallaha became a part of the British Forces but the later generations of the Jallaha were not content with the British rule did not serve the British in the armies, more famously Devinder Singh Jallah Gurdaspuriah formed an alliance with Subash Chandra Bose and raised a Sikh regiment in the unofficial Indian National Army and named it Maharaja Ranjit Singh Regiment after his Grandfather's King's name. Incidentally this regiment later was merged into the Sikh regiment of the Indian Army which was raised by Devinder Singh's great grandfather. After this mutainy by Devinder Singh, the official title awarded by the British was reversed. But the people of Gurdaspore and its neighbouring areas were loyal to the Jallaha. Thus after this act by the British, most of the Royal Sikh Regiment walked out of the army and protected the Jallaha and his family. This is one reason why the British never could take control of the official residence of the Jallaha, in fear of death by the very own men they trained. But this act greratly helped the Indian freedom movement. Firstly it weakened the British forces, and secondly it put many of trained men on the Indian side of the conflict.

After independence from the British was reached, the Jallaha never involved themselves in politics, and also never asked for the official declaration of their title. The descendants of Veer Singh still live in Gurdaspore, (Gurdaspur) and are sill referred to as Jallaha Gurdaspuriaha, with the title being handed down by the people of Gurdaspur to the first of them in the generation. The Jallahas still serve in the armed forces in India and form a part of the elite Regiments of the Army of the Republic Of India. They are cosidered to be masters of the martial art of Gatka. The People of Gurdaspore (Gurdaspur) consider them as the saviours of their land and honour.

Honours

A very popular nineteenth century British newspaper, Tit-Bits, wrote. "It is surprising how the important honour is to Sikhs, even when the last of them were being killed and defeated, a Sikh gave down his territory only if the honour of his people and his family was kept intact, which forced the mighty British royalty to bow down and give into his demands...and now the British who have to serve in his regiment have to wear his Uniform!"

Later Generations

Veer Singh's descendants live in his house in Gurdaspore.

The Jallahs of Gurdaspore still serve in the Army of the Republic Of India as a custom. They have been known as some of the best warriors of India and this falls true today. Also, they are the part of Elite Regiments in the Army of the Republic of India. The Jallahas have long stayed away from politics in India. The son of Devinder Singh was a war hero in the 1971 Indo-Pakistani conflict and has even won honours for the same, while his grandson is still actively serving in the Army of the republic of India and also played a role in the liberation of Freetown in West Africa on Behalf of the United Nations' forces. Even after the official title was abolished by the British the Jallhas remained one of the most powerful families in Gurdaspore and still continue as such.

Sawan Mal

Sawan Mal was the Khatri Diwan (governor) of Multan. He was originally from Gujranwala, the region where Maharaja Ranjit Singh's Misl, the Sukerchakias held sway. Along with Hari Singh Nalwa, he was one of the top commanders in Ranjit Singh's army. As a general under Ranjit Singh, he wrested the 'subah' (province) of Multan from the Durrani Afghans in 1823, after which he was made governor of the region, instituting improvements in agricultural production through irrigation schemes. He was succeeded to the governorship of Multan by his son, Mul Raj.

Inventor of the Sohan Halwa?

It is claimed that Sawan Mal invented a sweetmeat called *Sawan Halwa* or *Sohan Halwa* in 1750. This sweet was given as a gift to royal visitors and friends. It is now a popular confection in the Indian subcontinent. However this story may be of dubious authenticity since Diwan Sawan Mal was not even born in 1750. Perhaps there is an error in the date mentioned.

Descendants

Diwan Sawan Mal instituted vast improvement in agriculture, while his son, Diwan Mul Raj was instrumental in leading the revolt against the British to prevent the annexation of the Sikh Kingdom into East India Company territory. Diwan Sawan Mal's grandson, Harmohan Singh Rai Bahadur had betrayed the Lahore Durbar and joined hands with the regents of the British Crown and earned a Knighthood and the title of *Rai Bahadur* in the process. He was a general and the Jagirdar of Mithankot during the British Raj. They later migrated to India after the Partition. One of his Great Great Grandson is Believed to be living in Bangalore, by the name of Bakshi Yadavendra Singh Chopra. Diwan Mulraj's Grandson Diwan Sri Ram was the Governor of Gujranwala, Akalgarh, later migrated to India, Punjab after the partition. Another of his Great Grandson (son of Diwan Sri Ram) lived in Delhi, by the name of Diwan Bhim Sen-Om Prakash Chopra. He died in the year 2001 at the age of 91. His sons Pawan Chopra, Canadian national, is residing in Toronto, Canada and Dr. Arun Chopra in Hamburg, Germany. Dr. Deepak Chopra with his "The Chopra Centre-the path to wellness begins here" is living in San Diego, USA. Dr. Arun Chopra is instrumental in setting-up major

British, German, French and US-American companies in India and at the same time bringing Indian investors to these countries e.g. Dr. Arun Chopras "Planet Health-Worldwide Project". Thus Chopras are improving business, health care, educational and cultural relationship between Europe, USA and India on daily basis. There are four royal daughters namely Neha Chopra, Mallika Chopra, Sita Chopra and Sarah Chopra-Stari. The youngest of Chopra family's royal son Diwan Amit Chopra currently resides in Canada.

Trivia

There is a city in Punjab (Pakistan) called "Diwan Sawan Mal", which has been named after the Diwan

Sangat Singh Saini

Sangat Singh Saini served as a general in the army of Maharaja Ranjit Singh. He oversaw the operations in the Gurdaspur District. His headquarters were based in Batala. Sangat Singh was rewarded 300 acre estate from Maharaja Ranjit Singh for bravery in battle when Sangat Singh conquered a post in the Afghan region and brought back the Golden Sword of the Afghan ruler to Maharaja Ranjit Singh. The estate is now known as Sangatpur in Batala, Gurdaspur District, India.

General Zorawar Singh

Zorawar Singh Kahluria (1786-1841) was born in a village of Kahlur State (also called Bilaspur from its capital) in modern Himachal Pradesh, India.

His family belonged to the Kahluria clan of Rajputs—they migrated to the Jammu region where, on coming of age, Zorawar took up service under Raja Jaswant Singh of Marmathi (modern Doda district). In 1817 he joined the army of Maharaja Ranjit Singh, the state of Kashmir had become part of the Sikh Kingdom after a campaign against its Afghan rulers. Zorowar Singh was employed by the ambitious Maharaja Gulab Singh of Jammu and was placed under the commandant of the Reasi fort (Bhimgarh fort). While delivering a routine message to the Maharaja, Zorawar told him of the financial waste occurring in the fort administration and boldly presented his own scheme to effect savings. Gulab Singh was impressed by Zorawar's sincerity and appointed him commandant of Reasi. As promised, the Rajput youth fulfilled his task and his grateful ruler made him commissariat officer of all forts north of Jammu. He was later made governor of Kishtwar and was given the title of *Wazir* (prime minister). Like Kashmir, the Kingdom of Kishtwar was formed by a river valley (the Chenab flowing from Himachal Pradesh as the Chandrabhaga)—-the kingdom's ancient name was Kashtavat and it remained under Hindu rulers until the 17th Century when Raja Gairat Singh converted to Islam and received the title of *Raja Sa'adat Yar Khan* from the Mughal Emperor Aurangzeb.

Some of the people had also converted with their king but many remained true to their ancestral faith. Even though it was a newly conquered region Zorawar had no trouble in keeping the peace; many of the local Rajputs were recruited into his army. In 1835 the nearby region of Paddar was taken from Chamba (now in Himachal Pradesh) in the course of a battle. Paddar later became known for its sapphire mines. But this was a mere sideshow to General Zorawar Singh's more famous expeditions, on which he had already embarked in the previous year.

The Laddakh Campaigns

To the east of Kishtwar and Kashmir are the snow-clad mountains of the upper Himalayas — the rivers of Zanskar Gorge, Suru River, and Drass rise from these snows, and flow across the plateau of Laddakh into the Indus River. Several petty principalities in this region were tributary to the Gyalpo (King) of Laddakh. In 1834 one of these, the Raja of Timbus, sought Zorawar's help against the Gyalpo. Meanwhile the Rajput general had been burning to distinguish himself by expanding the territory of Raja Gulab Singh — also at that time, according to the Gulabnama, Kishtwar went through a drought that caused a loss of revenue and forced Zorawar to extract money through war.

The Rajputs of Jammu and Himachal have traditionally excelled in mountain fighting; therefore Zorawar had no trouble in crossing the mountain ranges and entering Laddakh through the source of the Suru River where his 5000 men defeated an army of local Botis. After moving to Kargil and subduing the landlords along the way Zorawar received the submission of the Ladakhis — however Tsepal Namgyal, the Gyalpo (ruler), sent his general Banko Kahlon by a roundabout route to cut off Zorawar's communications. The astute general doubled back to Kartse where he sheltered his troops through the winter. In the spring of 1835 he defeated the large Ladakhi army of Banko Kahlon and marched his victorious troops towards Leh. The Gyalpo now agreed to pay 50,000 rupees as war-indemnity and 20,000 rupees as an annual tribute.

Alarmed at the gains of the Dogras the Punjabi governor of Kashmir, Mehan Singh, incited the Ladakhi chieftains to rebel but Zorawar quickly marched back to the Himalayan valleys and subdued the rebels, now forcing the Raja of Zanskar to also pay a separate tribute to Jammu. But in 1836 Mehan Singh, who was in correspondence with the Lahore durbar, this time instigated the Gyalpo to revolt — Zorawar force-marched his army in ten days to surprise the Ladakhis and forced them to submit. He now built a fort outside Leh and placed there a garrison of 300 men under Dalel Singh — the Gyalpo was deposed to an estate and a Ladakhi general, Ngorub Stanzin, was made King. But the latter did not prove to be loyal hence the Gyalpo was restored to his throne in 1838.

Baltistan Campaign

To the northwest of Laddakh, and to the north of Kashmir, lies the region of Baltistan. Muhammad Shah, the son of the ruler of Skardu, Raja Ahmad Shah, fled to Leh and sought the aid of the Gyalpo and Zorawar against his father. But some of the Ladakhi nobles allowed Ahmad Shah to imprison his son and sought his aid in a general rebellion against the Dogras. After defeating the Ladakhi rebels Zorawar invaded Baltistan in the winter of 1841, adding a large contingent of Ladakhis to his army.

The advance brigade of 5,000 under Nidhan Singh lost its way in the cold and snow and was surrounded by the enemy; many soldiers perished from the cold. Then Mehta Basti Ram, a prominent Rajput from Kishtwar, established contact with the main force. On their arrival the Botis of Skardu were defeated and forced to flee. They were chased to the fort of Skardu which was invested by Zorawar for a few days. One night the Dogras scaled the steep mountain behind the fort and after some fighting captured the small fort on its crest. From this position the next day they began firing down at the main fort and forced the Raja to surrender. Zorawar built a fort on the banks of the Indus where he placed a contingent of his soldiers.

After placing Muhammad Shah on the throne for an annual tribute of 7000 rupees, a Dogra contingent under Wazir Lakhpat advanced westwards, conquered the fort of Astor and took its Darad Raja prisoner. However this Raja was tributary to Mehan Singh, the Punjabi Sikh governor of Kashmir, who was alarmed at the Dogra conquests since they only expanded the kingdom of Gulab Singh while not bringing any benefit to the Lahore durbar. His complaint at Lahore was forwarded to Raja Gulab Singh at Jammu and he ordered the Darad Raja to be released.

Tibet Expedition

With the Dogra ambitions clashing with the Punjabi empire in the west, Zorawar Singh turned his energies eastward, towards Tibet. As he had done in Laddakh, so too in the newly-conquered Baltistan, Zorawar recruited the Baltis in his army, which now had men from the Jammu hills, Kishtwar, and Laddakh. This five or six thousand strong army was divided into three columns that marched parallel into the unknown land of Tibet in May, 1841.

One column under the Ladakhi prince, Nono Sungnam, followed the course of the Indus River to its source. Another column of 300 men, under Ghulam Khan, marched along the mountains leading up to the Kailas Range and thus south of the Indus. Zorawar himself led 3,000 men along the plateau region where the vast and picturesque Pangong Lake is located. Sweeping all resistance before them, the three columns passed the Mansarovar Lake and converged at Gartok, defeating the small Tibetan force stationed there. The enemy commander fled to Taklakot but Zorawar stormed that fort on 6 September 1841. Envoys from Tibet now came to him as did agents of the Maharaja of Nepal, whose kingdom was only fifteen miles from Taklakot.

The fall of Taklakot finds mention in the report of the Chinese Imperial Resident, Meng Pao, at Lhasa:

On my arrival at Taklakot a force of only about 1,000 local troops could be mustered, which was divided and stationed as guards at different posts. A guard post was quickly established at a strategic pass near Taklakot to stop the invaders, but these local troops were not brave enough to fight off the Shen-Pa (Dogras) and fled at the approach of the invaders. The distance between Central Tibet and Taklakot is several thousand li...because of the cowardice of the local troops; our forces had to withdraw to the foot of the Tsa Mountain near the Mayum Pass. Reinforcements are essential in order to withstand these violent and unruly invaders.

Zorawar and his men now went on pilgrimage to Mansarovar and Mount Kailash. He had extended his communication and supply line over 450 miles of inhospitable terrain by building small forts and pickets along the way. The fort Chi-T'ang was built near Taklakot, where Mehta Basti Ram was put in command of 500 men, with 8 or 9 cannon. With the onset of winter all the passes were blocked and roads snowed in. The supplies for the Dogra army over such a long distance failed despite Zorawar's meticulous preparations.

As the intense cold, coupled with the rain, snow and lightning continued for weeks upon weeks, many of the soldiers lost their fingers and toes to frostbite. Others starved to death, while some burnt the wooden stock of their muskets to warm themselves. The Tibetans and their Chinese allies regrouped and advanced to give battle, bypassing the Dogra fort of Chi-T'ang. Zorawar and his men met them at the Battle of To-yo on 12 December 1841—-in the early exchange of fire the Rajput general was wounded in his right shoulder but he grabbed a sword in his left hand. The Tibetan horsemen then charged the Dogra position and one of them thrust his lance in Zorawar Singh's chest.

The Sino-Tibetan force then mopped up the other garrisons of the Dogras and advanced on Laddakh, now determined to conquer it and add it to the Imperial Chinese dominions. However the force under Mehta Basti Ram stood a siege for several weeks at Chi-T'ang before escaping with 240 men across the Himalayas to the British post of Almora. Within Laddakh the Sino-Tibetan army laid siege to Leh, when reinforcements under Diwan Hari Chand and Wazir Ratnu came from Jammu and repulsed them. The Tibetan fortifications at Drangtse were flooded when the Dogras dammed up the river. On open ground, the Chinese and Tibetans were chased to Chushul. The climactic Battle of Chushul (August, 1842) was fought and won by the Dogras who executed the enemy general to avenge the death of Zorawar Singh.

The Treaty of Chushul

"On this auspicious occasion, the second day of the month Asuj in the year 1899 we —-the officers of Lhasa, viz. firstly, Kalon

Sukanwala, and secondly Bakshi Sapju, commander of the forces of the Empire of China, on the one hand, and Dewan Hari Chand and Wazir Ratnu, on behalf of Raja Gulab Singh, on the other — -agree together and swear before God that the friendship between Raja Gulab Singh and the Emperor of China and Lama Guru Sahib Lassawala will be kept and observed till eternity; for the traffic in shawl, pasham, and tea. We will observe our pledge to God, Gayatri, and Pasi. Wazir Mian Khusal Chu is witness."

Estimate

Unlike so many other conquerors, General Zorawar Singh Kahluria was not despised or hated by the people whose lands he invaded. There is not a single word in any of the histories or traditional accounts about the rapacity or greed that comes naturally to most foreign invaders, and the same goes for his army. These Hindu invaders crossed the paths of people belonging to the Buddhist, Muslim, and Animist faiths and yet made no attempt to interfere with their religious practices. There were many monasteries filled with precious articles all through Laddakh and Tibet and yet there was not one instance of robbery or plunder.

Zorawar Singh's great military endeavours were balanced by a life of modesty and restraint. He was so honest that he would transfer to his master any gifts or tribute that came to him. This honest Rajput did not leave behind either vast properties or deep coffers for his descendants-— only a legacy of military achievement that caused the contemporary Europeans to term him the "little Napoleon of India".

Chattar Singh Attariwalla

General Chattar Singh Attariwalla, was a military commander and a member of the Sikh nobility during the period of the Sikh Empire in the mid-19th century in Punjab. He was also Governor of Hazara province and fought in the Second Anglo-Sikh War against the British. His son was General Sher Singh Attariwalla who with his army gave devastating blow to the British Army at Chillianwalah.

Balbhadra Kunwar

Balbhadra Kunwar was the commander of the Nepalese forces at the Battle of Nalapani in 1814 during the Anglo-Nepalese War.

Balbhadra Kunwar was handed responsibility of defending the area. Realizing he could not defend the town of Dehradun, he withdrew to the strategic hill fort of Khalanga with an army strength of 600 including women and children against the British stronghold of 3000. He turned down an incentive proposal of the British who would make him Governor of the Western Garhwal should he surrender or leave Nepal. The British attacked on October 31, but were repelled. Kunwar's marksmen killed General Gillespie and Colonel Alice of the British troops. They siege continued for a month until the British convinced that they could not win by military ways, blocked the source of water to the fort so that Nepalese would die of thirst. Ultimately after 4 days of thirst, without surrendering, Balbhadra emerged out of the fort with drawn kukris in his hands (along with other 70 survivors) and roared to the British-"You could have never won the battle but now I myself voluntarily abandon this fort. There is nothing inside the fort other than dead corpses of the children and women"! He and his party escaped into the hills on November 30, 1814. Later, Balbhadra retired to Punjab to the service of King Ranjit Singh and was ultimately killed in battle, by the Afghan artillery. The British commemorated his bravery with a stone inscription in Dehra Dun inscribing "in salute to our great opponent General Balbhadra and his brave Gurkhas......".

Mahan Singh Mirpuri

Sardar Raja Mahan Singh "Mirpuri" (also spelled Maan Singh "Mirpura"/"Mirpuria") was a famous General in the kingdom of Maharaja Ranjit Singh, and was the second-in-command to the famous General Sardar Hari Singh Nalwa. He was conferred by Maharaja Ranjit Singh the title of Raja for his conquests of Haripur, Nowshehra and Peshawar. The town of Mansehra derives its name from him.

Early Life

He was born a commoner in Gujranwala, in a Muhiyal family belonging to the Ambral branch of the Bali Clan. He was the grandson of Himmat Singh Bali, and his father Data Ram was a counsellor to Sultan Mukkarb Khan, the Gakhar Subedar of Gujrat.

Military Career and Later Life

While in Lahore in search of a job, he happened to participate in a hunting expedition of Maharaja Ranjit Singh, in which he caught the notice of the latter by single-handedly killing a leopard with his sword. Impressed by his valour, the Maharaja had him inducted into the army under the famous General Hari Singh Nalwa.

Mahan Singh played a key role in the battles of Peshawar and Kashmir, and in the 1818 siege of Multan, was seriously wounded two times. He went on to become second-in-command to Hari Singh Nalwa. In April 1837, he was the main defender of the Jamrud Fort, holding out against an invasion by Afghans. In the subsequent battle, Hari Singh Nalwa was done to death but Mahan Singh maintained the news secret until reinforcements arrived from Lahore.

Mai Desan, the widow of Hari Singh Nalwa, adopted Mahan Singh as her son and solemnized his marriage into a Mohan family of Gujranwala according to Muhiyal traditions.

Sardar Raja Mahan Singh he was murdered by his own soldiers in 1844, when mutiny broke out in the Sikh army.

Descendants

Mahan Singh had four sons, named Chhattar Singh, Himmat Singh, Sham Singh and Wadhawa Singh. His death at the hands of mutinying soldiers was avenged by Chhattar Singh, who was himself killed soon after. Himmat Singh's assistance to the British in the Indian Mutiny of 1857 on the orders of the Maharaja of Jammu fetched him awards from the latter. The widows of Chhattar Singh and Himmat Singh were later given pensions by the British government along with grants of agricultural land in Districts Jhelum and Gujranwala, and in Mirpur. Sardar Raja Mahan Singh's grandson Rai Sahib Bakshi Kartar Singh Bali was Vernacular Secretary in the Government of Kashmir under Maharaja Partap Singh, and President of the All India Mohyal Conference of 1906.

Jean-François Allard

Jean-François Allard (1785-1839), a French soldier and adventurer. Born in Saint Tropez, he became a soldier and was twice injured while serving in Napoleon's army. He was awarded the Legion d'honneur, and promoted to Captain of the 7th Hussars. After Waterloo, he drifted around and went to Persia where he visited Abbas Mirza to propose his services. He was promissed the position of a Colonel, but never actually received the troops corresponding to his function. In 1820, Allard left for Punjab, where he in 1822 entered the service of the Maharaja Ranjit Singh. He was commissioned to raise a corps of dragoons and lancers. On completion, Allard was awarded the rank of general, and became the leader of the European officer corps in the Maharaja's service.

Allard was a charming and gentle man, very different from some of the other European mercenaries in the Punjab. He also took the trouble learning Persian, and is said to have composed poetry in his new language.

In June 1834, Allard returned to France on leave, but returned 18 months later. He continued to serve the Maharaja until his death in 1839.

Another European taking service in the Punjab with Allard in 1822 was the Italian Jean-Baptiste Ventura. They were joined four years later by the Neapolitan Paolo Di Avitabile and the Frenchman Claude August Court. A Spaniard, Oms, also served with them for a while. Together, these officers drilled the Sikh army into a formidable force. Allard was awarded the Legion d'Honneur by Napoleon Bonaparte, and the Bright Star of the Punjab by Ranjit Singh. Allard was also an amateur numismatist and contributed greatly to the early study of Ancient Indian coins.

Jean-Baptiste Ventura

Jean-Baptiste Ventura (b. Giovanni Battista Reuben (also Rubino) Ventura in Finale Emilia near Modena, Italy ca. 1792-Toulouse, France ca. 1856) was a soldier, mercenary and adventurer who ended up in the Punjab.

Of Italian origin from Modena, Ventura, at the age of seventeen enrolled as a volunteer in the militia of the Kingdom of Italy, served with Napoleon's imperial army where he reached the rank of colonel of infantry. After Waterloo and the final downfall of Napoleon he returned to his home; but in 1817, yet known by the local authorities for his revolutionaries and Napoleonic sympathies owing to a dispute between him and a local member of the reactionary Ducal police, he was obliged to leave the country.

He went first to Triest, and then to Constantinople, where he was for a time a ship-broker.

Learning that Persia was seeking the services of European soldiers, he obtained an officer's commission, and helped to instruct the forces of the shah in European methods of warfare. He soon attained the rank of colonel. On the death of the shah in 1822, Ventura offered his services to his successor, 'Abbas Mirza. In the latter's service, however, were a number of English officers who were decidedly hostile to the French, with whom they classed Ventura on account of his having fought under Napoleon; and through their intrigues Ventura was dismissed.

He travelled east, ending in Lahore with Jean-François Allard in 1822. They took service with the Maharaja Ranjit Singh of Punjab, and soon got to prove their worth.

In March the following year, both Allard and Ventura held command in the Battle of Nowshera where a combined Afghan force was defeated, resulting in Punjab's capture of Peshawar.

A rebellion having arisen in Afghanistan, Ventura conducted successfully several campaigns of a difficult nature, and greatly enlarged the boundaries of the kingdom of Lahore.

Together with Allard, Paolo Di Avitabile and Claude August Court, Ventura formed the group of European mercenary officers responsible for the modernizing of the Sikh army, and the training and command of the Fauj-i-Khas, the European model brigade, with Ventura as its commander.

"...Jean Baptiste Ventura... reorganised the infantry into a formidable army including Gurkhas, Pathans, Biharis and Ooriyas."

He is also described as "the baron of the Fauj-i-Khas".

Ventura was highly thought of by the Maharajah, and in addition to the rank of General, he was also appointed *kazi* and Governor of Lahore. He rose rapidly in the Darbar and virtually became the Commander In Chief of the Darbar forces.

Ventura married an Indian (or a local Armenian according other sources) lady, by whom he had a daughter; but he was always desirous of returning to his native country. In 1837 he went on a diplomatic mission to Paris and London, but was recalled to Lahore before he had time to visit his family in Europe.

He spent his spare time in Peshawar exhuming Bactrian Greek and Kushan coins from Buddhist stupas in the Khyber Pass, making numerous excavations then sending the findings on to the Asiatic

Society of Bengal in Calcutta. On the death of Ranjit Sinh, Ventura took part in the contest for the succession, and remained in the service of the new raja, Dhulip Singh. During the reign of the latter, Ventura continued his career of conquest.

He served faithfully under Ranjit Sing and his successors Kharak Singh, Nau Nihal Singh and Sher Singh until his retirement in 1843. Taking his fortune with him, he lived out his days in comfort in Paris.

In France he presented King Louis Philippe with a set of ancient Greek coins which he had unearthed, and which were evidences of the march through that country of Alexander the Great.

In his later years he lost a part of his large fortune in unsuccessful commercial enterprises. According to Flaminio Servi, Ventura received baptism toward the end of his life.

Paolo Avitabile

General Paolo Bartolomeo Avitabile (*Abu Tabela*) (25 October 1791 – 28 March 1850) was an Italian soldier, mercenary and adventurer. A peasant's son born in Agerola, near Amalfi in Italy, he served in the Neapolitan militia during the Napoleonic wars. After Waterloo he drifted east like many other adventurous soldiers. He first served as a mercenary in Persia, before he was hired by the Maharaja Ranjit Singh of the Punjab.

Career in Europe

The young Avitabile served in the local levies of the Kingdom of Naples between 1807 and 1809, when he joined the artillery of the regular army. As a part of the Imperial Army, Avitabile served under Murat on several campaigns. In these campaigns he earned the rank of Lieutenant, as well as the command of the 15th Battery. After the fall of Napoleon and the defeat of Murat at Tolentino, Naples was restored to Ferdinand I of Sicily. Avitabile retained his rank and command and joined the army of the new Kingdom of Two Sicilies, where he joined the siege of Gaeta under the command of the Austrian general Delaver.

During this siege, he displayed great bravery and was wounded twice. The general recommended him for a promotion and a decoration, but was not heard. Avitabile was transferred instead to a position of lieutenant in a regiment of light infantry. It is said he quit in disgust over this treatment. His European career had come to an end.

In Persia

Having quit the army in Naples, Avitabile set his eyes on a career abroad. His initial idea was to, as many of his countrymen, seek fortune in America but this ended in a shipwreck off Marseille. Instead, he was advised to seek employment to the east. In Constantinople he was approached by an agent of the Persian Shah Fath Ali Shah recruiting European officers; in 1820, Avitabile took service with the Persian Shah. He remained in this employment for six years, during which period he rose to the rank of *khan* and a grade of colonel in the Persian army. Here he also met Claude August Court who would later accompany him on the travel to Punjab. Avitabile was rewarded for his services by two of Persia's highest decorations as Grand Commander of *The Lion and Sun* and of *The Two Lions and Crown*, but found the pay lacking. When he heard favourable notice from Jean-Baptiste Ventura of his employment in Punjab Ventura again broke up to travel further to the east.

In Punjab

Together with Court, Avitabile arrived in Lahore in 1827 and was hired by the Maharaja Ranjit Singh. While Court was given a position with the artillery, Avitabile was given a civilian position as governor of Wazirabad. It would seem he was an able administrator, as he held the position for the next seven years. He governed the city with a firm-at times, cruel-hand and managed to impose order and discipline. As a result, Wazirabad prospered.

In 1834 he was appointed governor of Peshawar, an area the Maharaja had conquered from the Afghans the previous year. Predominantly a Muslim Afghan province, the unruly region had proved too much of a task to govern for the Sikhs.

His rule of Wazirabad is described as just and rigorous, and his governorship of Peshawar as a rule of "gallows and gibbets".

With a ruthless, at times brutal, style of government, Avitabile established order in the province where he became known as Abu Tabela. Summary executions became usual, and it is said that he would have people executed by throwing them from the top of Mahabat Khan's mosque. While this brutality was shocking to visiting Europeans (in the words of Sir Henry Lawrence: *he acts like a savage among savage men, instead of showing them that a Christian can wield the iron sceptre without staining it by needless cruelty*), it proved both successful in maintaining order and even popular among the peaceful inhabitants.

His iron fist rule over Peshawar has made a place for him in local folklore. Even today unruly children in the city are brought to control by invoking Abu Tabela's name. In times of unrest, law-abiding citizens send a small wish for the return of an Abu Tabela to finally re-impose law and order.

As governor of Peshawar, Avitabile controlled the southern entrance to the Khyber Pass. The control of this strategic position, brought him in contact with the British army during the First Anglo-Afghan War (1839-42), where he was able to render vital assistance. During Elphinstone's advance in 1839, the British were well received in Peshawar and their officers received a princely treatment. Captain Havelock spent a month in Peshawar, and describes the splendour of Avitabile's court in his memoirs. He also gives a favourable characterization of the governor: *"He is, moreover, a frank, gay, and good-humoured person, as well as an excellent and skilful officer."*

Avitabile was also a scholar and an engineer, who worked very closely with the most brilliant Sikh engineer Lehna Singh Majithia.

When the British returned in 1842, to avenge the defeat of Elphinstone, they were given every possible assistance by Avitabile's government. In addition to supplies and transportation, he also personally advanced large sums of money to the British campaign treasury. By lending the British as much as ten lakhs (1 million) of rupees, he not only helped them paying their troops. He also managed to transfer a considerable fortune to safety in Europe.

Avitabile remained in the position of Governor during the First Anglo-Afghan War until he left in 1843. Having secured his retirement in Europe, he resigned his position to return home.

Back Home

As one of the few European adventurers in the area, he succeeded in building a fortune and getting away with it. He returned to Naples, where he built a grand home in San Lazzaro

(Agerola). He died soon after marrying a local girl: Enrichetta Coccia. The following legal battle over his inheritance, and the many distant relatives asserting their claims, made *Avitabile's cousin* something of a byword in Italy.

Descendants

Avitabile's family is spread throughout Naples and the United States, where his name was changed to "Avitable" by registrars at Ellis Island, who were misinformed by a typographical error on the passenger manifest from the Italian Steam Navigation Company.

Claude Auguste Court

Claude Auguste Court was a French soldier and mercenary.

He was hired by Maharaja Ranjit Singh of Punjab in 1827 to organize and train the artillery. He was promoted to the rank of General, and served as one of the leading European officers in the Khalsa.

Early Life

Court was born at Saint Cezaire, France, on 24 September 1793..He was educated at the Ecole Polytechnique in Paris

Military Career in French Army

In 1813, he joined the French army. After Napoleon's defeat at Waterloo in 1815 he was dismissed from service. He left France in 1818 for Baghdad and joined the Persian forces which were trained at Kermanshah by a handful of ex-officers of Napoleon's army including Ventura. While in Persia, he met another Neapolitan adventurer Avitabile and together they travelled on to Lahore reaching there in early 1827.

Military Services with Maharaja Ranjit Singh of Punjab

Maharaja Ranjit Singh gave Court employment in the artillery befitting his talents and scientific attainments. Court was responsible for the training of artillerymen, the organization of batteries and the establishment of arsenals and magazines on European lines. The Maharaja had his own foundries for casting guns and for the manufacture of shells. Court supervised these in collaboration with Sardar Lahina Singh Majithia. When Court produced the first shell at the Lahore foundry, the Maharaja bestowed upon him an prize of Rs 30,000, and when he produced the fuse, he was rewarded with an award of Rs 5,000. Court received a salary of Rs 2,500 per month, besides ajagir.

Expedition and Battles

He took part in the expedition of Peshawar (1834) and the battle of Jamrud (1837). He was promoted to general in 1836.

Role During Struggle for Succession of Ranjit Singh

Claude Auguste Court continued to serve the State after the death of Maharaja Ranjit Singh. After the death of Kanvar Nau Nihal Singh on 5 November 1840, Court along with Ventura sided with Sher Singh who was installed as Maharaja, with their help in investing the Fort of Lahore, on 20 January 1841.

Later Life and Death

After Maharaja Sher Singh's assassination in September 1843, he fled to Firozpur, in British territory, and, ultimately securing his discharge from the Sikh army, proceeded with his Punjabi wife and the children to France in 1844. He purchased an estate in the countryside and a residence in the city of Paris where he lived until his death in 1880.

Interest in Coin Collection

Court was one of the first Europeans to become interested in the coins of South Asia, which he collected from 1829. All trace of the collection vanished until 1994, however, when three albums came to light in an English book sale. They contain 627 rubbings, allowing many of Court's coins to be identified. These had been bought by Alexander Cunningham and entered the British Museum with his collection in 1888–94. Cunningham may also have owned the albums.

Alexander Gardner (Soldier)

Alexander Haughton Campbell Gardner (*Gordana Khan*) (1785-1877) was a soldier and mercenary. He travelled to Afghanistan and Punjab and served in various military positions in the region.

By his own accounts he was born in Wisconsin to a Scottish father and an Anglo-Spanish mother, but it has been alleged that he in reality was Irish, from Congloose. He was trained as an artillery gunner, most likely by the British army, and served most of his life as a mercenary in Central Asia. Originally, he had tried to secure a position in the Russian Army. Failing this, he drifted east and south, into Central Asia. Eventually, he reached Afghanistan and joined the rebel Habibullah Khan fighting against Dost Mahommed Khan. Gardner's wife, a local, and his baby were murdered by Dost Mahommed's forces. Gardner left Afghanistan as an outlaw for Punjab in August 1831, where he was appointed Commandant of Artillery. He served in this position for many years before he was transferred to the service of Maharaja Ranjit Singh, where he was one of between 32 and 100 Western soldiers in Ranjit's army. He later promoted to the rank of Colonel by Maharaja Ranjit Singh.

Gardner was involved in numerous gunfights and sword fights during his career. He was described as being six foot, with a long beard, an all around warrior and fighter. Gardner was known to have saved the City of Lahore in 1841 when his comrades abandoned him and he fired the guns that killed 300 enemies.

Gardner remained in the service of the Maharajas as they came and went, and witnessed the fall of the Punjab as a sovereign kingdom. This he vividly described in his book *The Fall of Sikh Empire*. In his old age he retired to Jammu then to Srinagar, where he died, well into his nineties.

Gardner's adventures are recounted in *Memoirs of Alexander Gardner: Soldier and Traveler* Edited by Major Hugh Pearse.

Gardner appears as a major supporting character in the novel Flashman and the Mountain of Light.

Conquests

Ranjit Singh's early conquests were minor and forgettable when he was a young misldar (baron) but by the end of his reign he had conquered vast tracts of territory, and in 1799, he even captured Lahore, (which is now located in Pakistan).

After the capture of Lahore, he rapidly annexed the rest of the Punjab. The war rose to a climax at the battle of Multan. Thereafter he was the undisputed ruler of Punjab, the Land of the Five Rivers. To secure his empire, he defeated the Pashtun militias and tribes of the tribal areas of Afghanistan. The Muslim Mughals, at this time, had already lost their empire due to their internal fightings, thus causing famous Rajput revolt, the re-establishment of the

Maharana of Mewar and the rising power of the Marathas during the 1700s. In the year 1819, Ranjit Singh successfully annexed Kashmir. Ranjit Singh lead the Sikh army and invaded Sewad (the Peshawar area) in 1818 wresting it from Afghanistan and making it a part of the Sikh Empire. In 1820 he annexed Hazara. In 1823, he defeated a large Afghan army at Nowshera, on the banks of the Kabul River.

Geography of the Sikh Empire

The Sikh Empire was also known as Punjab, the Sikh Raj, and the Khalsa Raj, was a region straddling the border into modern-day People's Republic of China and Islamic Republic of Afghanistan. The name of the region "Punjab" or "Panjab", comprises two words "Punj/Panj" and "Ab", translating to "five" and "water" in Persian.

When put together this gives a name meaning "the land of the five rivers", coined due to the five rivers that run through the Punjab. Those "Five Rivers" are Beas, Ravi, Sutlej, Chenab and Jhelum, all tributaries of the river Indus, home to the Indus Valley Civilization that perished 3000 years ago. Punjab has a long history and rich cultural heritage. The people of the Punjab are called Punjabis and they speak a language called Punjabi. The following modern day political divisions made up the historical Sikh Empire:

- Punjab region till Multan in south.
    - Punjab, India
    - Punjab, Pakistan
    - Haryana, India. Including Chandigarh.
    - Himachal Pradesh, India.
- Kashmir, conquered in 1818, India/Pakistan/China.
    - Jammu, India
    - Gilgit, Northern Areas, Pakistan (Occupied from 1842-1846).
- Khyber Pass, Afghanistan/Pakistan.
    - Peshawar, Pakistan (taken in 1818, retaken in 1834)
    - North-West Frontier Province and FATA, Pakistan (documented from Hazara (taken in 1818, again in 1836) to Bannu).
- Parts of Western Tibet (1841), China.

Legacy and Aftermath

After Maharaja Ranjit Singh died in 1839, after a reign of nearly forty years, leaving seven sons by different queens. He was cremated. His ceremony was performed by both Sikh and Hindu priests, his wife Maharani Mahtab Devi Sahiba, the Princess of Kangra, daughter of Maharaja Sansar Chand, the Empress of Punjab, committed Sati with Ranjit's body as Ranjit's head lay in her lap, some of the other wives also joined her and committed Sati. The throne went to his eldest son Kharak Singh, who was not entirely fit and prepared to rule such a vast empire. Some historians believe that the other heirs would have forged an even more durable, independent and powerful empire, had they come to the throne before Kharak Singh. However, the empire began to crumble due to poor governance and political infighting among his heirs. The princes died through internal plots and assassinations, while the nobility struggled to maintain power.

In 1845 after the First Anglo-Sikh War, Ranjit Singh's Empire was defeated and all major decisions were managed by the British East India Company. The Army of Ranjit Singh was reduced, under the peace treaty with the British, to a nominal force. Those who gave the stiffest resistance to the British were severely punished and their wealth confiscated. Eventually, Ranjit Singh's youngest son Dalip Singh, was crowned to the throne of Punjab in 1843 succeeding his brother, Maharajah Sher Singh. In 1849, at the end of the Second Anglo Sikh War, it was annexed by the British India from Dalip. Thereafter, the British took, Maharaja Dalip Singh, to England in 1854, where he was put under the protection of the Crown. Dalip Singh's mother, Maharani Jind Kaur, escaped and made her way to Nepal where she was given refuge by Sri Teen Maharaja Jung Bahadur Rana of Nepal, who then negotiated on her behalf to allow her to be reunited with her son. Maharani Jind Kaur and her son met at Spence's Hotel, Calcutta, on the 16th January 1861, after some thirteen and half years apart. She was granted permission to come to England. A residence was taken up at No. 1 Lancaster Gate (Now No.23).

Jind Kaur stayed for a short while at Mulgrave Castle, later she was placed in the charge of an English lady at Abingdon House, Kensington. On the morning of the 1 August 1863, Maharani Jind Kaur died peacefully. Her body was temporarily housed at London's Kensal Green Cemetery, and in the Spring of 1864, Duleep

Singh left for India and arranged for the cremation of her body. In the spring of 1864, Maharani Jind Kaur was cremated at Nasik in Bombay on the Panchvati side of the River. The authorities would not allow Dalip Singh to cremate his mother in the Punjab. On the left bank the Maharajah erected a small samadh built as a memorial in the memory of his mother. For a number of years the Kapurthala State Authorities maintained the memorial until 1924, when her remains were dug out and brought to Lahore by her granddaughter, Princess Bamba Sutherland and deposited at the Samadh of Maharajah Ranjit Singh.

Dalip Singh was converted to Christianity in his youth, upon reuniting with his mother during his adult years, he reconverted to Sikhism, he then petitioned the Crown to have his kingdom returned. He never received any justice or the respect he deserved. He died in 1893, Paris, France.

Maharajah Dalip Singh had three sons. The eldest Prince Victor was born on the 10 July 1866, followed by Prince Frederick in 1868, and then Prince Albert Edward Alexander Dalip Singh (died at the age of thirteen), who was born on the 20 August 1879.

Prince Victor Albert Jay Dalip Singh was Maharajah Dalip Singh's eldest son. He was honourable A.D.C. to Halifax, and was promoted to Captain in 1894, but his military career, however, was a shamble, his interest lied in other things and he resigned in 1898. During the First World War, he was ordered to remain in Paris and not to leave, but shortly after the war ended, Prince Victor died on the 7 June 1918, without any issue.

Princess Sophia, the youngest of the Maharajah's daughters. On the 22 August 1948, Princess Sophia died in her sleep. Her solicitor arranged for the cremation at Golders Green on the 26 August. It was her request that her ashes be taken to India for burial.

Princess Catherine was born on the 27 October 1871, and was named Catherine Hilda Dalip Singh. Princess Catherine died peacefully in her bed on the night of Sunday 8 November 1942 at her home in Penn, aged seventy-one. The cause of death was said to be heart failure. She was cremated.

Princess Ada Irene Helen Beryl Dalip Singh, born on 25 October, 1889. Tragically on the 8 October 1926, she committed suicide, local fishermen dragged her body out from the sea, off Monte

Carlo. She was apparently much aggrieved with the death of her brother Prince Frederick who had died two months earlier.

Princess Pauline Alexandrina Dalip Singh, born 26 December, 1887, her death was unrecorded, she disappeared in war-torn France during the Second World War

Princess Bamba Sutherland (Princess Bamba Sofia Jindan Dalip Singh) was born on the 29 September 1869 in London, a year after her brother Prince Frederick. In England, Princess Bamba began styling herself as the Queen of Punjab. She was truly her father's daughter and had her father's rebellious nature and seemed to be the more aggrieved one among her siblings. She was the most affected at the realisation of who she was and her ancestry. She was often visited by her cousin Karl Wilhelm, grandson of Ludwig Muller, at Hilden Hall, by which time she was already dreaming of going back to India in order to die there. In his memoirs Karl Wilhelm referred to Princess Bamba as 'the true heiress of Ranjit Singh' meaning that she was most conscious of the actual desperate situation of the whole family. 'She considered the Punjab and Kashmir as the lost possession of her family and was absolutely furious when the border between Pakistan and India was drawn right across the Punjab.' In Princess Bamba's eyes, Pakistan or India did not exist, there was just the Punjab and its capital Lahore. She met with distant relatives throughout her travels in India, trying to grasp one last glimpse of the glory that she was denied. She located the families of Wazir Ishwari Singh Katoch of Kangra and Hari Singh Nalwa, both residing in Nabha at the time. She met with the several Hindu and Sikh royal families in an attempt to prevent the division of her grandfather's empire.

On the 10 March 1957, Princess Bamba, the daughter of Maharaja Dalip Singh, died of heart failure at the age of eighty-nine. She had outlived her entire family and the final chapter of a tragic family was completed and finally laid to rest. Her funeral was conducted in a Christian ceremony in Lahore. Her rites witnessed by a select few Pakistani dignitaries, the Pakistani authorities did not allow for any of her distant relatives to attend, Sikh or Hindu, nor were any Sikhs in Pakistan allowed to attend her rites, thus there were sadly no Sikhs were present at Princess Bamba's funeral, the last of Dalip Singh's line. Maharaja Ranjit Singh is remembered for uniting the Punjab as a strong nation and his possession of the Koh-i-noor diamond. Ranjit Singh willed the

Koh-i-noor to Jagannath Temple in Orissa while on his deathbed in 1839. His most lasting legacy was the golden beautification of the Harmandir Sahib, most revered Gurudwara of the Sikhs, with marble and gold, from which the popular name of the "Golden Temple" is derived.

He was also known as Sher-e-Punjab which means the Lion of Punjab and is considered one of the 3 Lions of modern India, the most famous and revered heroes in Indian subcontinent's history. While Emperor Rajaraja Chola and Ashoka were the 2 most powerful Indian kings of history, they are not named among the 3 Lions. The other 2 Lions are Rana Pratap Singh of Mewar and Chhatrapati Shivaji, the legendary Maratha ruler. The title of Sher-e-Punjab is still widely used as a term of respect for a powerful man.

Captain Murray's Memoirs on Maharaja Ranjit Singh's Character

Ranjit Singh has been likened to Mehmet Ali and to Napoleon. There are some points in which he resembles both; but estimating his character with reference to his circumstances and positions, he is perhaps a more remarkable man than either. There was no ferocity in his disposition and he never punished a criminal with death even under circumstances of aggravated offense. Humanity indeed, or rather tenderness for life, was a trait in the character of Ranjit Singh. There is no instance of his having wantonly imbused his hand in blood."

Many famous folk stories about Maharaja portray a leader and the inspiration Maharaja Ranjit Singh was. In one famous incident, when Maharaja was about to cross the badly flooded river near Attock (now in Pakistan and called Kabul River). One of Maharaja's generals reported this fact to Maharaja, saying that the river cannot be crossed and it is now an Atak (an obstacle in Hindi) for us. Maharaja retorted *"eh Attock uhna lai atak hai, jehna de dillan wich atak hai"* or "This river Attock is an obstacle for those, who have obstacles in their hearts", then crossed the river successfully. The army and other generals followed his lead.

Another famous folk story about Maharaja is that he was accidentally hit by a stone thrown by a 5 year old boy, who actually wanted to hit a fruit tree to knock down some of its fruit. When he was brought before Maharaja, Ranjit Singh gave him a gold coin. He said, "How can I punish him for hitting me with a stone, when this tree will give him fruit for the same?"

Kharak Singh

Maharaja Kharak Singh was a Sikh ruler of the sovereign country of Punjab and the Sikh Empire. He was the eldest legitimate son of Ranjit Singh and Maharani Datar Kaur. He succeeded his father in June 1839. He was removed from power on 8 October 1839 and replaced by his son Prince Nau Nihal Singh. He became a prisoner and died from a slow poisoning on 5 November 1840.

Nau Nihal Singh

Maharaja Nau Nihal Singh (9 March 1821-6 November 1840) was a Sikh ruler of the sovereign country of Punjab and the Sikh Empire. He was the son of Maharaja Kharak Singh, himself eldest son and heir of Maharaja Ranjit Singh.

After the death of Ranjit Singh, Kharak Singh became king but was unable to keep control of the various factions within the kingdom. Prince Nau Nihal took control of the state himself.

Upon Kharak Singh's death, Nau Nihal Singh was in line to become king. However, whilst returning from his father's funeral, he was injured when a building collapsed upon him. His body was taken to a tent away from the courtiers, who were not allowed into the presence of the prince. Eyewitnesses described his initial injuries as being small blows to the head which knocked him unconscious. Later when the tent was opened Nau Nihal Singh was dead, his head having been smashed in, possibly with a rock. It is unclear whether the building's collapse was accidental or deliberate and who was responsible. The most likely culprits were the Dogra brothers, Gulab Singh and Dhian Singh is maintained by Sikh fundamentalists.

Maharaja Sher Singh (1807-1843)

Sher Singh Maharaja, Sikh sovereign of the Punjab from January 1841 until his death in September 1843, was the son of Maharaja Ranjit Singh, born on 4 December 1807 to Mahitab Kaur, the Maharaja's first wife. Sher Singh grew up into a handsome, broad-chested young man. His soldierly mien made him popular with the army. He loved hunting and hawking, and devoted attention to cultivating European interests and hobbies in the company of foreigners serving at the Sikh court. In 1829, Maharaja Ranjit Singh conferred upon him civil and military honours and the privilege of sitting on a chair in the Darbar. Sher Singh took part in many of the campaigns undertaken by the Maharaja for the expansion of his kingdom. In May 1831, he defeated at Balakot, in Hazara district the turbulent Sayyid Ahmad Barelavi who had started a *jihad* against the Sikh rule. From 1831 to 1834 he acted as governor of the province of Kashmir. He was one of the army commanders who led in 1834 forces in Peshawar and who finally seized the city from the Afghans.

In the political vacuum cretaed by the deaths in November 1840 successively of Maharaja Kharak Singh and his son Kanvar Nau Nihal Singh, Sher Singh staked his claim to the throne of the Punjab. Another major contestent was Rani Chand Kaur, Kharak Singh's widow, who sent for Gulab Singh Dogra from Jammu to counteract the influence of his brother, Raja Dhian Singh, who had declared support for Sher Singh. Dhian Singh suggested several compromises. Chand Kaur could marry Sher Singh or, being childless could adopt Sher Singh's son Pratap Singh as her son. However, Chand Kaur asserted that Nau Nihal Singh's widow was pregnant and might give birth to a rightful successor. Ultimately an arrangement was arrived at under which Chand Kaur was to act as regent for her expected grandson, while Sher Singh would function as vice-regent and head of the council of regency, and Dhian Singh as the principal minister. But the triumvirate failed to work in unison. A few days later, two powerful Sandhanvalia Sardars, Atar Singh and Ajit Singh, collaterals of the royal contenders for the throne, arrived in Lahore and took over control. On 2 December 1840, Chand Kaur was proclaimed the Maharani of the Punjab, with the title of Malika Muqaddasa, emperess immaculate. The next day Sher Singh left Lahore for his estate in Batala. A month later, Dhian Singh Dogra was compelled to quit the capital, and Chand Kaur and the Sadhanvalias gained complete control of the administration.

Sher Singh still had the support of the army and most of the crack regiments had gone over to his side. The European officers were with him too. In January, 1841, he arrived in Lahore with at the head of a considerable force. Chand Kaur had appointed Gulab Singh Dogra as commander-in-chief and charged him with defending the city. She cleared the soldiers arrears of pay for four months, and lavished presents of gold bangles, necklaces and shawls on the officers. She issued orders to the city bankers forbidding them to lend money to Sher Singh. But the situation turned decisively in favour of Sher Singh, when regiments stationed outside the city-walls joined him in a body. He finally had with him 26,000 infrantry, 8,000 horses, and 45 guns, whereas Chand Kaur was left with only 5,000 men, a few guns and a limited quantity of gunpowder.

Sher Singh forced his way into the city, and made a proclaimation assuring safety of life and property to the citizens and offering pardon to those who would come over to him. The leading courtiers made their submission and forwarded a joint appeal to Chand Kaur and Gulab Singh Dogra to lay down arms. The Maharani, however chose to fight. For two days, Sher Singh's artillery shelled the fort, but with little effect. On the evening of 17 January 1841, Dhian Singh Dogra arrived and secured a ceasefire. Chand Kaur was persuaded to accept a jagir and relinquish her claim to the throne. At midnight Gulab Singh dogra and his soldiers evacuated the Fort, taking with them all the State's hoard of gold and jewels. From among the Sandhanvalia supporters of Chand Kaur, Ajit Singh fled to seek help from Mr. Cler, British political agent in Ludhiana, and, on his refusal to receive him, he proceeded to Calcutta to see the Governor-General. Ajit Singh's uncle, Atar Singh, also sought asylum in the British territory.

Sher Singh occupied the fort and ascended the throne on 20 January 1841, though the formal tilak (anointment) ceremony was performed a week later on 27 January by Baba Bikrama Singh Bedi of Una. His son Kanvar Pratap Singh, received a Khillat as heir apparent and Dhian Singh Dogra as Wazir or minister. In the second half of July, Sher Sigh married the daughter of the Raja of Suket. Known in the palace as Rani Dukno, she earned fame as one of the most beautiful women of her time. The match was made on the recommendation of Lahina Singh Majithia woh conducted the preparatory negotiations.

Sher Singh forbore from taking any reprisals and treated generously even those who had opposed him. Through a proclamation by the beat of drum, he assured the people of Lahore peace and security. The army was warned not to molest the citizens in any manner, and the commanders were cautioned exercise maximum vigilance to this end. But since the Maharaja was not able to redeem his promises of rewards to the troops(as Gulab Singh Dogra had stole and carried away the state treasury to Jammu), they went berserk, killing regimental accountants and officers, who they suspected of having embezzled their wages or having dealings with the English, and plundering the city. As the prestige of the Darbar declined, the men of the army arose to have their voice heard in matter of state. The one institution with which they were familiar was the *Panchayat* the council of elders which regulated the affairs in their villages. The system was imported into the army, and each regiment began to elect his own panches whose duty was to deliberate on the orders of the commanding officer and then to make their recommendations to the men. This seriously affected discipline in the army.

The British from across the border might have intervened in the affairs of Maharaja Sher Singh's administration, but they were prevented from doing so by a sudden turn of events in Afghanistan which British had occupied earlier with the active help of the Sikhs under the Tripartite Treaty of 1938, placing Shah Shuja on the throne of Kabul. In a bloody rising in Kabul in the autumn of 1841, Shah Shuja was murdered and the British army of occupation was annihilated. For the recovery of Afghanistan, Lord Ellenborough, the governor-general, sought (spring 1842) the cooperation of the Sikhs. Reassured that the Sandhanvalia refugees in the British territory would not be allowed to disturb his reign, Sher Singh was persuaded to assist. The purchase of grain and hire of carriage cattle in the Punjab were facilitated, and a division of 5,000 Sikhs helped force the Khyber pass. Sher Singh allowed Dost Mohammad Khan, with whom the Sikhs crossed swords in many battle and whom the British were escorting to Kabul for the installation as they new king. The Lahore Darbar signed a separate treaty with Dost Muhammad Khan as the Amir of Afghanistan.

A notable event during Sher Singh's reign was the conquest of the Laddakh valley which was strategically very important and which made the frontier secure against expanding influence of China. A Sikh expedition under the Dogra General Zorawar Singh, marched towards Tibet. Garo and Rudok wre occupied and Lhasa armies attacked. Although the expedition did not make much headway owing to premature snowfall and difficult and unfamiliar terrain, a treaty of peace was signed on 17 September 1842 between the representative of Khalsa darbar and the representative of the

Chinese emperor. It was agreed that the traditional boundaries of Laddakh and Tibet would be considered inviolable by both parties and trade, particularly of tea and *Pashmina* wool, would, as in the past, pass through Laddakh.

In March 1842, Mr. Clerk of the Ludhiana political agency had led a diplomatic mission to Amritsar to condole with Maharaja Sher Singh on the death of his predecessor and congratulate him upon his accession. He also took the oppurtunity of interceding on behalf of the Sandhanvalias, Atar Singh and Ajit Singh, who had formallly sought the Maharaja's permission for returning to the Punjab. In September 1842 a letter was received from Ajit Singh announcing "his intention to come to Lahore for presenting himself before the Shahzada (Sher Singh)." Sher Singh gave his approval for the return of the fugitives. Baba Bikram Singh of Una placed them under solemn oaths. On his standing surety for them, Sher Singh pardoned them. Ajit Singh arrived in Lahore on 17 November 1842, followed by Atar Singh. Amnesty was also extended to Lahina Singh Sandhanvalia and Kehar Singh Sandhanvalia who were released from confinement in the Mukerian Fort.

Although Sher Singh had shown magnamity in allowing Atar Singh and Ajit Singh to return to the Punjab and to resume their accustomed positions at the court, they were not reconciled to him. Their original nominee for the throne of the Punjab, Mai Chand Kaur, whose cause they had persistently espoused even after crossing over to the British territory, was now dead (9 June 1842), yet they continued to nurture a feeling of hostility towards Sher Singh. This culminated in a murderous plot. On 15 September 1842, the Maharaja rode out of the city early in the morning, that being a *sankrant* the first day of the Bikrami month, there was no darbar for him to attend. He alighted near Tej Singh's garden where tents were put up for his son, Kanvar Partap Singh. To fulfil the morning's engagement, he moved on the Shah Balaval where sittingin the *baradari* or pleasure house, he witnessed wrestling-bouts, with Diwan Dina Nath and Buddh Singh, his armour-bearer, in attendance. After he had dismissed the wrestlers with due charity, the Sandhanvalia Sardars, who had followed him with 150 horse and 300 foot, requested him to inspect their troops. Totally without suspicion, Sher Singh agreed and came out of the room. After the parade, Ajit Singh sought his permission to show him a carbine he had obtained from an Englishman in Calcutta. As the Maharaja who was a great lover of weapons put forth his hands to take hold of the rifle, Ajit Singh pressed the triggers and emptied the loaded barrels into his chest. "Oh, Sardar, What deception?" was all the Maharaja could say as he dropped to the ground dead. Ajit Singh rushed forward and cut off his head with a single blow of the sword. The shots that killed Sher Singh were a signal for the elder Sandhanvalia, Lahina Singh, to pounce upon the 12-year old Son of Maharaja Sher Singh, in the nearby Tej Singh garden, and hack off his head.

Sher Singh was survived by his son Sahdev Singh, born to Rani Dukno in 1843, who, after the annexation of the Punjab in 1849, accompanied the deported king, Duleep Singh, to Fatehgarh in Uttar Pardesh. Descendants of Sahdev Singh, his son Basdev Singh and daughter Harbans Kaur (later married to the Rana of Dhaulpur), lived at Rae Bareli.

Dalip Singh Sukerchakia

Maharaja Dalip Singh Sukerchakia (a.k.a. Maharaja Dalip Singh), (Black Prince of Perthshire), GCSI (6 September 1838 in Lahore, Sikh Empire-22 October 1893 in Paris, France) was the last Maharaja of Sikh Raj. He was the youngest son of the legendary "Lion of the Punjab" (Maharaja Ranjit Singh) and the "Messalina of the Punjab" (Maharani Jind Kaur), and came to power after a series of intrigues, in which several other claimants to the throne and to the Koh-i-Noor diamond killed each other. After his exile to Britain at age 13, he was befriended by Queen Victoria, to whom the Kohinoor Diamond was also presented through him by Lord Dalhousie in June 1850 after it was confiscated by the British Raj following the British annexation of the Punjab, India, after the British had defeated the Sikhs, from that date the diamond became part of the Crown Jewels, set in the Crown of Queen Elizabeth, and on display in the Jewel House in the Tower of London.

He was much admired by Queen Victoria who is reported to have written "Those eyes and those teeth are too beautiful" about the Punjabi maharajah, she was also the godmother to several of his children.

Today he is considered as Britain's first Sikh settler, having been exiled to its shores in 1854, after being dethroned and his country annexed by the British Raj in 1849.

Early Years

Dalip Singh was crowned to the throne of Punjab in 1843 succeeding his half-brother, Maharajah Sher Singh. After the close of the Second Anglo-Sikh War and the subsequent annexation of the Punjab on 29 March 1849, he was deposed at the age of eleven by the East India Company under Governor-General Hardinge and was separated from his mother, who was imprisoned. He was put into the care of Dr. John Login and sent from Lahore to Fatehgarh on 21 December 1849.

The British took, in controversial circumstances, the Koh-i-Noor diamond along with other items of his family's personal estate, country and religious property (most items were sold by public auction) to Queen Victoria as reportedly part of the terms of the conclusion of the war and the 250th anniversary of the East India Company on 3 July 1850. His health was reportedly poor, and he was mostly in quasi-exile in Fatehgarh and Lucknow after 1849, with tight restrictions on who he was allowed to meet. No Indians, except trusted servants, could meet him in private. As a matter of British policy, he was to be anglicised in every possible respect. While no specific information was released about his health, he was often sent to the hill station of Landour near Mussoorie in the Lower Himalaya for convalescence, at the time about 4 days' journey. He would remain for weeks at a time in Landour at a grand hilltop building called The Castle, which had been lavishly furnished to accommodate him.

Legality of the Koh-i-noor being Acquired by the British

The Kohinoor diamond was then given by Dalip Sing as Maharaja Ranjit Singh's successor (who owned it) to Queen Victoria, Indian historians argue that Prince Dalip Singh was only a minor then, and could not have given the diamond away without coercion from his British advisors. Record also says that the confiscated diamond was presented to the Queen-mother by Lord Dalhousie in 1850 through the young exiled Prince.

Conversion to Christianity

In 1853, under the tutelage of his long-time retainer Bhajan Lal (himself a Christian convert) he converted to Christianity at Fatehgarh with the approval of the Governor-General Lord Dalhousie. His conversion remains controversial, having been effected in unclear circumstances before he turned 15. He was also heavily and continuously exposed to Christian texts under the tutelage of the devout John Login. His two closest childhood friends were both English, one being the child of Anglican missionaries. In 1854, he was sent into exile in Britain.

Life in Exile

London: Dalip Singh's arrival on the shores of England in 1854 threw him into the European court. Queen Victoria showered affection upon the turbaned Maharajah, as did the Prince Consort. Dalip Singh was initially lodged at Claridge's Hotel in London before the East India Company took over a house in Wimbledon and then eventually another house in Roehampton which became his home for 3 years. He was also invited by the Queen to stay with the Royal Family at Osborne, where she sketched him playing with her children and Prince Albert photographed him, while the court artist, Winterhalter, made his portrait, He eventually got bored with Roehampton and expressed a wish to go back to India but it was suggested by the East India Company Board he take a tour of the European continent which he did with Sir John Spencer Login and Lady Login.

Scotland

On his return from Europe in 1855 he was given an annual pension, and was officially under ward of Sir John Spencer Login and Lady Login, who leased Castle Menzies in Perthshire, Scotland for him. He spent the rest of his teens there but at 19 he demanded to be in charge of his household. Eventually, he was given this and an increase in his annual pension. In 1858 the lease expired and Dalip Singh rented the house at Auchlyne from the Earl of Breadalbane. He was remarkable in the area as the first Indian prince to visit Scotland, and soon had the nickname, the "Black Prince of Perthshire". He was known for a lavish lifestyle, shooting parties, and a love of dressing in highland costume. (At the same time, he was known to have gradually developed a sense of regret for his circumstances in exile, including some inner turmoil about his conversion to Christianity and his forced departure from the Punjab). His mother stayed in Perthshire with him for a short time, before he rented the Grantully Estate, near Aberfeldy. Following the deaths of his mother and John Login in 1863, he returned to England.

Mulgrave Castle

Dalip Singh took on a lease at Mulgrave Castle in Yorkshire in 1858 and enjoyed the English countryside while there.

Elveden Estate

Dalip Singh bought (or the India Office purchased for him) a 17,000 acre (69 km^2) country estate at Elveden on the border between Norfolk and Suffolk, close to Thetford, in 1863. He fell in love with Elveden and the surrounding area and restored the church, cottages, and school. He transformed the run-down estate into an efficient game preserve and the house into a quasi-oriental palace where he lived the life of a British aristocrat. Dalip Singh was accused of running up large expenses and the estate was sold after his death to pay his debts. Today, Elveden is owned by descendants of the Guinness family of brewing fame; it remains an operating farm and private hunting estate.

Re-initiated into Sikhism

While in exile, he sought to learn more about Sikhism and was eager to return to India. Though previous efforts were thwarted by his handlers, he reestablished contact with his cousin Sardar Thakar Singh Sandhawalia, who on 28 September 1884, left Amritsar for England along with his sons Narinder Singh and Gurdit Singh and a Sikh granthi (priest), Partab Singh. He also brought a list of properties held by Dalip Singh in India, all this renewed his connection with Sikhism.

The British Government decided in 1886 against his return to India or his re-embracing Sikhism. Despite protests from the India Office, he set sail for 'home' on 30 March 1886. However, he was intercepted and arrested in Aden, where the writ of the Raj began. He could not be stopped from an informal re-conversion ceremony in Aden, far less grand and symbolic than it would have been in India, done by emissaries sent by Sardar Thakar Singh Sandhawalia, who was earlier planning the *Pahaul* ceremony at Bombay. Dalip was forced to return to Europe.

Death

Dalip Singh died in Paris in 1893 at the age of 55, not having seen India (let alone the Punjab) again after he was 15, except for two brief, tightly-controlled visits in 1860 (to bring his mother to

England) and in 1863 (to scatter his mother's ashes). Dalip Singh's wish for his body to be returned to India was declined, in fear of unrest given the symbolic value the funeral of the son of the Lion of the Punjab may have caused, given growing resentment of British rule. His body was brought back to be buried according to Christian rites, under the supervision of the India Office in Elveden Church beside the grave of his wife Maharani Bamba, and his son Prince Edward Albert Duleep Singh. The graves are located on the west side of the Church.

A life-size bronze statue of the Maharajah showing him on a horse was unveiled by HRH the Prince of Wales in 1999 at Butten Island in Thetford, a town which benefited from his and his sons' generosity.

A film titled, *Maharaja Duleep Singh: A Monument Of Injustice* was made in 2007, directed by P.S. Narula. In an auction at Bonhams, London on 19 April 2007, the 74 cm high white marble portrait bust of Maharajah Duleep Singh by Victorian sculptor John Gibson RA in Rome in 1859, fetched £1.7 million (£1.5 million plus premium and tax).

Heraldry

A coat of arms was granted, commissioned by Prince Albert.

Family

Dalip's mother, Maharani Jind Kaur, was in exile in Nepal. In 1860 he was allowed to return to India and he decided to bring his mother back to England. She died in England in 1863.

Dalip Singh married twice, first to Bamba Muller and then to Ada Douglas Wetherill. He had eight children in total, six from his first marriage to Bamba:

- Prince Victor Duleep Singh
- Prince Frederick Duleep Singh
- Prince Albert Edward Duleep Singh
- Princess Bamba Sutherland
- Princess Catherine Duleep Singh
- Princess Sophia Duleep Singh.

He also had two children from his second marriage to Ada Douglas Wetherill:

- Princess Pauline Alexandra Duleep Singh
- Princess Ada Irene Beryl Duleep Singh.

All the eight children died without issue, ending the direct line of the Sikh Royalty. There is a memorial at Eton College in England to Princes Victor and Frederick, Maharajah Duleep Singh's two sons who studied at Eton in the 1870s.

Maharani Bamba Muller

Maharani Bamba Muller was an Arabic-speaking, part-Ethiopian, part-German girl, whose father was a German banker and whose mother was an Abyssinian Coptic Christian slave. She and Dalip met in Cairo in 1863 on his return from scattering his mother's ashes in India; they were married in Alexandria, Egypt on 7 June 1864. The Maharani died in London on 18 September 1887.

Ada Douglas Wetherill

Some sources describe Ada Douglas Wetherill as a French princess. In fact, she was neither French nor a princess. This is very likely a fiction created to give her some legitimacy later in life. Wetherill had been Dalip's mistress before he decided to return to India with his family, and upon being stopped in Aden by the British authorities he abandoned his family and moved to Paris, where she joined him. She stayed with him through his years in Paris and also travelled with him to St. Petersburg, Russia, where he failed to persuade the Czar of the benefits of invading India through the north and reinstalling him as ruler.

Queen Victoria and Maharaja Dalip Singh reconciled their differences before he died. Out of loyalty to Maharani Bamba, the Queen refused to receive Ada, who she suspected had been involved with the Maharaja before Maharani Bamba's death in 1887.

Possible Descendant

It has been claimed that Dalip Singh may be the great-great-grandfather of Bob Goddard, a British debt collector for Halifax. Genetic evidence suggests that Goddard has an unusual combination of minor blood groups that is rare among the white British population but common among Asians. The genealogical history of Goddard's family suggests his grandfather, Charlie Goddard, was born in 1888 as the illegitimate child of an English maid serving at Breckles Hall in Norfolk. It was rumoured that the father may have been an Indian prince, believed to be Prince Frederick Duleep Singh, who was a resident at Breckles Hall when Charlie was born.

End of Empire

After Maharaja Ranjit Singh's death in 1839, the empire was severely weakened by internal divisions and political mismanagement. This opportunity was used by the British Empire to launch the Anglo-Sikh Wars.

First Anglo-Sikh War

The First Anglo-Sikh War was fought between the Sikh Empire and the British East India Company between 1845 and 1846. It resulted in partial subjugation of the Sikh kingdom.

Background and Causes of the War

The Sikh kingdom of Punjab was expanded and consolidated by Maharaj Ranjit Singh during the early years of the nineteenth century, about the same time as the British-controlled territories were advanced by conquest or annexation to the borders of the Punjab. Ranjit Singh maintained a policy of wary friendship with the British, while at the same time building up his military forces to deter aggression both by the British and by the Afghans under Dost Mohammed Khan. He hired American and European mercenary soldiers to train his artillery, and also incorporated contingents of Hindus and Muslims into his army.

Events in the Punjab

Ranjit Singh died in 1839. Almost immediately, his kingdom fell into disorder. Ranjit's unpopular legitimate son, Kharak Singh, was removed from power within a few months, and later died in prison under mysterious circumstances. It was widely believed that he was poisoned. He was replaced by his able but estranged son Kanwar Nau Nihal Singh, who also died within a few months in suspicious circumstances; he was crushed by a falling archway at the Lahore Fort while returning from his father's cremation. There were at the time two major factions within the Punjab contending for power and influence, the Sikh Sindhanwalias and the Hindu Dogras. The Dogras succeeded in raising Sher Singh, the eldest illegitimate son of Ranjit Singh, to the throne in January 1841. The most prominent Sindhanwalias took refuge on British territory, but had many adherents among the Army of the Punjab. The army was expanding rapidly in the aftermath of Ranjit Singh's death, from 29,000 (with 192 guns) in 1839 to over 80,000 in 1845 as landlords and their retainers took up arms. It now proclaimed itself to be the Khalsa, or embodiment of the Sikh nation. Its regimental panchayats (committees) formed an alternate power source within the kingdom, declaring that Guru Gobind Singh's ideal of the Sikh commonwealth had been revived, with the Sarbatt Khalsa or the Sikh as a whole assuming all executive, military and civil authority in the State, which British observers decried as a "dangerous military democracy". British representatives and visitors in the Punjab described the regiments as preserving "puritanical" order internally, but also as being in a perpetual state of mutiny or rebellion against the central Durbar (Court). In one notorious instance of unrest, Sikh soldiers ran riot, looking for anyone who looked as if they could speak Persian (the language used by the clerks who administered the Khalsa's finances) and putting them to the sword.

Maharajah Sher Singh was unable to meet the pay demands of the Khalsa, although he reportedly lavished funds on a degenerate court. In September 1843 he was murdered by his cousin, an officer of the Khalsa, Ajit Singh Sindhanwalia. The Dogras took their revenge on those responsible, and Jind Kaur, Ranjit Singh's youngest widow, became Regent for her infant son Duleep Singh. After the Vizier Hira Singh was killed while attempting to flee the capital with loot from the Royal Treasury (Toshkana), by troops under Sham Singh Attariwala, Jind Kaur's brother Jawahir Singh became Vizier in December 1844. He apparently spent his term of office in a state of terror, trying to bribe the Khalsa with promises of treasure which could not be met. At an army parade in September 1845, he was butchered to death in the presence of Jind Kaur and Duleep Singh.

The Khalsa nevertheless did not take over the kingdom at this point. Although Jind Kaur publicly vowed revenge against her brother's killers, she remained Regent. Lal Singh became Vizier, and Tej Singh became commander of the army. Sikh historians have stressed that both these men were prominent in the Dogra faction. Originally high-caste Hindus from outside the Punjab, both had converted to Sikhism in 1818 (like the majority of the Sikhs in Punjab at that time).

British Actions

Meanwhile, immediately after the death of Ranjit Singh, the British East India Company had begun increasing its military strength, particularly in the regions adjacent to the Punjab. In 1844, they annexed Sindh, to the south of the Punjab. They had also established a military cantonment at Ferozepur, only a few miles from the Sutlej River which marked the frontier between British-ruled India and the Punjab.

The actions and attitudes of the British, under Governors-General Lord Ellenborough and his successor, Sir Henry Hardinge, are disputed. By most British accounts, the main concern was that the Khalsa, now without strong leadership to restrain them, was a serious threat to British territories along the border. Sikh and Indian historians have countered that the military preparations made by these Governors-General were offensive in nature; for example, they prepared bridging trains and siege gun batteries, which would be unlikely to be required in a purely defensive operation. The British attitudes were affected by reports from their new Political Agent in the frontier districts, Major George Broadfoot, who stressed the disorder in the Punjab and recounted every tale of corrupt behaviour at the court. For some British officials, there was a strong desire to expand British influence and control into the Punjab, as it was the only remaining formidable force that could threaten the British hold in India and the last remaining independent kingdom not under British influence. The kingdom was also renowned for being the wealthiest, the Koh-i-Noor being but one of its many treasures. Despite this, it is unlikely that the British East India Company would have deliberately attempted to annex the Punjab had the war not occurred, as they simply did not have the manpower or resources to keep a hold on the territories (as proven by the outbreak of the Second Anglo-Sikh War). Nevertheless, the unconcealed and seemingly aggressive British military build-up at the borders had the effect of increasing tension within the Punjab and the Khalsa.

Outbreak and Course of the War

After mutual demands and accusations between the Sikh Darbar and the East India Company, diplomatic relations were broken. An East India Company army began marching towards Ferozepur, where a division was already stationed. This army was commanded by Sir Hugh Gough, the commander in chief of the Bengal Army, and was accompanied by Sir Henry Hardinge, the British Governor General of Bengal, who placed himself beneath Gough in the military chain of command. The "British" army consisted of formations of the Bengal Army, with usually one British unit to every three or four Bengal infantry or cavalry units. Most of the British artillery consisted of light guns from the elite Bengal Horse Artillery.

In response to the British move, the Sikh army began crossing the Sutlej on 11 December 1845. Although the leaders and principal units of the army were Sikhs, there were also Punjabi, Pakhtun and Kashmiri infantry units. The artillery consisted mainly of units of heavy guns, which had been organised and trained by European mercenaries.

The Sikhs claimed they were only moving into Sikh possessions (specifically the village of Moran) on the east side of the river, but the move was regarded by the British as clearly hostile and they declared war. One Sikh army under Tej Singh advanced towards Ferozepur but made no effort to surround or attack the exposed British division there. Another force under Lal Singh clashed with Gough's and Hardinge's advancing forces at the Battle of Mudki on 18 December. The British won an untidy encounter battle.

On the next day, the British came in sight of the large Sikh entrenchment at Ferozeshah. Gough wished to attack at once, but Hardinge used his position as Governor General to overrule him and order him to wait for the division from Ferozepur. When they appeared late on 21 December, Gough attacked in the few hours of daylight left. The well served Sikh artillery caused heavy casualties among the British, and their infantry fought desperately. On the other hand, the elite of the Sikh army, the irregular cavalry or ghodachadas (alt. gorracharra, horse-mounted)s, were comparatively ineffective against Gough's infantry and cavalry as they had been kept from the battlefield by Lal Singh.

By nightfall, some of Gough's army had fought their way into the Sikh positions, but other units had been driven back in disorder. Hardinge expected a defeat on the following day and ordered the state papers at Mudki to be burned in this event. However, on the following morning, the British and Bengal Army units rallied and drove the Sikhs from the rest of their fortifications. Lal Singh had made no effort to rally or reorganise his army. At this point, Tej Singh's army appeared. Once again, Gough's exhausted army faced defeat and disaster, but Tej Singh inexplicably withdrew.

Operations temporarily halted, mainly because Gough's army was exhausted and required rest and reinforcements. The Sikhs were temporarily dismayed by their defeats and by their commanders' actions, but rallied when fresh units and leaders joined them, and Maharani Jind Kaur exhorted 500 selected officers to make renewed efforts. When hostilities resumed, a Sikh detachment crossed the Sutlej near Aliwal, threatening Gough's lines of supply and communications. A division under Sir Harry Smith was sent to deal with them. Sikh cavalry attacked Smith continually on his march and captured his baggage, but at the Battle of Aliwal on 28 January 1846, Smith won a model victory, eliminating the Sikh bridgehead.

Gough's main army had now been reinforced, and rejoined by Smith's division, they attacked the main Sikh bridgehead at Sobraon on 10 February. Tej Singh is said to have deserted the Sikh army early in the battle. Although the Sikh army resisted as stubbornly as at Ferozeshah, Gough's troops eventually broke into their position. The bridges behind the Sikhs broke under British artillery fire, or were ordered to be destroyed behind him by Tej Singh (ostensibly to prevent British pursuit). The Sikh army was trapped. None of them surrendered, and the British troops showed little mercy. This victory effectively broke the Sikh army.

Aftermath

Maharaja Dalip Singh, entering his palace in Lahore, escorted by British troops after the *First Anglo-Sikh War* (1845-46)

In the Treaty of Lahore on March 9, 1846, the Sikhs were made to surrender the valuable region (the Jullundur Doab) between the Beas River and Sutlej River. The Lahore Durbar was also required to pay an indemnity of 15 million rupees (1.5 crore). Because it could not readily raise this sum, it ceded to the East India Company, as equivalent for one crore of rupees, Kashmir, Hazarah and all the forts, territories, rights and interests in the hill countries situated between the Rivers Beas and Indus. In a later separate arrangement (the Treaty of Amritsar), the Raja of Jammu, Gulab Singh, purchased Kashmir from the East India Company for a payment of 7,500,000 rupees (75 lakh) and was granted the title Maharaja of Jammu and

Kashmir. Maharaja Duleep Singh remained ruler of the Punjab and at first his mother, Maharani Jindan Kaur, remained as Regent. However, the Durbar later requested that the British presence remain until the Maharaja attained the age of 16. The British consented to this and on December 16, 1846, the Treaty of Bhyroval provided for the Maharani to be awarded a pension of 150,000 rupees (1.5 lakh) and be replaced by a British resident in Lahore supported by a Council of Regency, with agents in other cities and regions. This effectively gave the East India Company control of the government. Sikh historians have always maintained that, in order to retain their hold on power and maintain the figurehead rule of Duleep Singh, Lal Singh and Tej Singh embarked on the war with the deliberate intent of breaking their own army. In particular, Lal Singh was corresponding with a British political officer and betraying state and military secrets throughout the war. Lal Singh's and Tej Singh's desertion of their armies and refusal to attack when opportunity offered seem inexplicable otherwise. Although the Khalsa was indeed weakened by the war, resentment at British interference in the government led to the Second Anglo-Sikh War within three years.

Treaty of Lahore

The Treaty of Lahore of March 9, 1846, was a peace treaty marking the end of the First Anglo-Sikh War. The Treaty was concluded, for the British, by the Governor-General Sir Henry Hardinge and two officers of the East India Company and, for the Sikhs, by the seven year old Maharaja Duleep Singh Bahadur and seven members of the Lahore Durbar acting on his behalf.

The terms of the Treaty were punitive. Sikh territory was reduced to a fraction of its former size, losing Jammu, Kashmir, Hazara, the territory to the south of the river Sutlej and the forts and territory in the Jalandhar Doab between the rivers Sutlej and Beas. In addition, controls were placed on the size of the Lahore army and thirty-six field guns were confiscated. The control of the rivers Sutlej and Beas and part of the Indus passed to the British, with the proviso that this was not to interfere with the passage of passenger boats owned by the Lahore Government. Also, provision was made for the separate sale of Kashmir by the East India Company at a later date to Gulab Singh, the Raja of Jammu.

Bibliography

Adikaram, E. W.: *Early History of Buddhism in Ceylon,* D. S. Puswella, Migoda, 1946.

Agrawala, V. S.: *Shiva Mahadeva: The Great God,* Veda Academy, Varanasi, 1966.

Ahmad, Imtiaz: *State and Foreign Policy: India's Role in South Asia,* Vikas, New Delhi, 1993.

Ahmad, Jamil-ud-din: *Some Recent Speeches and Writings of Mr. Jinnah,* Lahore, Ashraf, 1952.

Aiyar, R. Krishnaswami: *Outlines of Vedaanta,* Chetana, Bombay, 1978.

Archer, W. G.: *The Kama Sutra,* Unwin Hyman, London, 1990.

Ashton, S.R. : *British Policy Towards the Indian States, 1905-1939,* London, Curzon, 1982.

Aurobindo, Sri: *Vyasa and Valmiki,* Acharya Press, Pondicherry, 1956.

Avalon, Arthur and Ellen: *Hymns to the Goddess,* Ganesh and Co., Madras, 1964.

Aziz, Ashraf: *Light of the Universe: Essays on Hindustani Film Music,* Three Essays Collective, New Delhi, 2003.

Bagchi, P. C.: *Studies in Dharmashastra,* University of Calcutta Press, Calcutta, 1939.

Bahadur, K.P.: *The Wisdom of Vedaanta,* Sterling Publishers Private Limited, New Delhi, 1996.

Banerjea, J. N.: *Pauranic and Vedanta Religion,* University of Calcutta, Calcutta, 1996.

Bankimchandra, C.: *Essentials of Dharma,* Sanskrit Book Depot, Calcutta 1979.

Basu, Manoranjan: *Dharmashastra: A General Study,* Shrimati Mira Basu, Calcutta, 1976.

Beaumont, Roger : *Sword of the Raj: The British Army in India, 1747-1947*, Indianapolis, Bobbs-Merrill, 1977.

Benjamin, Joseph : *Scheduled Castes in Indian Politics and Society*, New Delhi, Ess Ess Publications, 1989.

Bhattacharyya, B.: *Nispannayogavali of Mahapandita Abhyakara Gupta*, Oriental Institute, Baroda, 1949.

Borchert, Bruno: *Mysticism: Its History and Challenge*, Samuel Wiser, York Beach, 1994.

Bose, D. N.: *Dharmashastra: Their Philosophy and Occult Secrets*, Kali Press, Calcutta, 1965.

Bowle, John: *The Imperial Achievement: The Rise and Transformation of the British Empire*, Little, Brown, 1974.

Brockington, J. L.: *Righteous Rama: The Evolution of an Epic*, Oxford, London, 1984.

Bromley, D.: *Krishna Consciousness in the West*, Bucknell University Press, Lewisburg, 1989.

Brooks, E.: *The Original Analects: Sayings of Confucius and His Successors*. Columbia University Press, New York, 1988.

Bruhn, Klaus: *The Jina-Images of Deogarh*, MacMillan, Leiden, 1969.

Burke, Mary Louise: *Swami Vivekananda in America: New Discoveries*, Advaita Ashrama, Calcutta, 1966.

Chaudhary, M.: *Partition and the Curse of Rehabilitation*, Calcutta, Bengal Rehabilitation Organization, 1964.

Chaudhuri, Nirad: *Thy Hand, Great Anarch! India: 1921-1952*, London, Chatto & Windus, 1987.

Coomeraswamy, Ananda K.: *Buddha and the Gospel of Buddhism*, MacMillan, London, 1928.

Crawford, Cromwell S.: *Ram Mohan Roy: His Era and Ethics*, Acharya Press, New Delhi, 1984.

Dalton, Dennis : *Gandhi's Power : Nonviolence in Action*, New Delhi, OUP, 2001.

Danielou, Alain: *The Complete Kama Sutra*, Park Street Press, Rochester, 2000.

Dasgupta, Shahana: *Rani Lakshmibai: The Indian Heroine*, Rupa & Company, Calcutta, 2002.

Datta, V.N.: *Sati: Widow Burning in India*, Manohar, New Delhi, 1990.

David, M. D.: *John Wilson and his Institutions,* Mumbai, 1957.

De Bary: *Self and Society in Ming Thought,* Columbia University Press, New York, 1970.

De, Sushil Kumar: *Ancient Indian Erotics and Erotic Literature,* Firma K. L. Mukhopadhyay, Calcutta, 1959.

Deak, Istvan: *The Lawful Revolution: Louis Kossuth and the Hungarians 1848-1849,* Columbia University Press, 1979.

Dhar, Niranjan: *Vedanta and Bengal Renaissance,* Minerva Associates, Calcutta, 1977.

Dikshit, D.P. *Political History of the Chalukyas of Badami.* New Delhi: Abhinav, 1980.

Donat, K.: *Meditate the Tantric Yoga Way,* George Allen and Unwin, London, 1973.

Doniger, W.: *The Rig Veda: An Anthology,* Penguin, New York, 1981.

Duboi, Abbe: *Hindu Manners, Customs and Ceremonies,* Fifth Indian Impression, CUP, 1985.

Dwivedi, M.: *The Principal Upanishads,* Adyar Library, Madras, 1931.

Eaton, Richard M.: *Sufis of Bijapur, 1300-1700: Social Roles of Sufis in Medieval India,* Princeton University Press, Princeton, 1978.

Edwardes, Michael: *Battles of the Indian Mutiny,* London; B. T. Batsford Ltd., 1963.

Erickson, Erik H.: *Gandhi's Truth: On the Origins of Militant Nonviolence,* Norton, New York, 1970.

Farquhar, J.N.: *Modern Religious Movements in India,* Munshiram, New Delhi, 1967.

Fay, Peter Ward: *The Opium War, 1840-42,* University of North Carolina Press, 1975.

Fisher, Michael H.: *The Politics of British Annexation of India - 1757-1857,* Oxford, 1996.

Frauwallner, E..: *History of Indian Philosophy,* Motilal, Delhi, 1973.

Gambhirananda, S.: *Brahma Sutra Shamkar Bhasya,* Adavita Ashrama, Calcutta, 1977.

Gambhirananda, Swami: *Brahma Sutra Shamkar Bhasya,* Adavita Ashrama, Calcutta, 1977.

Gandhi, M. K.: *The Story of My Experiment With Trust,* Washington, Public Affairs Press, 1948.

Garbe, R.: *The Philosophy of Ancient India,* Chicago University Press, Chicago, 1899.

Goradia, Nayana: *Lord Curzon: The Last of the British Moghuls,* New Delhi, Oxford University Press, 1993.

Goudriaan, T.: *Ritual and Speculation in Early Tantrism,* State University of New York Press, New York, 1992.

Gough, A.E.: *The Philosophy of the Upanisads and Ancient Indian Metaphysics,* MacMillan, London, 1882.

Grant, G. P.: *Philosophy in the Mass Age,* Copp Clark, Toronto, 1959.

Grisenold, H.D.: *Insights into Modern Hinduism,* Oxford, New York, 1934.

Growse, F. S.: *The Ramayana of Tulasidasa,* Motilal Banarsidass, Delhi, 1995.

Gurumurthy, S. : *Hindu Heritage, Assimilative, Not Divisive,* Vigil, Madras 1993.

Haich, E.: *Sexual Energy and Yoga,* Aurora Press, New York, 1982.

Hasan, Murhirul: *Legacy of a Divided Nation: India's Muslims Since Independence,* New Delhi, Oxford, 1997.

Hasan, Mushirul: *India's Partition: Process, Strategy and Mobilization,* New Delhi, Oxford UP, 1993.

Heifetz, Hank: *The Origin of the Young God: Kalidasa's Kumara-sambhava,* University of California Press, Berkeley, 1985.

Heimann, Betty: *Facets of Indian Thought,* Geroge Allen & Unwin, London, 1964.

Heinsath, Charles: *Indian Nationalism and Hindu Social Reform,* Princeton University Press, Princeton, 1964.

Heschel, J.: *God in Search of Man: A Philosophy of Judaism,* Noonday Press, New York, 1997.

Hirschman, Edwin: *White Mutiny: The Ilbert Bill Crisis in India and the Genesis of the Indian National Congress,* New Delhi, Heritage, 1980.

Hixon, L.: *Mother of the Universe: Visions of the Goddess, Tantric Hymns of Enlightenment,* Quest Books, Wheaton, 1994.

Hopkins, J.: *Kalachakra Tantra Rite of Initiation,* Wisdom Publications, Boston, 1982.

Hopkirk, Peter: *The Great Game: The Struggle for Empire in Central Asia,* Kodansha, 1992.

Hume, R.E.: *The Thirteen Principle Upanishads*, Oxford University Press, London, 1971.

Hutchins, Francis: *Spontaneous Revolution: The Quit India Movement*, New Delhi, Manohar, 1971.

Irene, S.: *Vedic Heritage Teaching Program*. Arsha Vidya Gurukulam, Coimbatore, 1994.

Iyar, K.: *Vedanta: The Science of Reality*, Ganesh and Co., Mardas, 1930.

Iyengar, B.K.S.: *Light on the Yoga Sutras of Patanjali*, Aquarian Press, London 1993.

Jacob, K.: *Religion and Ethics in Advaita*, C.M.S. Press, Kottayam, 1982.

Jafar, Malik Muhammad: *Jinnah as a Parliamentarian*, Lahore, Afzar Publications, 1977.

Jain, Kailash Chand, *Lord Mahavira and His Times*, Saraswati Press, Delhi, 1974.

James, Lawrence: *The Rise and Fall of the British Empire*, St. Martin's, 1997.

James, Robert Rhodes: *The British Revolution, 1880-1939*, New York, Knopf, 1976.

Jean, M.: *Tantrik Yoga*, The Aquarian Press, Wellingborough, 1970.

John, B.: *Mantras: Sacred Words of Power*, George Allen and Unwin, London, 1977.

John, Elsner: *Pilgrimage: Past and Present in the World Religions*, Harvard University Press, Cambridge, 1995.

John, K.: *The Origin and Development of the State Cult of Confucius*, Paragon Book, New York, 1966.

Karmarkar, D.: *Sankara's Advaita*, Karnatak University, Dharwar, 1976.

Kaushik, Asha : *Globalization, Democracy and Culture : Situating Gandhian Alternatives*, Jaipur, Pointer, 2002.

Kaviraj, G.: *Aspects of Indian Thought*, University of Burdwan, Calcutta, 1966.

Kavlekar, K.K. : *Non-Brahmin Movement in Southern India, 1873-1949*, Kolhapur, Shivaji University, 19790

Keith, A.B. : *Rigveda Brahmanas*, Harvard University Press, Cambridge, 1920.

Keith, Arthur Berriedale: *The Religion and Philosophy of the Veda and Upanishads*, MacMillan, Delhi, 1925.

Kishwar, Madhu : *Religion at the Service of Nationalism, and Other Essays*, OUP, Delhi, 1998.

Klaus, K.: *A Survey of Hinduism*, State University of New York Press, Albany, 1989.

Knipe, M.: *Hinduism: Experiments in the Sacred*, Harper, San Francisco, 1991.

Knott, K.: *Hinduism, A Very Short Introduction*, Oxford University Press, New York, 1998.

Kosambi, D. D. : *The Culture and Civilisation of Ancient India in Historical Outline*, London, Routledge and Kegan Paul, 1956.

Kottackal, Jacob: *Religion and Ethics in Advaita*, C.M.S. Press, Kottayam, 1982.

Kuiper, F.B.J. : *Aryans in the Rigveda*, Rodopi, Amsterdam, 1991.

Kuppuswamy, Sastri S.: *Compromises in the History of Advaitic Thought*, Kalyani Press, Madras, 1940.

Louis, Fischer: *Essential Gandhi: An Anthology of His Writings*, Vintage, New York, 1983.

Low, D. A. and Brasted, Howard: *Freedom, Trauma, Continuities: Northern India and Independence*, New Delhi, Sage Publications, 1998.

Maheshwari, Shriram: *Rural Development in India: A Public Policy Approach*, New Delhi, Sage, 1995.

Makhan, L.: *The Ramayana of Valmiki*, Munshiram Manoharlal, New Delhi, 1978.

Mathew, Arnold: *Culture and Anarchy*, The University Press, Cambridge, 1935.

Mayer, A. : *Caste in an Indian Village: Change and Continuity 1954-1992*, Delhi, OUP, 1996.

Mazumder, Sukhendu : *Politico-Economic Ideas of Mahatma Gandhi: Their Relevance in the Present Day*, New Delhi, Concept Pub., 2004.

Mearns, David J.: *Shiva's Other Children: Religion and Social Identity amongst Overseas Indians*, Sage, Walnut Creek, 1995.

Mearns, J.: *Shiva's Other Children: Religion and Social Identity amongst Overseas Indians*, Sage, Walnut Creek, 1995.

Mehra, Parshotam: *A Dictionary of Modern Indian History, 1707-1947*, New Delhi, Oxford University Press, 1985.

Metcalf, Thomas R.: *The Aftermath of the Revolt: India, 1857-1870*, Princeton, Princeton University, 1964.

Mohan, K.: *The Mahabharata*, Munshiram Manoharlal, Delhi 1997.

Mookerjee, Ajit: *Kali The Feminine Force*, Thames and Hudson, London, 1988.

Mookerji, Satkari: *Modern Polity and Vedanta*, Sanskrit College, Calcutta, 1972.

Moon, Penderel: *The British Conquest and Dominion of India*, London, Duckworth, 1989.

Morris-Jones, W.H.: *The Government and Politics of India*, London, Hutchinson, 1971.

Nanda, B. R. : *Gandhi and His Critics*, Oxford University Press, Delhi, 1993.

Neale, Walter C.: *Economic Change in Rural India: Land Tenure and Reform in the United Provinces, 1800-1955*, New Haven, 1962.

Nevile, P.: *Lahore: A Sentimental Journey*, New Delhi, Penguin, 1993.

Oddie, G.A. : *Hindu and Christian in South-East India*, London, Curzon Press, 1991.

Pathak, Dr S.P.: *Jhansi during the British Rule*, Ramanand Vidya Bhawan, Delhi, 1987.

Preston, Diana: *The Boxer Rebellion*, Berkley Books, 2000.

Raimundo Panikkar: *The Vedic Experience: Mantramanjari*, Longman Todd, London, 1977.

Raja, C. Kunhan : *The Taittiriya Sarvanukramani of Yaska*, Madras, 1931.

Ramamurti, A.: *Advaitic Mysticism of Sankara*, Visvabharati, Santiniketan, 1974.

Ranajit Guha: *A Construction of Humanism in Colonial India*, CASA, Amsterdam, 1993.

Renou, Louis: *The Nature of Dharmashastra*, Walker and Co., New York, 1997.

Robson, Brian: *Sir Hugh Rose and the Central India Campaign*, Sutton Publishing Ltd for the Army Records Society, UK, 2000.

Satyapal Verma: *Role of Reason in Sankara Vedanta*, Parimal Publication, Delhi, 1992.

Savarkar, Vinayak Damodar : *The Indian War of Independence* 1857 Rajdhani Granthagar, Delhi, 1988.

Scheftelowitz, Isidor : *Die Kasmirische Rezension von Katyayanas Sarvanukramani,* Zeitschrift fur Indologie und Iranistik, 1922.

Shukla, D. N.: *Vastu-Shastra,* Motilal Banarsidass, Delhi, 1966.

Singh, Birendra Kumar: *Early Chalukyas of Vatapi, circa A.D. 500 to 757*, Delhi, Eastern Book Linkers, 1991.

Smith, Col. J. T. : *Silver and the India Exchanges,* Effingham Wilson, London, 1876.

Strauss, L.: *Political Philosophy,* The Bobbs Merrill Co., New York, 1975.

Swami Vishnu Tirtha: *Devatma Shakti,* Swami Shivom Tirth, Rishikesh, 1962.

Talageri, Shrikant : *Aryan Invasion Theory and Indian Nationalism,* Voice of India, Delhi, 1993.

Tejomayananda, Swami: *Hindu Culture: An Introduction,* Chinmaya Publications, Piercy, 1993.

Thapar, Romila : *Ashoka and the Decline of the Mauryas,* London, Oxford University Press, 1961.

Thompson, Edward: *The Making of the Indian Princes,* Oxford University Press, London, 1943.

Trautmann, Thomas R.: *Kautilya and the Arthasastra: A Statistical Study,* Leiden, Brill, 1971.

Trimingham, J.: *Sufi Orders in Islam,* Oxford University Press, New York, 1998.

Utpat, V.N.: *Riddles of Buddha and Ambedkar,* Itihas Patrika Prakashan, Thane 1988.

Vable, D.: *The Arya Samaj. Hindu without Hinduism.* Vikas Publ., Delhi, 1983.

Vedalankar, Pandit Nardev : *Basic Teachings of Hinduism,* Veda Niketan, Durban, 1978.

Visvantha, K.: *Essentials of Hinduism,* Narosa Pub. House, New Delhi, 1989.

Wendy Doniger: *Siva: The Erotic Ascetic,* Oxford University Press, Delhi, 1998.

Zaidi, A. Moin: *Evolution of Muslim political Thought in India,* New Delhi: S. Chand, 1975.

Index

D

E

F

G

H

I

J

K

L

M

N

O

P

R

S

T

U

V

W

Y

□□□